Luminos is the Open Access monograph publishing program
from UC Press. Luminos provides a framework for preserving and
reinvigorating monograph publishing for the future and increases
the reach and visibility of important scholarly work. Titles published
in the UC Press Luminos model are published with the same high
standards for selection, peer review, production, and marketing as
those in our traditional program. www.luminosoa.org

Local Color

Local Color

Reckoning with Blackness in the Port City of Veracruz

———

Karma F. Frierson

UNIVERSITY OF CALIFORNIA PRESS

University of California Press
Oakland, California

© 2025 by Karma F. Frierson

Suggested citation: Frierson, K. F. *Local Color: Reckoning with Blackness
in the Port City of Veracruz*. Oakland: University of California Press, 2025.
DOI: https://doi.org/10.1525/luminos.246

Library of Congress Cataloging-in-Publication Data

Names: Frierson, Karma F., author
Title: Local color : reckoning with blackness in the port city of Veracruz /
    Karma F. Frierson.
Description: Oakland, California : University of California Press, [2025] |
    Includes bibliographical references and index.
Identifiers: LCCN 2025008192 | ISBN 9780520413399 (cloth) |
    ISBN 9780520413405 (paperback) | ISBN 9780520413412 (ebook)
Subjects: LCSH: Black people—Mexico—Veracruz (Veracruz-Llave)—
    History | Black people—Race identity—Mexico—Veracruz
    (Veracruz-Llave) | Black people—Mexico—Veracruz (Veracruz-Llave)—
    Social life and customs | Veracruz (Veracruz-Llave, Mexico)—
    Ethnic relations
Classification: LCC F1392.B55 F75 2025 | DDC 305.896/07262—
    dc23/eng/20250416

LC record available at https://lccn.loc.gov/2025008192

GPSR Authorized Representative: Easy Access System Europe,
Mustamäe tee 50, 10621 Tallinn, Estonia, gpsr.requests@easproject.com

34 33 32 31 30 29 28 27 26 25
10 9 8 7 6 5 4 3 2 1

For Adrenée, Lillie, and Tina

CONTENTS

List of Illustrations   ix
Acknowledgments   xi

Prologue: A View from the Port   1

Introduction: Blackness a la Veracruzana   5

1. Veracruz and Its Jarocho   30

Interlude: Tenacious Roots   47

2. The Living Past   48

Interlude: Mother and Child   72

3. Practicing Innateness   74

Interlude: Day and Night   94

4. Affectations   96

Interlude: A Hand to Hold   117

5. Sanguine Blackness   119

Conclusion: The Jarocho and the Afro-Mexican   137

Epilogue: New Views in the Port   149

Notes   153
Bibliography   171
Index   183

ILLUSTRATIONS

FIGURES

1. An advertisement for the 2012 International Afro-Caribbean Festival in the process of being hung from the side of the Veracruz Institute of Culture (IVEC) *21*
2. Awaiting the start of an event taking place in the City Museum for the 2011 International Afro-Caribbean Festival *56*
3. Members of the son music group Pregoneros del Recuerdo playing onstage in the Plazuela de la Campana as part of the Festival to the Traditional Veracruzan Son with a Cuban Root *59*
4. Taller members practicing the son jarocho song "El Toro Zacamandú" *64*
5. Son jarocho taller members practicing a son on their jaranas while other members practice the accompanying dance, the zapateado, on the tarima *83*
6. A group of danzón enthusiasts practicing choreography onstage in the Plazuela de la Campana in preparation for a competition and performance *87*
7. Members of a danzonera club wear matching outfits and dance freestyle in the zócalo among other enthusiasts while tourists look on *107*
8. The early stages of setting up the tables in the Plazuela de la Campana in preparation for a night of free live music and dancing *108*
9. Regulars enjoy a Sunday afternoon in the Plazuela de la Campana as the danzonera plays onstage *113*

X   ILLUSTRATIONS

10. Street art modeled after the Cerveza Indio campaign featuring La Huaca as
one of the iconic neighborhoods in Mexico   *132*

MAPS

1. Veracruz in relation to Mexico and Cuba   *xv*
2. Veracruz dancing and cultural sites   *xv*

ACKNOWLEDGMENTS

My deepest gratitude to the many people who have made this book possible, from those who gave of their time and energy during my fieldwork, to those who offered their ideas and feedback on early drafts, to those who encouraged me to keep going and expressed enthusiasm for the work. Thank you all. Words cannot express how impactful you have been and how grateful I am for your generosity and investment.

Para comenzar, agradezco a todas las personas en Veracruz que me han acogido desde el primer momento en que llegué allí. Gracias por recibirme en sus vidas, por escuchar mis preguntas, ofrecerme sus perspectivas y por desafiar mi visión del mundo. Gracias por las innumerables tazas de café, nieves, limonadas y bailes. Si observas tu nombre o te reconoces por tu seudónimo: gracias! Si no logras reconocerte aquí, te agradezco de igual forma. Cada una de las interacciones que he tenido en Veracruz ha contribuido a este libro y tu generosidad es altamente apreciada. Quiero agradecer públicamente a aquellos que me han abierto sus puertas y me han abierto puertas como Francisco Moran, Gustavo Vergara, Ricardo Cañas, Óscar Hernández, Rafael Vázquez, Gilberto Gutiérrez, José Rosales, Ignacio Hernández y Julio Torres. Agradezco de forma personal a Jonás (QDEP), Chava, Angelica, Eric y Linda Langner, y las yogis de la cancha por su invaluable amistad y su apoyo.

I arrived at the University of Chicago undecided between two vaguely conceived ideas and was only able to develop a research agenda due to the guidance and mentorship of the faculty and the stimulating fellowship among my cohort and fellow graduate students. I count myself immensely fortunate to have spent my formative years among such inspiring company.

To my chair, Stephan Palmié, thank you for your generosity as a thought partner, mentor, and friend. You encouraged me to take my half-baked idea and let it cook under the warm sun of Veracruz and in the process changed my life. I'm forever grateful for your guidance and encouragement. To Shannon Dawdy, thank you for believing in me more than I believed in myself at times and for challenging me to be more. You were always there when I needed you, in the big moments and the quiet ones. To Justin Richland, thank you for your pragmatism, advice, and constant reminders to look for the difference that makes a difference. Even without the formal relationship of being committee members, I would also like to specifically thank Joe Masco for being a fount of wisdom and cheerleader when I needed it and François Richard for supporting me as a mentor and friend both at Chicago and in Mexico and for telling me when I was doing too much. Of course, I thank Anne Ch'ien for her optimism, support, practicality, and efficacy. If I become half as accomplished as Anne, I would count myself a success.

My graduate studies peers sustained me and inspired me. I could not have done this without you all and am glad I did not have to. I can only attempt to express the depth of my gratitude for my writing group: Ella Butler, Molly Cunningham, and Kaya Williams. You've read so many versions of this, I'm confident you know it—and Veracruz—better than I do. Thank you for letting me join your friend group all those years ago. You have strengthened this work, but more importantly you have strengthened me. Where would I be without my Cats? I was fortunate to enter graduate school in the company of extraordinary thinkers who became amazing friends. My entire cohort has been inspirational, and I want to especially thank Meghan Morris, Jenny Hua, Andrea Ford, Azara Krovatin, Christien Tompkins, Maira Hayat, Cameron Hu, and Martin Doppelt for being true friends through the years. The advantages of large cohorts, long times to completion, and workshop culture mean you get to be in the company of extraordinary people beyond your cohort, people like Jamie Gentry, Adela Amaral, Agnes Mondragon, Kristen Simmons, Kate Mariner, Emily Bock, LaShaya Howie, Kai Parker, Hannah Chazin, Tania Islas, Stefanie Graeter, and Adela Zhang.

I have had the distinct honor of developing as an academic within three departments—the Center for Latin American Studies at Rutgers University-New Brunswick, the Department of African & African-American Studies at Washington University in St. Louis, and recently in the Department of Black Studies at the University of Rochester. I have grown and learned a lot from each of these communities and have developed into a more expansive, rigorous, and creative scholar of both Latin American and Black studies from the conversations, mentorship, and examples set. I would especially like to thank Ulla Berg for being a wonderful mentor and organizing the invaluable book manuscript workshop where she, Aldo Lauria-Santiago, and Isar P. Godreau so generously gave of their time. To Shanti Parikh, Geoff Ward, Kia Caldwell, Dillon Brown, Bret Gustafson,

Ignacio Sánchez Prado, and especially Tim Parsons, thank you for your mentorship, encouragement, and advice. The transition from dissertation to book and from graduate student to colleague was stewarded by your hands, and I am deeply appreciative. To Gerald Early, Adrienne Davis, Rafia Zafar, Michelle Purdy, Rebecca Wanzo, Sowande' Mustakeem, and Wilmetta Toliver-Diallo thank you for being role models and setting such high standards. To Samuel Shearer, Robin McDowell, Raven Maragh-Lloyd, Zachary Manditch-Prottas, Jonathan Fenderson, Samba Diallo, Lauren Eldridge Stewart, Esther Kurtz, Miguel Valerio, Paige McGinley, Talia Dan-Cohen, Kenly Brown, John Mundell, and Shelley Mitchom, thank you for being true friends, generous interlocutors, and provocative questioners. To my new colleagues, thank you for being engaged and for your enthusiastic support of my work, especially Jeffrey McCune, Jordache Ellapen, and Pablo Sierra Silva. Thank you also to Jean Allman for helping me see both the forest and the trees when I felt lost in the wilderness.

I have been fortunate to receive feedback on iterations of this work from myriad people throughout the years. I deeply appreciate everyone who has given their time and energy toward improving this work. Thank you to participants at various venues, including the Workshop on Latin America and the Caribbean, US Locations Workshop, and the Center for the Study of Race, Politics and Culture at the University of Chicago; the Mellon Mays community; the CLAS community at Rutgers; the Ethnographic Theory Workshop and the Center for the Study of Race, Ethnicity & Equity at Washington University in St. Louis; the Dangerous Subjects Workshop at the University of Washington, and especially to María Elena García for taking me under her wing and being such a generous mentor; and the NEH Summer Institute on Transnational Dialogues in Afro-Latin American and Afro-Latinx Studies, with special thanks to Michele Reid-Vazquez, Satty Echeverria, Jacqueline Lyon, and Ashley Agbasoga. I am also indebted to Briana Toole and Sandra Ayoo for their encouragement and motivation. Special thanks to my editor Kate Marshall for being a champion of this project from the dissertation stage to today, to the anonymous readers whose critical engagement greatly improved this work, and to Chad Attenborough for assisting me in the final stages.

This project would not have been possible without the generous support of various organizations and centers, including the Mellon Mays Undergraduate Fellowship; the National Science Foundation Graduate Research Fellowship; the Tinker Foundation; the COMEXUS-Fulbright García Robles Scholarship; the University of Chicago's Center for the Study of Race, Politics and Culture and Center for Latin American Studies; Washington University in St. Louis's Center for the Study of Race, Ethnicity & Equity, Center for the Humanities, and Provost's Office; and the ACLS/Marwan M. and Ute Kraidy Centennial Fellowship in the Study of the Arab World and Latin America. Thank you to the Humanities

Center at the University of Rochester for providing the resources for this work to be published open access.

Most crucially, thank you to my family, without whom none of this would be possible. To my uncle, Gregory J. Glover, who taught me that jargon is slang and the value of rigor; to my sister, Savannah J. Frierson, the original writer in the family, who has given so generously her writerly and editorial expertise on requests both large and small; to my dad, the late Matthew C. Frierson, who was so invested in the completion of this book and a constant motivator; a Juan Carlos Cerecero y Teresa Olivera, mis suegros, por su interés, consejos, y apoyo incondicional. To Miguel Angel Cerecero Olivera, mi joyita, you've been there through every part of this journey. You are, without a doubt, the best part.

MAP 1. Veracruz in relation to Mexico and Cuba. Map by Ben Pease / Pease Press Cartography.

MAP 2. Select dancing and cultural sites in Veracruz. Map by Ben Pease / Pease Press Cartography.

Prologue

A View from the Port

Ricardo and I share a table in the Café La Merced, leaning a bit close to hear each other over the hissing cafeteria machines and the clink of stainless-steel spoons against thick-walled glasses—a local custom to call the attention of waiters carrying kettles of warm milk and black coffee.[1] The patrons around us watch the sports highlights on muted, lofted television screens, chat over sweet bread and sweeter drinks, or read a local newspaper—some of which carry the masthead of my coffee companion's place of employment. Amid this slice of everyday life, Ricardo and I arrive at the topic that changed our chance encounter at a cultural event about the Afro-Caribbean culture of Veracruz into an agreed-upon meeting here: *los negritos*, Black people.

Ricardo's bodily comportment works to transform hearsay into fact as he makes a confidential lean forward before fluidly shifting into a confident lean back. I would not find Black people in the Gulf Coast port city of Veracruz, also known as simply El Puerto, or the Port. For that, he reveals, I would have to go to the nearby town of Yanga. By now, I am used to the confidence with which these tellers tell such tales. They often preface their stories with "Dicen que . . . ," or "They say that . . . ," as they ironically add their voice to this nebulous and anonymous "they." Ricardo, like so many of his ilk, had little firsthand experience with the elsewhere to which he pointed. He had never been there.

Despite his conspiratorial affect in La Merced, the town of Yanga, located just one hundred kilometers from the Port, is a common locale in the quest to find Black people in the state of Veracruz. Because of its history as a settlement formed by self-liberated, formerly enslaved people known as maroons, the otherwise small town is famous. Known as "The First Free Town in the Americas," Yanga was officially recognized as a site of memory and commemorated by UNESCO; its storied history as an undefeated maroon settlement makes it a key place in the narration of Mexico's Black past. Throughout my time in the city, many people like Ricardo would helpfully recommend other places where I might find *negros*, or, as they were more commonly referred to, *gente de color*, which literally translates to "people of color." A popular choice in the Actopan region of northern Veracruz is the town of El Coyolillo, with its sign proclaiming it an "Afromestiza community" and its famous Carnival featuring iconic bovine masks.[2] Other destinations are more niche. To the south, in the isthmus, there is Chacalapa, which at its founding was exclusively for people of African descent.[3] To the west, along the border with Oaxaca, is Amapa.[4] It is there where the first attempt to apply a colonial technique called a *reducción* to Black maroons occurred.[5] Some residents of the Port would point to nearby Alvarado, with its strong reputation as having Black people. There are also the many small towns scattered throughout the state with names that "sound African" or reference Africa and therefore carry the expectation of being where Black people are to be found. Among those locales are places such as La Matamba, Mandinga, Mozomboa, or Mozambique.[6]

At first, these places were siren calls as I searched for Afro-descendants with whom to engage. When I first traveled to Veracruz, in 2011, I had been interested in studying how such peoples experienced the increased recognition of their presence in and contribution to Mexico. I wanted to explore the possibilities afforded by the recent multiculturalist agenda to include Afro-descendants after decades of exclusion and marginalization. Upon my arrival, more than one person sought to disabuse me of the notion that there were still communities of *negros* in the city. However, they—like Ricardo—were eager to help and offered other towns as possible places to find *gente de color*. These suggestions seemed to align with the urban/rural divide sociologist Jennifer Anne Meri Jones delineated in which rural residence led to "strong Afro-Mexican identification" while urbanites disavowed mention of race.[7] In those early days of casting about for a field site, I would leave the Port to journey to a few of these rural places in search of those folk who in Jones's experience "asserted not only a black identity based on history and phenotype, but also an Afro-diasporic one."[8]

As it would turn out, I was inadvertently treading a similar path as another anthropologist, Anthony Jerry, who engaged in what he terms "chasing Blackness" a few years before me and on the opposite coast. His chase took him from the Costa Chica of Oaxaca to the interior of the state's isthmus and back, to artisans and activists alike. The experience led him to focus on subject positions rather than identities as such—especially since the identities did not yet exist at the time of his investigation.[9] He likened this experience to that of another ethnographer, Christina Sue, who referred to her research on Black identity and meaning in the Port as a "wild goose chase."[10] The metaphor of a chase resonates with my own experience in Veracruz, especially when I was intent on studying "Black people."

However, whereas Jerry transformed the fluidity and movement of a chase into his methodology and Sue interpreted the chase as a manifestation of racial distancing, the chase and its implications did not arrest my attention. While the Yangas, Mandingas, and Coyolillos promised to be concrete places for ethnographic attention to a subject position that would eventually be encompassed by the term *Afro-Mexican*, what ultimately intrigued me was what the discourse on Blackness itself was doing for people in the port city. In the city, there was no need to chase Blackness at all. Its occurrence was both regularly scheduled and happenstance. Attending to Blackness rather than Black people created the opportunity to understand people like Ricardo better—people who spend their leisure time learning how they personally are connected to an Afro-Caribbean heritage even while locating *negros* somewhere else.

The simultaneous impulse to spatialize Black people in rural areas while racializing their hometown as Afro-Caribbean is the contradiction at the heart of Veracruz.[11] As a result, many locals have unmoored their Blackness from the need, desire, or compulsion to adopt a Black identity. Instead, they have made it a trait they possess and share *as* locals in the port city of Veracruz—locals known as *jarochos*. This makes the Port an interesting site in which to dwell despite the constant gestures away from it. Thus, while the hinterland beckoned, this book is an ethnographic study of Blackness in the port city of Veracruz.

Dwelling in the Port required me to reckon with both my interlocutors' and my own preconceptions of Blackness. It compelled me to grapple with my expectations of what Blackness means and looks like. It demanded a reassessment of what recognition means beyond self-recognition as Black. It required understanding identification *with* one's Blackness as distinct from but no less potent than identifying *as* Black. Although I first arrived in Veracruz in search of Black people, I came to realize the questions I had—about the consequences of acknowledging Mexico's Blackness on one's lived experiences—were not limited to Black Mexicans. That is to say, equally fascinating is what people who do not self-identify as Afro-Mexican do with the narrative that their place of residence and local practices are manifestations of what is known in Mexico as *la tercera raíz*, or the third root. The third root refers to not just the presence of Afro-descendants in Mexico but also the African contributions to Mexican history and culture broadly.

The cultural and political climate has evolved since I first arrived in Veracruz. The primary and eclipsing change has been the official political recognition of Afro-descendant Mexicans as their own ethnic group, captured by the umbrella term *Afro-Mexican*. The first major milestone was the 2015 mid-census survey—the first time the modern Mexican state asked its citizens whether they self-identified as Black or Afro-Mexican. In 2019 came a constitutional change on the federal level to include language specific to Afro-Mexicans. This momentum continued with the full census count of 2020, which enumerated 2.2 percent of the Mexican populace as Afro-Mexican. *Local Color*, however, is not their story.

Instead, this is the story of people like Ricardo, people who may not identify as Afro-Mexican but who nevertheless are curious and knowledgeable about Mexican Blackness. It is about people in the racialized space known as Veracruz as they reckon with what the third root means for them. It is about those who are working over the received knowledge of their Black heritage in their hands, in their feet, in their affect. It is about residents in the port city of Veracruz who have articulated and embraced the Blackness of their regional identity—*jarocho*—irrespective of their personal racial identity claims or subject positions. It is about residents who, in trying to be more *jarocho*, have come to understand their inherited Blackness as requisite to such an endeavor.

It is an ethnography of a city and its recreation of Blackness in its own image. Rather than chasing Black or Afro-Mexicans mythologized as belonging to the hinterland, *Local Color* dwells in the city that has developed a robust discourse about the so-termed third root, which is to say the too-long-ignored contributions of Africans and their descendants to the making of Mexico. It involves not bus trips to the rural regions to the north, west, or south of the city, but rather chats over coffees, cultural workshops, public talks and presentations, dancing, and everyday life in the Port of Veracruz. It is an account of how people who may be identified as Black are an absent presence, but how narratives about African and Afro-Caribbean retentions and influences make Blackness palpable—a spectral presence that does not quite haunt but rather animates the city and its citizens' understanding of themselves. As a result, it is an account of Blackness a la Veracruzana, or Veracruzan Blackness, which is an iteration of Mexican Blackness. It is a view from the Port.

Introduction

Blackness a la Veracruzana

When I first arrived in Veracruz in the summer of 2011, I did not intend to conduct research in the city. Like the countless travelers over the centuries who had disembarked in Veracruz on the way to other parts of Mexico, I thought the city would be a place I passed through. An introduction to Mexico, a place to visit, but not my destination. Armed with book knowledge and rusty Spanish, I left the airport for the language immersion school I had enrolled in with the intention to relearn the language and get the lay of the land. I became interested in Blackness in Mexico after seeing the traveling exhibition *The African Presence in México: From Yanga to the Present* at the Oakland Museum of California in 2009. I remember leaving the exhibition with the impression that the Gulf Coast state of Veracruz had a rich Black past, but it was the Pacific Coast that had the robust contemporary presence. I wanted to know what that historical discourse about Veracruz was doing in today's Veracruz. What was *that* region's Black present? I wondered. I thought the geographic divide of the exhibition intriguing and had enrolled in graduate school with curiosity more than with a question. I hoped this preliminary field visit would help me develop my research plan.

Inspiration would come one afternoon while on a language school field trip. We had entered through the big, imposing doors of the City Museum, seeking refuge from the heat. While the building is not air-conditioned, its wide halls ring the courtyard, offering protection from the sun if not the heat. Industrial fans keep the air circulating as visitors travel clockwise through the chronologically organized exhibitions. The museum displays a range of artifacts, dioramas, photographs, and printed information. At the threshold between two rooms, just to the left, stands a panel that would convince me to dwell in the city and consider what Blackness does in Mexico and for Mexicans. It presented a narrative elision, a puzzle I would want to unpack. The panel explains the regional identity known as *jarocho* (ha-RO-cho), asking, "Where was 'the jarocho' born?"

Spend any amount of time in Veracruz, and you will encounter the term. It is both noun and adjective. It is a way of life, a point of pride, and a set of cultural practices. In the national imaginary, the jarocho is dressed in white—the women in white lace dresses with a black embroidered apron, gold jewelry, and red stole and a flower in their hair, the men in a white linen guayabera, red neckerchief, and four-cornered hat atop their head. This typical dress is not contemporary, but you will see it in today's Veracruz, under archways as dancers perform for tourists, on the open-air tour buses that will take you around the historic center of Veracruz, as the entertainment for cultural events where dancers will perform for dignitaries and onlookers alike. In the city of Veracruz, you are inundated with the word and the associated image. Jarocho. But where was the jarocho born? Where does it come from?

The City Museum has answers for the questions you may have never asked. In the casta society of the eighteenth century, it tells its visitors, particularly in the central coastal region of the Gulf Coast, the word *jarocho* was "a pejorative term for people of Indian and Black mixture." The panel offers etymological origins of the term and informs the reader that the word alluded to "the activity most characteristic of afromestizos" in the region, which was cowboy culture. The panel then makes explicit mention of these afromestizos' role as defenders of the port city and insurgent participants in the War for Independence. Toward the end of the eighteenth century and into the nineteenth, the word ceased to be derogatory and became more expansive. It was used for the "mestizos of the Veracruz countryside of European, African, and indigenous roots, with a predominant Black aspect." This is also when the "jarocho" began to be recognized for its "happy and boisterous character." The panel concludes by informing the viewer that from the 1930s onward, *jarocho* was applied—especially by outsiders—to the inhabitants of the city of Veracruz, not just those in the Papaloapan River basin and southern plains, hence the nickname of the city, the "Puerto Jarocho" (Jarocho Port).[1]

To illustrate the panel, the curators included reproductions of mid-nineteenth-century lithographs by the Frenchman P. P. Blanchard and the Italian Claudio Linati, both of whom famously captured everyday life from their travels through Mexico. There are images labeled as a *mestiza* (Euro-Indigenous person), a *mulata* (Afro-European person), and a *costeño* (person from the coast); tableaus of women and children; and two of well-dressed couples with the caption *tipos populares* (popular types). The costeño, mulata, and one of the depicted children are dark skinned, while the rest of the people are various shades of brown, and some are pale in complexion. None of the images are labeled as *jarocho*, and none of them are dressed in the typical attire now associated with the regional type. From its explicit mention of the "predominant Black aspect" to its implicit avoidance of the popular imagery associated with the jarocho, this panel textually and visually disavowed the prevailing assumptions about one of Mexico's most iconic folk characters.

Although the City Museum is free and open to the public, it is not necessarily a bustling location. I have no idea how many people have seen this panel or if those who have seen it were taken aback by its narrative. I can speak only for myself in saying that this small summary in a museum dedicated to the centuries-long history of Veracruz intrigued me. Originally, I was most struck by the passive voice throughout the text. These connotational shifts were nonagentive; they simply occurred. What was once Afro-Indigenous became generic; what was once racial became regional.

At first, I wanted answers to questions like how and why this term became deracinated. You have at the onset a strong declaration about the Blackness of the regional type—the jarocho. The museum panel goes into detail on the historical significance of the jarocho, always centering its Blackness. Then, there is a shift in the twentieth century when the jarocho is deracialized and instead regionalized. There is no analysis of this change. The specificity of the eighteenth and nineteenth centuries gives way to an unexamined statement of fact regarding the broadening and whitening of the term. The lack of curiosity about this change made me even more intrigued.

However, as I spent more time among these contemporary jarochos, I began to reconsider this panel. Rather than asking questions of its narrative, I was fascinated by the panel's very existence. I came to see the panel as an example of how the jarocho has been Blackened in recent years. The term *jarocho* remains a broad regional label, yet its Blackness is integral. I became curious as to why this story is told in this way and what possibilities arise from its telling. What does this "retroactive significance," as Michel-Rolph Trouillot would put it, tell us about power?[2] How does it impact our understanding of Blackness itself?

To study Blackness in Mexico is to grapple with slippages. Both the panel and its elisions are products of the temporal slippage between the existence of Afro-descendants and their political recognition. Such a misalignment has created the opportunity for Blackness to accrue significance beyond the racial identification framework. For while people of African descent have existed in Mexico for over five hundred years, their modern-day enumeration first occurred in 2015.[3] In the expansive time between existence and categorization, Mexicans have developed various understandings of Blackness both within the dominant ideology of *mestizaje* (racial mixture) and outside of it. While there has been rich discourse on how self-identifying Mexicans of African descent have made sense of their existence in the penumbra of Mexican nationalism, theirs is not the only response to the treatment of Blackness within Mexicanness.[4]

There, too, is the slippage between cultural and political recognition. State recognition of African heritage in Mexico—captured by the phrase *la tercera raíz* (the third root)—predates the recognition of Afro-Mexicans by three decades, with the former occurring in the late 1980s and the latter in the mid-2010s. The third root discourse valorized the African and Afro-diasporic heritage of the Mexican, but not necessarily Afro-descended Mexicans. There are those who have critiqued this approach as an ineffectual form of multiculturalism because it did not make material changes in the lives of Afro-descended Mexicans.[5] From this perspective, the third root could be viewed as a multiculturalism that is little more than "rhetorical gestures" at the "level of recognition and celebration."[6] While this critique has been leveled by scholars and activists alike, not enough attention has been paid to the generative aspects of this early wave multiculturalism. Rather than focusing on what it did not produce—that is, formal recognition of Afro-Mexicans—it is worthwhile attending to what it did create. Within this interstitial moment, there were those who used their Blackness as a resource for other, nonracial group identities more salient to them. This book is about such people.

Among such people, Blackness becomes noticeable whenever it serves as the difference that makes Veracruz and its jarochos different and regionally distinct. It is a story about why the "where are they?" question is never dismissed outright, and about what can be learned when you listen beyond the assertion that "Ya no encuentras negros en Veracruz." What does it mean to say "you will no longer encounter Black people in Veracruz," especially when the person saying it is one of the staunchest proponents of third root discourse? What is to be done with this unmooring of Blackness from Black people? And more importantly, what can this teach us about studying the legacy of the African diaspora in Latin America and beyond?

Over the past few decades, Afro-Latin Americans have made significant progress in gaining recognition and collective rights as minoritized populations within their countries; yet this success has overdetermined what we understand the contemporary legacy of the African diaspora in Latin America to be. By focusing on groups identifying and identified as Black, we overlook alternative manifestations of Blackness in the region. Just as anthropologist Stephan Palmié has argued that "Africanity" and "Blackness" do not necessarily need to map onto each other, neither do Blackness and Black identity.[7] This holds true not only in analyses but also in practice. This is what makes Veracruz such an interesting place. It is a city where cultural politics celebrating Blackness have taken root, nurtured by expectations, nostalgia, and academic research. The fruit it has borne, however, is not a large population that identifies itself as Black; rather, it is a population that identifies with Blackness, proclaiming it a local cultural resource that makes them more jarocho rather than necessarily Black.

As Stuart Hall argues, identification is a process rather than a fait accompli.[8] This is especially important to consider in Latin America, where national narratives have historically overlooked the presence of Afro-descendants and their contributions to national and regional cultures. To assume that self-recognition as Black is the only valid or valuable manifestation of Blackness is to overlook the historical contexts that in many places disallowed the formation of group identity around Blackness. Moreover, it gives short shrift to the holistic impact of Afro-descendants in the formation of the Americas. It invites the presumption that contemporary identifying and identifiable Afro-Latin Americans are the only relevant inheritors of the impact Afro-descendants have made in this hemisphere. It also makes it easier to marginalize that impact along with Afro-descendant populations.

What constitutes evidence of that inheritance varies as locals create the contours of their collective Blackness. At times, evidence is familial, imagined in the stature, hair texture, or facial features of ancestors past or progeny yet to come. Other times, people find proof in their delight in music and dance, their enjoyment of Afro-Antillean rhythms, or their predilection for friendliness, double entendre, and the good life. Most times, tracing the contours of their collective Blackness means emphasizing the Afro-Caribbean contribution to their culture—a contribution popularly captured by the phrase *la tercera raíz*, the third root.

LOCATING MEXICAN BLACKNESS

In this book, you will find familiar words such as *Blackness, Black, Afro-Caribbean, Afro-Mexican,* and *Afro-descendant.* You will also find words perhaps less familiar to you—primarily the term *jarocho* and the phrase *la tercera raíz.* Convention would have me define the latter terms but not the former ones, with the assumption that the first are understood because of their common usage. This is an error. It is true I will commit much of the book to unpacking the word *jarocho* (see chapter 1) and the phrase *la tercera raíz* (see chapter 3).

However, the meanings of the first list of words, although they are written in English, are not as self-evident as we may want them to be. Firstly, we must be on guard for what Lorgia García Peña has called "hegemonic blackness," which universalizes the US context and Anglophone experience. "Hegemonic blackness," García Peña argues, is a distorted lens through which global Black experiences are "understood, analyzed, engaged, and translated around the world."[9] The universalizing tendency is the "cultural imperialism" Pierre Bourdieu and Loïc Wacquant warned against.[10] Yet while their intervention stresses the need to historicize how language and concepts such as race and racism travel across contexts, it is equally important to understand these concepts are not merely the product of "research carried out by Americans and by Latin Americans trained in the USA," but are also particular—and lived—realities.[11]

Secondly, while words like *Blackness, Black, Afro-Caribbean,* and *Afro-descendant* shade into each other, they are not wholly interchangeable. Slippages exist in both practice and analysis, within and across scholarly literature, not to mention in everyday life. Sometimes, words on the page fail to capture the context and the messiness of lived experience. In Veracruz, for example, people who—based on context clues—are speaking about the same phenomenon will use different words to reference it. A new list of words: *lo afro, lo negro, lo caribeño*. In this phrasing *lo*, when translated into English, becomes the turn of phrase "that which is," making those phrases read "that which is Afro," "that which is Black," "that which is Caribbean," respectively. "Afro," "Black," and "Caribbean" also overlap to large degrees, but they are not the same, either. For example, "Afro," whose usage aligns with Africanity in that it includes not just Africa but also its diaspora, sometimes references heritage, but other times references people. This slippage complicates the meaning of "Afro," and it is not a trivial distinction.

Heritage, as this book argues, is a cultural resource that is not necessarily appropriable to a racialized group. To use the same term to identify a category or type of people moves away from a heritage framework toward an identity one. While there are Mexicans who may identify or be identified as "Afro," taking for granted their existence as a group is a form of what Rogers Brubaker called "groupism." It is the tendency to treat such people as a collective entity with attributable interests and agency.[12] While Brubaker cautions against groupism more generally, it is certainly not practicable in Mexico, where official recognition of Afro-Mexicans as an ethnic category has only existed since the mid-2010s.[13] But even when not taking for granted the existence of such a group, sometimes called Black Mexican, other times Afro-Mexican, there remains the presumption that such a group *ought* to exist. The rhetorical move to use *afro* and similar terms as both heritage and identity not only conflates the two but presupposes the fixedness of Afro-Mexican or Black subjecthood.

The ethnographer Christian Rinaudo calls this tendency toward groupism a characteristic "paradox" of Afro-Mexican studies. The absence of an "ethnic sense" among Black populations in Mexico animates much of the scholarship, yet such a group still serves as the object of study.[14] While some scholars focus on the cause of this absence, others attend to its consequences. As an alternative, Rinaudo advocates attention to "the work of ethnicity" and to how ethnic categories emerge and under what circumstances and contexts they become useful. As he argues, focusing on categories instead of groups allows one to analyze "the emergence, diffusion, appropriation, or rejection of categories like 'negro,' 'moreno,' 'afromestizo,' 'afromexicano,' 'afrodescendiente,' 'afroandaluz,' 'afrocaribeño,' not to mention categories that designate local belonging such as 'jarocho,' to cite just one example."[15]

In *Local Color*, I follow both Brubaker, in his insistence that we move away from such reifying moves and instead focus on processes, and Rinaudo, in his intervention that new avenues of thinking are available in Afro-Mexican studies when we look beyond "groups," "populations," "communities," and "identities." This means, rather than thinking of race, ethnicity, or nation, we consider racialization, ethnicization, and nationalization, respectively. It requires, as Brubaker advocates, a shift from groups to groupness and a commitment to "treating groupness as variable and contingent rather than fixed and given."[16] Rather than trying to limit "that which is *afro*" to those who are Afro- or Black Mexican, *Local Color* focuses on the ways and the consequences of identifying certain Mexican cultural forms as related to *lo afro*.

What is more, "that which is *afro*" very often is "that which is Caribbean" in Veracruz. Interlocutors would more commonly identify something as *afro* while discussing a cultural form or antecedent that they trace to the Caribbean. This is partly because the third root discourse on the national level references Africa while its local iteration focuses on the Caribbean.[17] However, the association between the Caribbean and Blackness predates the multicultural turn and its inclusion of the third root in the narration of Mexico, Mexicans, and their culture.

In so doing, I build upon the work of Latin Americanist scholars more broadly, who have grappled with the variability and contingency of "Black" in other contexts, especially when translating from the Spanish word *negro* to the English word *Black*.[18] A major source of confusion lies in the slippage between *negro* as a color label and *negro* as a racial identity. As Tanya Golash-Boza has explored in her work based in Peru, race and color are materially distinct in their ability to foment feelings of groupness. She distinguishes the two by observing how race is a social category imposed from the outside and constitutive of a group, while color is a label that does not create group-based identity.[19] The former is mutually exclusive and references a group with common physical, cultural, and ancestral traits. The latter lacks mutual exclusivity and describes a phenotypic spectrum.

Despite these analytical distinctions, in ordinary conversations individuals use the term *negro* as both identity and a color label, often in the same sentence or conversation. Sociologist Christina Sue has argued that their entangled and interconnected relationship means that, in order to understand racial dynamics, one must address color—which is shorthand for a range of phenotypic markers such as skin tone, hair texture, eye color, and facial features. Ultimately, Sue argues, because identity and color are so enmeshed, color must be treated as a manifestation of race.[20] However, this entanglement does not make the two interchangeable.

Treating color as if it were always race by another name presumes that color labels or descriptors always foment a sense of group identity. In my experience, this is not reliably the case. While I agree with Sue that color is particularly important in Mexico because race purportedly is not, I am less than convinced, as I make evident in the chapters that follow, that inconsistent color labeling signifies racial fluidity. The translational slippage between *negro* as a color label and *negro* as a racial category requires great caution. An articulation of one's color is neither a proclamation nor a disclamation of one's racial identity.

Even within Spanish-language scholarship, the question of terminology is contested. Mexican anthropologist and public scholar María Elisa Velázquez has identified four main lexical camps for referring to the same population and topic.[21] When Gonzalo Aguirre Beltrán, the founding father of Afro-Mexican studies, began his research in the mid-twentieth century, he used *negro o mulato* as a single phrase as well as the term *afromestizo*, alongside its analogues *euromestizo* and *indiomestizo*. Velázquez associates the phrase *tercera raíz* with another prominent figure in the field, the historian Luz María Martínez Montiel. As the first Mexican Africanist scholar, Martínez Montiel has worked to disseminate knowledge about the Africanisms present not only in Mexico but also throughout Latin America and the Caribbean.[22] Without Martínez Montiel's academic and public scholarship, the third root would not be the common turn of phrase it is today. However, despite the recent conflation of the third root with the political aspirations of Afro-Mexicans, these were not always synonymous terms. Velázquez notes that the term *afromexicano* (Afro-Mexican) began to gain traction only in the 1990s, and by the end of that decade, historians and other scholars began to employ *poblaciónes de origen africano* (populations of African origin) or *afrodescendientes* (Afro-descendants). Thus, while the early scholarship used *negro, mulato*, or *afromestizo*, by the turn of the twenty-first century, new terms were added to the conversation. Crucially, no terms were supplanted. Instead, all these words—not to mention regionally or temporally specific language—have been in use to describe the same referent. *Local Color* embraces this multiplicity of terms.

While individuals' racial identity is not a primary concern of this book, the term *Black* appears throughout this text. When used as a color label, it will be orthographically represented in lowercase—that is, *black*. When I use the word to refer to an ethnoracial sensibility, it is capitalized as *Black*. Rarely is the word used as a noun. Instead, it is adjectival—for example, Black heritage. Locals tend to use *lo afro* and *lo negro* interchangeably, while *lo africano* specifically refers to something they perceive as African and *lo caribeño* refers to Afro-Caribbean ties. Both to capture the fuzziness and to mark the distinctions, I have chosen to use *Black* rather than *African* as the modifier to encompass both Africa and its diaspora. *African* and *Afro-Caribbean* will be used when the distinction is intentionally made. This is an analytical choice, not a reflection of everyday language use among jarochos.

I do not endeavor to contribute to the erasure of that which is African in Mexico, but rather to recognize that some people make ties to the African continent while other people go only as far as the Caribbean. I will at times refer to the "African contribution," particularly when discussing national-level discourse and concerns since the original intention of the third root movement was to celebrate African retentions and Afro-descendant peoples. In Veracruz, this mission has highlighted the Afro-Caribbean heritage specifically, which would be lost if I translated everything as *African*. I have made every effort to reflect the intentions of my interlocutors as I perceived them, but I recognize that in the slipperiness of this language, I may have misunderstood those blurred distinctions.

During the time I conducted the bulk of my research (2014–15), the neologism *Afro-Mexican* was rarely used among my interlocutors. Anthony Jerry, an anthropologist who is interested in questions of citizenship and recognition, offers a clear critique of the term, calling "the project for recognition [of the Afro-Mexican] . . . a methodology of *mestizaje*."[23] In the chapters that follow, I use *Afro-Mexican* to signal state projects of categorization and enumeration. In a move akin to Jerry's, I use *Black Mexican* as a contrast to *Afro-Mexican*, with the former indicating people of African descent in Mexico and the latter a project of "making up people" that aligns with state interest.[24]

Scholarly debates and conventions aside, what struck me most at the time of my research in the mid-2010s was the fact that there was no consistency in usage among my interlocutors. Indeed, based on the wording of censual tools, the federal government itself is still working out the official position on whether, when, or how terms such as *Afro-Mexican, Black*, or *Afro-descendant* should be glossed as the same thing. With that said, this book is not about people who identify as Black, Afro-Mexican, or Afro-descendant. Instead, *Local Color* is about how people identify with what I broadly refer to as "Blackness." I have turned to this term as an umbrella descriptor, which can encompass the various slippages and shades of meaning of "that which is Black," "that which is Afro," "that which is Caribbean," and "la tercera raíz" (the third root).

I am not alone in this move. The word *Blackness* has become quite popular in English-language Afro-Mexican studies over the past decade. Christina Sue, for example, lists Blackness alongside race mixture and racism in the subtitle of her book *Land of the Cosmic Race* (2013), while Jerry titles his book *Blackness in Mexico* (2023), though his subtitle reveals that he is focused on Afro-Mexican recognition and citizenship. These ethnographies published a decade apart and focused on opposite coasts of Mexico both unpack the ideological relationship between Blackness and Mexicanness. Sue investigates how everyday people grapple with their "Blackness" within a national ideology, which is partly but foundationally based on "nonblackness"—"the marginalization, neglect, or negation of Mexico's African heritage."[25] Because of nonblackness, Sue argues, color must be considered as a proxy for race, and we must attend to themes of racial identity and group boundaries, as well as racial discrimination and inequality.[26] Like Sue, Jerry is also interested in the lived consequences of the ideological erasure of a Black presence in Mexico. However, Jerry details how the creation of the idealized Mexican, which he refers to as "the non-Black Mestizo," necessarily relies on the Black subject position within Mexico.[27] He argues against the assumption that Blackness has been inconsequential to the development of Mexican national ideology and instead calls it a "specter in Mexican society" and a type of "dark matter" around which other subject positions develop.[28]

Although these works are distinct in their interests and analyses, both consider Blackness as a conceptual and ideological foil to Mexico's national ideology known as *mestizaje*. While having "multiple, sometimes dissonant, understandings," mestizaje in its broadest strokes was a political ideology developed to create national identity in postrevolutionary Mexico.[29] In creating this identity, elites looked to the colonial *casta* character of the mestizo—the product of Euro-Indigenous mixture—as the avatar of the new nation. Historically, mestizaje has imagined the national community as homogeneous, and therefore, as Sue and Jerry point out, non-Black.

Recently, scholars have challenged this broad view, arguing for a more nuanced consideration about difference within sameness. Anthropologist Peter Wade has argued for a "mosaic" approach to mestizaje, which I find resonates with Mexico's emphasis on regionalized popular culture.[30] Ben Vinson III, in his recent work *Before Mestizaje* (2018), echoes Wade in his assessment that mestizaje "may have opportunistically preserved and created both blackness and indigeneity" in Mexico.[31] Similarly, historian Theodore Cohen tells the story of "how blackness became Mexican after the Revolution of 1910" in his book *Finding Afro-Mexico* (2020), which pushes against the assumption that Mexican nationalists uniformly erased Mexico's African heritage.[32] My use of the term *Blackness* follows these interventions in that it is concerned with heritage, particularly as *los veracruzanos* (Veracruzans) look to the Caribbean.

Since the adoption of the third root discourse in 1989, cultural politics in Veracruz have highlighted its importance within the Afro-Andalusian Caribbean. By approaching Blackness through an emphasis on the port city's Caribbean nature, I cast Blackness as cultural practice and as historical legacy. Following Diana Taylor's argument that identity-as-difference needs to be performed to be seen and Manuel Cuellar's theorization about embodiment and its role in symbolic, material, and physical production, Blackness, as I encountered it and as I explore it, is less about phenotype or political subject position and more about performance and heritage.[33] The performance of Blackness in Veracruz, along with local understandings of it as unique in the context of a broader Mexican heritage, intertwines Mexico's "African root" with transculturated practices from across the Caribbean, but particularly from Cuba. For this reason, Blackness in Veracruz is best understood as local color.

LOCAL COLOR

The title of this book, *Local Color*, is both a play on words and an argument for focusing on the locality of Blackness. The US literary genre of the same name aimed to vividly represent reality through an attention to characteristic features such as manners, dress, and speech. Writers of this late nineteenth-century movement were particularly interested in the environment, the setting, the place itself.[34] They were committed to depicting the influences a place has on the people inhabiting it and were "devoted to capturing the nuances of a particular region . . . and focusing on the distinguishing particularities of that environment."[35] Literary scholar Donald Dike defines local-color writing as "writing that insists upon the special context of the events and characters with which it deals, that insists upon the primary importance of that special context to its meaning."[36] I found a similar insistence on context and place reflected how cultural producers in Veracruz gave primacy to the city's location as a Caribbean port city in Mexico.

The genre's critics often point to its superficiality and sentimentality, but as one of the leading scholars on local color, Robert D. Rhode, argues, the literary movement was both fundamentally romantic, due to its interest in the strange and picturesque, and fundamentally realistic, with its preference for the minute and immediate.[37] While ethnography is not fiction, the ethos of the local colorist resonated with me as I was analyzing my fieldwork. In many ways, local color is reminiscent of that famous anthropological adage of making the strange familiar and the familiar strange. When thinking about race or racial matters, local color and its commitment to context helps one navigate the "fault lines" of this uncanniness especially as it relates to ideas related to race.[38]

When scholars state that race is a social construction, the argument carries with it the understanding that "its significance and the ways in which it is recognized, projected, or contested changes continuously, both historically and in particular locales," as anthropologist John Hartigan has noted.[39] What this book concerns itself with is not quite race, but it is part of the racialization process, part of that social construction. It is groupness, not groupism. And it is deeply imbricated with time and place. Place has a profound impact on processes of racialization, particularly in Mexico. In the absence of official or popular recognition of Blackness in Mexico, locality has been of utmost importance in how people fashion Mexican Blackness. For example, anthropologist Laura Lewis has written extensively on how Afro-descended people in the Costa Chican town of San Nicolás on the Pacific Coast of Mexico use their Indianness to tie them to the nation, as a way to counteract the "otherness" of Blackness.[40] There, locals—who prefer the term *moreno* rather than *negro*—process their identification as a hybrid racial and cultural category through the lens of their community. In other words, they ground themselves in place when they think through their Blackness.

It is not inconsequential that the two coasts of Mexico—both racialized as Black spaces in the national imaginary—have deeply local conceptions of that Blackness. Their parallel reckonings suggest that we consider racial localization as a response to the broader invisibility and denial of Afro-descendants and their contribution in Mexico on the national scale. Racial localization and its various iterations on Blackness also demands critical reflection as the nation moves forward in establishing an Afro-Mexican type intent on hailing these different, locally based consequences of racialization. However, the strategy Lewis observed among the San Nicoladenses would not suit the Veracruzanos in the Port. Firstly, the centrality of Veracruz as a major port city has guaranteed it is always imagined as integral to the nation-state. Secondly, San Nicolás's interethnic tension rooted in land claims is not present in Veracruz. Indeed, indigeneity and Indigenous peoples are less salient to the reputation and image of Veracruz. It is why some question the ordinal number "third" of the third root as misleading. Blackness, many would tell me, should be the first root.

This is not a new phenomenon, nor is it merely a response to recent cultural politics. Take, for example, the impressions of Veracruz in 1939 as written by the Spanish poet and exile Juan Rejano in his book *La esfinge mestiza*, which was published in 1945. Even as he wrote of its Mexican essence, he makes mention of the evident "mulata charm, the wit, the glimmer of Black blood" of the city, commenting, "There are moments, without knowing why, one has the impression that Veracruz is the entrance to a country where the *mestizaje* has been done not by the Indians but by Black people."[41] Indeed, Rejano's observations are more akin to *mulataje* than mestizaje. If the latter presupposes a Euro-Indigenous mixture, the former takes as its base the *mulato*, the offspring of African and European parentage. As mestizaje is the organizing ideology of Mexico, mulataje is "a particularly Caribbean response to the cult of *mestizaje*."[42] Nowadays, the Caribbean aspect, or *lo caribeño*, of contemporary Veracruz is largely cultural and cultivated. One still gets the impression that mestizaje in the city was done with Black people because of that cultivation. Veracruz's inclusion in the Caribbean is the lens through which its Blackness is read. Therefore, Blackness, which is normally understood as racial, becomes regional in this context.

The city of Veracruz understands its Black heritage to be simultaneously local and cosmopolitan rather than rural and, consequently, Afro-Caribbean rather than Afro-Mexican. The Afro-Caribbean and Afro-Mexican differentiation further distinguishes the jarocho from the other types of persons imagined as Black in Mexico. In other words, Veracruz's role as a major port city has dictated its Blackness. As Angela Castañeda has characterized it, Veracruz is "an open window to the Caribbean."[43] Yet for decades, it was an even wider threshold—an open-access port through which goods and people flowed, creating intimate relationships and fictive kin between jarochos and other Caribbean populations.

Whereas Paul Gilroy conceives of the Black Atlantic as ships in motion, we must also consider ships in port, both metaphorically and literally. For it was not through the crisscrossing of the Atlantic alone that these transatlantic ties were forged. The ships, he argues, were "the living means by which the points within the Atlantic world were joined. They were the mobile elements that stood for the shifting spaces in between the fixed places they connected."[44] However, mobile as they are, ships do not always move; and the fixity of their ports of call vis-à-vis the ships does not mean a fixity within the port cities themselves.

The dynamism of these fixed places delimiting the Black Atlantic makes for a unique ethnographic stage from whence to view Blackness. Anthropologist Henk Driessen muses that port towns have been underexamined in anthropology because the "passage, transience, openness, and flux" of such places run counter to the discipline's "emphasis on regularity, continuity and tradition, on the orderly and circumscribed, and on small-scaleness."[45] Yet developing a "sense of place," a practice of dwelling in such flux, is still possible. Dwelling, as Keith Basso expounds, emphasizes the "lived relationships" people develop with places and through which spaces become meaningful.[46] These relationships manifest in the stories we tell ourselves, the built environment we traverse, and the activities in which we engage with regularity and in community. Basso argues these actions not only conjure one's sense of place; they also inform one's sense of self.[47] Place-making and self-making, in short, are co-constitutive. They are also processual.

Processes of attachment and place-based association are part of the broader phenomenon of racializing place. Race is in practice a local affair. Anthropologist Jacqueline Nassy Brown has noted that the pursuit of diaspora through place and localness deserves more attention.[48] Whereas localness among Brown's inter-locutors in Liverpool—another port city—often conjures past realities to make contemporary claims to place through race, localness serves a different function in Veracruz. There are no specific sites in Veracruz where one can find Black people or commemorate Black culture—though the neighborhood of La Huaca has attempted to take that mantle. Instead, Blackness is constantly instantiated through the actions of individuals in the city. These actions occur in specific loca-tions, to be sure, but the sites themselves do not conjure recollections of past Blackness. Rather, the city as a whole carries a dispersed, reputational Blackness that colors how people reckon with their own relationship to it.

In treating place as foundational to understanding race, *Local Color* builds on the important work of numerous scholars of Afro-Latin America who highlight the mutually co-constitutive relationship between race and space.[49] It follows what George Lipsitz has described as "The lived experience of race [having] a spatial dimension, and the lived experience of space [having] a racial dimension."[50] For example, Juliet Hooker has demonstrated how the racialization of a region within a nation as Indigenous or Black has contributed to that region's reputation as infe-rior or savage. At the same time, the spatialization of race designates particular regions as the location of specific races, thus purifying the rest of the nation.[51] We see both of these processes at play in Veracruz. The city has been racialized as open, carefree, and sensual—all traits that are also associated with (Afro) Carib-beanness. Likewise, because Afro-descended peoples in Mexico have been spatial-ized as coastal folks, the coastal regions have been the focus of third root discourse efforts (see chapter 3).[52] In Veracruz we see how the spatialization of race and the racialization of space influence each other. The expectation that Veracruz is a key site of Mexican Blackness has created the conditions that have made possible its commitment to valorizing Afro-Caribbean practices, which in turn serve as justi-fication for its reputation.

This "looping effect" makes evident the process of invention and social con-struction.[53] As anthropologist Isar Godreau demonstrates in *Scripts of Blackness* (2015), local and institutional representations are political and intentional rather than neutral and natural.[54] In a critical intervention on the anthropological scholarship of Afro-Latin America, she exposes the danger in tying Blackness to particular places, a tendency she refers to as "emplacement." She argues this inclination "circumscribes" Blackness to place and as a result renders it pure, homogeneous, and outside the nation.

While *Local Color* gives primacy to place, it is not about emplacement. Instead, it captures what develops in response to state and scholarly efforts to emplace Mexican Blackness within the city itself. If emplacement tracks the top-down implementation of the spatialization/racialization dynamic, *Local Color* focuses on its uptake as a dialectic and discursive process. Specifically, it considers how these narratives facilitate a project of belonging, rather than how they serve as discursive technique of othering.

By using Blackness in the service of claims to local belonging in a port city, people in the Port construct it not merely as a quality but as *qualia*. By qualia, I follow Lily Hope Chumley and Nicholas Harkness's rumination on the term and their insistence not on the physical and material properties of things (qualities), but rather on how those qualities matter to people, how they experience and reflect on what they perceive those qualities to be (qualia).[55] Blackness as an abstraction is not inherently local, but in this context, it functions as qualia in that it takes the "embodied, conventional, and experienceable" form of localness in the city.[56] In other words, the way jarochos in the Port think about their Blackness could not have developed elsewhere in Mexico.

In essence: Veracruz matters. My decision not to "chase" Blackness into the hinterland, but rather to attend to the local fruit borne of the third root discourse, elevated Veracruz from mere setting to critical context. It would be impossible to anonymize the location because the location is integral to the phenomenon in question. While Blackness exists throughout the Mexican Republic, the third root discourse through which jarochos in the Port came to understand their Blackness was tailored to the specific historical legacies and cultural practices of Veracruz. The state-sponsored narrative painted Veracruz as a "Black place" not because it had "Black people," but rather because it had a strong Afro-Caribbean character. Discourse located and naturalized these Afro-Caribbean traits in behaviors (such as irreverence, happiness, openness, and laziness) and customs (such as dance and musical acumen) associated with Veracruz. In the process, these characteristics served regionalized ends while retaining their racialized reputations. This transformation allowed Veracruz to embrace Blackness as something one identifies *with* rather than as something one identifies *as*.

How scholars have sought to make sense of Afro-Mexico, and of the processes of localizing race and racializing the local, has been bifurcated along geographic and disciplinary lines, according to historian Theodore Cohen. Whereas historians tend to focus on the port cities of the Gulf and Caribbean coasts, ethnographers have traipsed to the Pacific Coast.[57] Cohen traces the beginning of this intellectual genealogy to Gonzalo Aguirre Beltrán, who could only have imagined the proliferation of the field when he wrote his first text on Afro-Mexico, *La población negra de México, 1519–1810*, in 1946. In the intervening years, scholars in Mexico and from around the world, representing a wide range of disciplines, have contributed to our understanding of Afro-descendants in Mexico and their impact on the making of Mexico across time and throughout the country. Historian Ben Vinson III has argued that the expansion of Afro-Mexican studies can be schematized along three tracks. One track uses the Mexican case study to think broadly on themes such as slavery, freedom, and Blackness. Another, he argues, seeks to understand how Blackness meshed with colonial and postcolonial hierarchies. He characterizes the third track as a continuance of the path Aguirre Beltrán carved nearly a century ago—an attempt to "understand how blackness fits into the larger, postrevolutionary national discourse of *mestizaje*."[58] Vinson describes this track as one in which scholars emphasize "the spaces for the survival and transformation of African cultures" through a transcultural and syncretic lens.

Vinson conceived of this three-track schema when considering historical studies, yet the heuristic is generative for thinking ethnographically as well. Because these three tracks have dominated the scholarship on Afro-Mexico, they have also influenced the narratives disseminated as public history. The most dominant track in public discourse is arguably the emphasis on how Blackness fits within mestizaje. This is, after all, the political promise of the third root discourse. However, because the third root discourse in Veracruz relies heavily on presenting scholarship to the local population, the division of labor Cohen observes between historical and ethnographic inquiry is actually reproduced in the public programming on offer in the port city. Through ethnography, *Local Color* is able to examine how those narratives travel across a broad popular audience.

ENGAGING JAROCHO PUBLICS

Not everyone from Veracruz thinks about Blackness in a meaningful way. The city, after all, is the largest municipality in the state, with a population of over half a million residents. Amid this vibrant and growing populace, there are self-selecting communities of people who seek out social interactions where they can learn, perfect, perform, and reflect on cultural practices and norms associated with the jarocho stereotype. I call these affinity groups "jarocho publics," and they are the communities on which this work focuses.

Jarocho publics cohere around either places or practices. Such places include public squares and cultural centers, both independent and state sponsored (see map 2). They also form around practices such as musical, dance, and festive traditions. As such, jarocho publics are both concrete audiences bound by an event or a physical space and individuals sharing a discursive language in common. This language often focuses on themes associated with the city, such as Afro-Caribbean musical genres or folkloric tradition. The circulating discourses are at once academic and popular, its authors ranging from poets and aficionados, chroniclers and scholars, to musicians and maestros, dancers and bystanders. In a cosmopolitan and dynamic city such as Veracruz, jarocho publics are a way to conceptually frame the fluid communities that consist of regular attendees, occasional visitors, and spectators.

In Veracruz, where the festival schedule is perennial, the fandangos monthly, and the free live music nearly daily, there is a lot to draw one's attention. It is in the air, carried on the breeze traveling through old *callejones* (alleyways), flanked by buildings made of coral. It is on the airwaves emitting from the XEU radio tower, on vinyl signs draped in view of major thoroughfares, on the biweekly calendars of events posted by the tourism office (figure 1). It is on the tips of both fingers and tongues, as those in the know share an irregularity in the schedule of events that is otherwise filled with standing engagements. Despite this pervasiveness, there are those who live, work, and love in the port city who consider themselves jarochos but do not actively participate in these "jarocho publics." Nevertheless, they cannot avoid passively participating in the Afro-Caribbean discourse. Moreover, belonging to a public, as Michael Warner argues, can be as simple as merely paying attention and need not be a permanent state of being. There are countless opportunities to pay attention—however fleetingly—in Veracruz. The Port is a place that constantly tells itself and others about itself. It ranks among what anthropologist Shannon Dawdy calls "antique cities."[59] Like New Orleans and the Port's sister city, Havana, part of its appeal is its remnants of an older way of life in contrast to modernism. These cities' imagined communities are quite declarative, fashioning themselves as "a package of self-reinforcing representations and practices."[60]

Jarocho publics manifest where those affinity groups who practice and support the cultural activities considered to be iconic to the Port gather. They are the public spaces in which the jarocho-ness of Veracruz is on display for tourists' eyes and those who participate in spaces organized around self-reflective discourse about their jarocho-ness. Jarocho publics constitute overlapping communities in Veracruz. In public spaces, for example, music foments the connection. Places like the Veracruz Institute of Culture and its sponsored events generate their own publics, as do the various workshops where people can learn how to play the music or perform the dances most associated with the Port's culture. Such publics are at once concrete audiences, bound by an event or a physical space, and spaces of discourse that are circularly organized by the discourse itself.[61] This public-making discourse simultaneously centers on the musical genres and members of the public who recognize themselves in the music. For example, the emphasis on Afro-Caribbean music that jarochos laud as distinctive to the region works to racialize the city itself and consequently provides an avenue for individuals to access what they perceive to be their Blackness. The most prominent centers of gravity for jarocho publics include *son jarocho*, Afro-Antillean genres, and public programming and events.

FIGURE 1. An advertisement for the 2012 International Afro-Caribbean Festival in the process of being hung from the side of the Veracruz Institute of Culture (IVEC), as seen from the street. Photo by the author.

Tracking the discourse about Blackness in Veracruz—as opposed to search-
ing for Black Veracruzanos—led me to public spaces and public talks and to four
main affinity groups. Those groups include *fandangueros, danzoneros,* culture
enthusiasts, and dancers. Fandangueros are enthusiasts of the folkloric tradition
of son jarocho. Danzoneros are dancers dedicated to the Afro-Cuban ballroom
dance the *danzón.* Both groups regularly interface with third root discourse as
they practice their respective artistic pursuits. Regular attendees of festivals and
academic forums organized by the state and private interests consume narratives
about the Blackness of Veracruz and actively participate and supplement those
stories. Dancers both knowingly and unwittingly affirm that the third root is not
just in the past but is also thriving in the present. Through their actions, these
participants constantly instantiate and presence the Afro-Caribbean heritage of
the Gulf Coast city.

Jarocho publics engage in the *rescate* of Blackness in all its multivalence. The
Spanish verb *rescatar* alternately means to rescue or save, to recover, to retrieve,
and to revive. Jarocho publics have rescued Blackness from the obsolescence
all too commonly associated with mestizaje; recovered and retrieved their local
Blackness through archival resources; and revived the long-standing association of
jarochos with Mexico's Black popular culture. Consequently, the Afro-Caribbean
heritage serves as a cultural resource to better practice the expected jarocho character; to make them distinct within the Mexican nation; and to make them a part
of the larger Afro-Andalusian Caribbean. As a result, Blackness is integral to the
jarocho. In this way, the third root has deeply implanted in Veracruz, and through
the labor of such enthusiasts, it continues to bear fruit.

These jarocho publics presence their Blackness through the reiterative nature
of practice, be it narrative recitation or corporeal repetition. Through practice,
Blackness becomes familiar to both practitioners and their audiences. This in
turn strengthens the locals', visitors', and scholars' expectations to find Blackness
in the port city. While many of these publics have a performance facet through
shows, competitions, and presentations, jarochos manage their expected Blackness beyond the performance space. While performative, the idea of performance
itself suggests a fleetingness, as it "becomes itself through disappearance."[62] In
contrast, Blackness in Veracruz becomes itself through its various repetitions and
recitations. The narratives of the jarocho's character, genealogies of cultural practices, and liberating structure of collective music and dance all recover, recuperate, and revitalize an afromestizo past, and in so doing presence it and project it
into the future.[63] By grounding Blackness in this way, jarochos make it available
to everyone engaged in jarocho publics. You may not become Black, but you can
become jarocho.

The places where people most commonly discuss Blackness are regularly
scheduled gatherings, even if the explicit mention of the third root is unpredict-
able. Jarocho publics organize around scenarios where references to Blackness

may arise without notice, but always within context. These scenarios make sense as sites to study Blackness in Veracruz because they are where jarochos make sense of their third root. According to Diana Taylor, the scenario is a "meaning-making paradigm" that not only "structures social environments, behaviors, and potential outcomes" but also serves as a "portable framework" that through its cumulative repetitions "makes visible, yet again, what is already there: the ghosts, the images, the stereotypes."[64] These scenarios in Veracruz span fandangos, public dancing, and festivals. They gather people and presence Blackness. They are where I focused my attention.

The bulk of my research occurred between 2014 and 2015. However, my first encounter with the city was in 2011 and my most recent in 2024, while finishing this book. My long association with the city has impacted my perspective on the events immediately preceding and following national recognition. For three summers prior to my long-term fieldwork, I established my presence in a son jarocho workshop space, familiarized myself with the public spaces of Veracruz, and developed relationships with the cultural promoters in the city. In the fieldwork between 2014 and 2015, I added the danzonero community to my field of activities. On my return visits post-2015, I continued to participate in the communities where I met my interlocutors. At first, especially between 2016 and 2017, I was interested in the impact the 2015 mid-census survey may have had on my interlocutors. However, I eventually realized the historical specificity of that moment is an integral part of the analysis. Therefore, while my personal connection to Veracruz and its jarochos has given me a deep understanding and appreciation of local practices and the changes across time, the analysis cleaves closely to the time before and after 2015.

The warp and weft of social relations within the city's cultural scene dictated my encounters. As someone interested in how people received and used the third root discourse, I sought out spaces and communities where that discourse prevailed. My comportment in such portable frameworks involved engaging with the third root as the jarochos did. For example, at public talks I was an audience member; at fandangos I was a musician adding my instrument to the convivial space. In classes I was a fellow student who followed the teacher's instructions, and in public spaces I watched the action.

Often, my association with prominent members led to quick acceptance among the broader community members. Likewise, simply showing up consistently to the same space led to familiarity among regulars that evolved into conversations. For example, I first encountered the son jarocho scene through an introduction by mutual acquaintances to a well-regarded musician. Based on his suggestion, I attended a *taller* (son jarocho class) that met twice weekly during one of my preliminary fieldwork visits. For two summers, I would return to that group to practice *sones* (musical pieces) and socialize (see chapter 3). Based on that familiarity, I was already a known entity when I rejoined the group full time during my long-term field work from 2014 to 2015.[65] The regulars of this group became my core interlocutors, though I met a wide variety of son jarocho enthusiasts through the fandango scene. Some of these regulars were also how I came to be familiar with and within the public space known as La Plazuela de la Campana (see chapter 4). Every Thursday after class we would get a *cafecito* before heading to the Plazuela—or La Campana, as it's colloquially known—to hear the Pregoneros del Recuerdo play their set.[66]

I also entered the danzonero scene as a student, though I joined without sponsorship. As with the son jarocho group, I opted to stay primarily with one group rather than shallowly engaging with a wide variety of groups. This was for two reasons. First, the class schedule was the primary mode of engagement. By consistently attending class and learning choreography together, I was able to build rapport. Secondly, because allusions to the third root are often contextual, "deep hanging out" with the same people both provided the opportunity to be present for such spontaneous discussions and built the intimacy needed to discuss racial matters on a personal level.[67] However, like the fandango scene, enthusiasts of the danzón regularly meet for both social dances and competitions.[68] As someone who learned the danzón, I was able to integrate into these situations and was invited to social gatherings outside of the hobby space.

In addition to these personal relationships, my time in Veracruz consisted of observing and recording public speech acts. Because I was interested in official discourse and its reverberations, much of my schedule followed the cultural programming by the Veracruz Institute of Culture (IVEC). My first visit to the city, in 2011, coincided with that year's International Afro-Caribbean Festival. Through attending events, I met staff members of IVEC, who would go on to sponsor my research, inform me of events, and introduce me to other scholars, academics, and cultural producers. By becoming a regular attendee of events, I was able to meet citizens interested in learning about their local culture and history.

Whether learning chord progressions or choreography, gossiping and people watching at open-air night scenes, or actively listening to presentations, questions, answers, and discussions, jarocho publics unfolded through everyday (night) life. My approach derived from a commitment to groupness rather than groups themselves. If I were studying Black Mexicans, I would be interested in groups and taking for granted the existence of such a collective. However, in studying Blackness, this "Blackness without Black people," I was studying a groupness formed around jarocho identity. Such an approach treats groupness as contingent and allows us to think of groupness as "an event," as something that "happens."[69] In this way, Blackness becomes something that facilitates that feeling of cohesion among jarocho publics. Individuals access their Black heritage while performing their jarocho identity, be it through consuming Afro-Caribbean narratives about Veracruz or participating in the revitalization and continuation of folkloric or popular practices. In other words, Blackness becomes a perspective on their world, a way to interpret and represent their regional character.[70] It is Blackness within the paradigm of mestizaje.

ON WRITING THE BEFORE IN THE AFTER TIMES

I wrote *Local Color* in a post-2015 world, but its contents recount Blackness in a time and place uninvolved with the categorization and enumeration of Afro-Mexicans. The 2015 mid-census survey, state and federal constitutional changes, and the full census count of Afro-Mexicans in 2020 have ushered in new possibilities for what it may mean to be Black, Afro-Mexican, or Afro-descendant in the mestizo nation.[71] This shift was not on the horizon for either me or my interlocutors. Instead, the book focuses on cultural politics valorizing Black heritage in its maturation and prior to its evolution.

While what it means to be Afro-Mexican is currently a work in progress, discourse on Mexican Blackness in Veracruz was well-established at the time of my research. The new political possibilities have unsettled these familiar approaches. The sensation is not unlike the feeling you get when you stand planted in the overly saturated, silken sand at water's edge. As the tide goes in and out around you, the sea alternately robs you of and gives you sand, taking the ground from under you and depositing new layers atop you. The waters giveth and they taketh away. You have not moved, but the world has moved around you. You sink into shifting sands.

The "ethnographic problem" of Blackness in Mexico has indeed shifted radically from the conception of this project to its fruition. As anthropologist Stephan Palmié has observed, ethnographic problems lead curious dual lives in which not only they themselves change but also the epistemic moment in which we approach them changes. Palmié implores us to embrace the fact that ethnographic inscription is "the situated and contingent crafting of representations of a no-less-situated and contingent world out there."[72] What is more, these situated and contingent representations are consumed in epistemic moments beyond our control or ken.

As political discourse increasingly treats the third root as proprietary to self-identifying Afro-Mexicans, it is important to embrace the radical nature of what people in Veracruz did with the received knowledge of their Black heritage. In the absence of self-identifying Afro-descended *groups*, the port city recreated Blackness in its own, collective image. The Blackness could not be disentangled from the jarocho. It was foundational. Now, as politicians court constituent groups of their own making, the Blackness within Veracruz is something to be "protected," as if it were in danger (see conclusion). On the contrary, it was quite well supported by social fact and state-based programming. What was overlooked were self-identifying Black Mexicans, not Mexican Blackness. Therefore, while the discourse and political animus has shifted toward what is to be done after enumeration "made visible" millions of Mexicans now able to proclaim themselves Afro-Mexican, it is important to hold space for what came before it.

Local Color is an ethnographic study of jarocho publics in the interstitial moment between two different multiculturalist agendas regarding Mexican Blackness—an established approach of valorizing Blackness as a cultural contribution and a growing call to quantify and recognize Afro-Mexicans as a population entitled to collective rights and reparative justice. This unique moment provides the opportunity to critically address how cultural producers and their audiences shape what Blackness can and does mean. Whereas most research on contemporary Afro-Latin America focuses on self-identifying Afro-descendant communities, *Local Color* examines what conceptions of Mexican Blackness do for individuals as they construct their regional identity within the hegemonic narratives of mestizaje. It does so by giving attention to communities of people who identify with their Blackness, but do not necessarily identify as Black. In the process, it challenges two opposite interpretations: that they are either engaging in inappropriate appropriation of a culture that is not their own or that such individuals are in denial, engaged in racial distancing, or merely acting expediently within the neoliberal frameworks of multiculturalism. Instead, it ethnographically tracks how individuals make sense of their locale and their place within it through ideas about collective Blackness. It delves into the conditions that made possible the encounter recounted in the prologue, one in which a jarocho chose to spend his leisure time learning about the Blackness of his city yet located Black people elsewhere.

In short, *Local Color* is a study of how living in a racialized space conditions the ways in which locals vivify, reference, and appropriate their Black past to constitute themselves as regionally distinct within their nation. It builds on literature about the racialization of place and the spatialization of race in Latin America, while intervening in the methodological assumption that only Black communities can teach us how Blackness functions in Latin America today. Delimiting research on the contemporary legacy of the African diaspora in Latin America to groups who currently self-identify or present as Black disregards the long history of individuals grappling with the tension between Blackness and Latinness. Engaging with communities like the jarochos in Veracruz provides a critical lens for understanding both the significance of Blackness beyond Black identity and the dialectic between state and regional cultural politics. It argues that the slippage between expectations and self-conception provides a unique perspective on alternative manifestations of Afro-Latin America.

Although the nation officially recognized its Afro-descendant population only in the 2010s, people of African descent have lived, thrived, struggled, and died in the place we now call Mexico for over five hundred years. For the past few decades, this fact has undergirded an important thread of the port city's cultural politics. Still, while the prevailing assumption in Latin America has held that valorizing Blackness would curtail anti-Blackness and ultimately lead to self-identification as

Black, the jarochos in Veracruz challenge this narrative. After years of celebrating *lo afro, lo negro,* and *la tercera raíz,* which I have collectively glossed as Blackness, many people in the port city refer to and claim their Afro-Caribbean heritage with ease. Such persons exceed the quantified population who affirmatively identified as Afro-Mexican for census workers.[73] Many jarochos are curious and knowledgeable about the Blackness embedded in their history, culture, and tradition. What is more, they treat it as integral to what makes Veracruz regionally distinct. From official narratives to self-reflective ones, Blackness functions as one of the features and peculiarities unique to the city and its inhabitants. It has become the difference that makes a difference. Therefore, while other locations in the state may have more *gente de color* than the port city, it is nevertheless the case that in the city of Veracruz, Blackness is a force to be reckoned with.

ORGANIZATION OF THE BOOK

This ethnography places jarochos' racial reckonings with their third root in conversation with the nation's changing orientation toward Blackness. Unbeknownst to my interlocutors and me at the time, the federal government was shifting its attitude toward Mexican Blackness in a way that—while beholden to late twentieth-century concepts of the third root—reoriented toward a more ethnoracial and rights-based approach. This research therefore captures a city and way of life right before its moment of reckoning—the 2015 mid-census survey, which was the first step toward enumerating Afro-Mexicans. It asked, "Based on your culture, history, and traditions, do you consider yourself to be Black, which is to say Afro-Mexican or Afro-descendant?" In order to capture both the similarities and the differences in these two multicultural orientations, the book takes the 2015 mid-census survey question as an organizing framework to emphasize how they overlap and divide.

The book uses this question as a guide, with each chapter unpacking the state's criteria in order to argue that jarochos understand their Blackness as culturally, historically, traditionally, and ancestrally shared, regardless of whether individual jarochos self-identify as Black or Afro-descendant. This convergence of criteria with divergent ends—regional versus racial identification—demonstrates how jarochos made use of Blackness in response to previous multicultural policies and beyond the intentions of current agendas.

Chapter 1, "Veracruz and Its Jarocho," traces the long relationship between the local regional figure of the jarocho and conceptions of Blackness in Mexico. This history contextualizes why the turn toward valorizing Blackness in Mexico was successful in Veracruz. It includes analyses of state documents, travelogues, literary arts, tourism materials, mass media, and popular culture from the colonial period to the present. It demonstrates how Blackness and its relationship to Veracruz has waxed and waned, but never disappeared, throughout major shifts in Mexican racial politics, including independence, the postrevolutionary nation-building project of ideological mestizaje, and the late twentieth-century adoption of multiculturalism. This chapter argues that this enduring affiliation has created expectations that Veracruz and her jarochos are avatars of Mexican Blackness, while it explores how jarochos have reckoned with this expectation by transforming Blackness into a collective, regional quality.

The second chapter, "The Living Past," is a deep exploration of the third root concept and explains the political contexts of its creation, development, and full fruition. It argues that the Black past of Veracruz has become a resource for present conceptions of collective jarocho character. The chapter demonstrates how the tendency to situate Blackness in "the Past" is not a technique jarochos use to distance themselves from Blackness. Rather, it is a strategy to localize the national-level discourse on Mexican Blackness and safeguard it for future implications. This chapter highlights public and private occurrences, when locals explicitly and intentionally center Afro-descendant peoples in the narration of Veracruz's past. It reveals how state-sponsored public programming uses history as a cultural resource for articulating regional identity. In this chapter, I emphasize how the robust discourse about the third root has made Blackness present in the everyday lives of jarochos, despite the lack of collective identity as Black Mexicans.

Chapter 3, "Practicing Innateness," delves into the work involved in performing jarocho stereotypes. It juxtaposes two jarocho publics—fandangueros and danzoneros—in the *taller* (workshop) space to illustrate how academic discourse travels among laypeople with an interest in the origins of their story. I consider *talleres* as sites where the embodied practice and discursive iterations of jarochos' regionalized, collective Blackness converge. The chapter is based on my longtime participation in social settings where jarochos pay for lessons in the folkloric tradition of son jarocho or the Afro-Cuban ballroom dance complex the danzón, to learn how to be "more jarocho." Because of the vibrant interchange and overlap between scholarly interest in the third root and revitalization of local culture, individuals interested in learning jarocho practices have simultaneously learned about the Black heritage integral to those art forms. As key sites where locals articulate their relationship to their Black heritage, *talleres* are crucial encounters where jarochos construct alternative forms of embodying Mexican Blackness not as Black people but rather as jarochos.

The fourth chapter, entitled "Affectations," continues the focus on the work and effort of being oneself beyond the *taller* paradigm. It treats happiness as a racial script and tracks efforts to achieve it. The chapter analyzes leisure practices locals consider jarocho culture—specifically, public dancing to Afro-Antillean musical genres and personal affectations and strivings toward happiness—to argue how everyday practices become evidence for and instantiations of a thriving third root. This chapter focuses on public spaces such as a small plaza with near-nightly live dancing music; the *zócalo*, or main plaza, where tourists consume leisure as regional performance; and state and private cultural centers to argue individuals' personal yet public strivings toward happiness contribute to the racialization of Veracruz as an Afro-Caribbean space.

In the fifth chapter, "Sanguine Blackness," I unpack the use and usefulness of metaphorical "Black blood," as it scales from the familial to the collective. It examines how individuals take the reputational Blackness of the archetypal jarocho and make it specific to their family history as jarochos. Through intimate conversations on genealogical inheritances, I analyze the local concept of the *pringa*, which is both a drop and a stain, to argue that Black ancestry functions as a cultural resource affixed to the jarocho regional type. This chapter interprets how contemporary jarochos project Black ancestry into their past and future and demonstrates how previous metaphors of blood and ancestry found in the hegemonic conceptions of *limpieza de sangre* (blood purity) and *mestizaje* (intercultural and interracial mixture) endure in the contemporary multicultural moment.

The conclusion, "The Jarocho and the Afro-Mexican," is a reflection on how the post-2015 world is a turn in broader understandings of what Blackness means and looks like in Veracruz. I argue the national shift toward counting and politically recognizing self-identifying Afro-Mexicans is significant in both Mexican multiculturalism and racial reckonings with Blackness itself. The conclusion grapples with the new political landscape in which Mexicans can self-identify as Black and ruminates on whether and how jarochos will reconcile their alternative approach to Mexican Blackness with this new emphasis on Black Mexicans. It ends with a question: how will the jarocho reckon with the Afro-Mexican?

In the spirit of the local colorists, in between the chapters I have interspersed short ethnographic anecdotes of encounters I experienced while living in Veracruz. Given that a central premise of the local color genre is the edict that place matters, these interludes serve to give the reader a sense of the place known as the port city of Veracruz. While the interludes themselves are thick description with little analysis, they resonate with the chapters they precede. My intention, through observations about public space or encounters taking unsuspecting turns, is for these anecdotes and character sketches to set the tone for their paired chapters.

With these snapshots—some banal, others singular—I hope to prime you for the substantive analysis that follows. They are, together, ways of reckoning with Blackness. They answer, in their own way, the question "What is Blackness?" It is recognition, yes, but it is more than that. Sometimes, it is a reputation that precedes you. Sometimes it is conjured through divination. It is effort and it is convention. It is romantic and realistic. It is many things, all of them lived and learned locally.

1

Veracruz and Its Jarocho

The city of Veracruz is not the capital of the state that shares its name. Nevertheless, the city and state have a synecdochical relationship that at times results in connotative ambiguity. While I will clarify when I mean the state rather than the city, locals do not always extend that same courtesy. At times, it is difficult to discern when the Veracruz in question is the city or the state. This slippage has contributed to the city's reputation for Blackness. The state has several *pueblos negros* (Black towns), but the city is not one of them. Nevertheless, the cognitive association between Veracruz and Mexican Blackness paints the city with the same brush. This, added to its enduring relationship to the broader Caribbean, has created a city where the reputational strength of Blackness resonates irrespective of demographics.

The port city of Veracruz is a liminal space, betwixt and between the Caribbean region that birthed it and the Mexican nation it helped to birth (see map 1). Rather than considering themselves peripheral to either region to which they lay claim, contemporary Veracruzanos emphasize and center the simultaneity of their Caribbean and Mexican history and culture. By not choosing between the two, Veracruzanos have celebrated both the historical importance of the port city to Mexico and the cultural contributions the Caribbean has given the city. This positionality makes for a rich area to think ethnographically about Blackness and its manifestations in a national context characterized by its absence.

To understand the local significance of Blackness in Veracruz, one must first understand two key things: one, Veracruz's historical and cultural position vis-à-vis the nation and the region; and two, the evolution of the local regional type known as the jarocho. The Port is unlike other regions of the country where

Blackness is presumed to reside. Rather than a rural or marginal location, the city of Veracruz is both a historically significant city and a major domestic tourism destination. Both qualities have fomented a tendency for Veracruzanos to tell themselves and others about themselves. This discursive practice has intensified the impulse to highlight their particularities—their local color. Drawing on their rich history and Caribbean character has made Blackness one avenue toward that distinctiveness. In other words, Blackness has become one of the ways to celebrate their differences. The aim of this chapter is not to provide a comprehensive history of the city or the jarocho. Rather, it interrogates those histories in order to demonstrate how and why contemporary associations of Blackness in the city have been successful.

THE "TYPICAL JAROCHA"

An interesting philosophical disagreement unfolded in the comments section of a 2017 public Facebook post. A mover and shaker in the culture scene I will call "El Vate Veracruzano" used his personal social media account to ask "the artistic community of the Port of Veracruz" to help him find a protagonist for a video he planned to make in commemoration of the city's five hundredth anniversary. The casting call sought a young woman "between fifteen and twenty-five years old, with brown skin and curly hair," who would embody "the typical jarocha."[1] As a poet, dancer, musician, producer, and promoter, El Vate is a known character among many members of the city's jarocho publics, and his ambitions include creating spaces to emphasize the city's Afro-Caribbean character. He has done so through his own civil association, which I will call Artists and Representatives of Edu-cultural Themes (Artistas y Representantes de Temas Educativos, ARTE A.C.), and in collaboration with other organizations and entities such as the Neighbors' Association of La Huaca (la Asociación de Vecinos del Barrio de La Huaca) or the Veracruz Institute of Culture (Instituto Veracruzano de la Cultura, IVEC). For these reasons, his participation in the commemoration effort was unsurprising. However, the Facebook post prompted an unexpected dialogue. Rather than answering the casting call, another well-known personality in the culture scene, who is an academic, raised a concern about El Vate's approach.

In the comments, the academic asked plainly, "Why look for the typical jarocho? Why not show the diversity of ways of being, thinking, feeling, or appearing jarocho or jarocha?"[2] He went on to argue that El Vate himself was as jarocho as anyone else. Implicit in the comment was the fact that El Vate, with his pale skin and russet hair, was the opposite of the image he was curating. As such, perpetuating the jarocho stereotype would be counterproductive to the broader project people like El Vate have dedicated their efforts to celebrate. He concluded his remarks by arguing that one's appearance should form neither a limit nor a requirement for the planned project, reiterating that he was only sharing his opinion, and wishing El Vate success with the enterprise.

In response, El Vate reaffirmed that everyone had a place in the commemorative efforts while also defending the specificity of the casting call on artistic grounds. The video would be a visualization of his poem, which described a woman with the sought-after features. More interestingly, he emphasized that the video would "celebrate also the Afro-descendancy that has little space in visual media and ironically not in videos of Veracruz either."[3] After conceding the academic's point about typicality, El Vate maintained, "we would have maaany [sic] criticisms if the lead were blonde . . . you get me?"[4] In closing, he invites the academic—who *is* brown-skinned—to join them for the filming. While the academic's darker features were not the reason for this invitation, his presence would have served El Vate's visual aims quite well.

This was no mere interaction on Facebook. The crux of the disagreement between the poet and the academic speaks to a broader point about the jarocho figure and its relationship with Blackness. While the original request sought a woman who visually represents an image celebrating Afro-descendancy, no one disagreed that there is much diversity within the jarocho regional type. Their difference of opinion focuses on what is "typical" for this ethnoregional identity marker.[5] Central to this question is whether and how Blackness factors into that portrayal. Both men understand that jarochos are a diverse group of people; both also know representation—especially in a commemorative frame—matters. It is as scholar B. Christine Arce theorized when considering Mexican Blackness and the tendency for Mexico's "nobodies," which is to say Afro-Mexican women, to appear and disappear in the national imaginary. Arce focuses on the aesthetic as a "realm of paramount importance in the production of knowledge and the crafting of history" because it is a space afire with possibility.[6] El Vate, in writing and casting a jarocha with features associated with Blackness, sought to harness the commemorative moment to make an implicit argument about the Blackness of Veracruz. Despite the seemingly crosswise efforts to either typify or diversify the jarocha, both the poet and the academic were well aware of the significance the jarocho figure plays in any telling of the city's story.

The idea of Veracruz began on the wide, level beach called Chalchihuecan, where the conquistador Hernán Cortés landed one Good Friday over five hundred years ago, in 1519. Historian William Prescott remarked of the event, "Little did the Conqueror imagine that the desolate beach on which he first planted his foot was one day to be covered by a flourishing city, the great mart of European and Oriental trade, the commercial capital of New Spain."[7] And while Afro-descendants numbered among those who first disembarked on the beach across from the islet San Juan de Ulúa, it is also doubtful any in that party would have imagined that bustling metropolis would carry with it a reputation for Blackness.[8] San Juan de Ulúa became the permanent site of a deep water port for the Spanish, but the city would move three times in its first century of existence.⁹ Since its return to its original location in 1599, Veracruz has been a vibrant port city.

Colonizers, enslaved Africans, refugees, immigrants, sailors, and visitors have all passed through this main Atlantic port of entry. For centuries, the formerly walled city has served as the introduction to Mexico for many visitors.¹⁰ The nineteenth-century German botanist Carl Sartorius, for example, wrote of his first impressions: "Everything is strange here, the language, dress and complexion of the inhabitants, and the town with its Andalusian-Moorish trappings."¹¹ Another European, the Marquesa of Calderón de la Barca, had a more critical first impression of Veracruz "in all its ugliness" and noted "the sadness of the aspect of this city."¹² The diplomat's wife expressed this sentiment in a private letter from December 1839 that was later published in her famed travel memoir *Life in Mexico* (1843).¹³ Despite her unimpressed opinion of the city, Calderón de la Barca mentioned that "those who have resided here any length of time, even foreigners, almost invariably become attached to it; and as for those born here, they are the truest patriots, holding up Vera Cruz as superior to all other parts of the world."¹⁴ While the "ugliness" and "sad aspect" were attributable to a postwar moment (she arrived months after the Pastry War with France), the patriotism and particularity she observed among inhabitants persists to this day. Indeed, the city of Veracruz is known as Heroica Veracruz (Heroic Veracruz) and holds the designation as four times heroic.¹⁵

Reflections on the city, such as those by Sartorius and Calderón de la Barca, have lives beyond the archive. In 1992 the state government published an eleven-volume compilation of one hundred travelers' impressions of Veracruz state, *Cien viajeros en Veracruz: Crónicas y relatos*, spanning from 1519 to 1983. (Volume 5 has an excerpt from Calderón de la Barca's *Life in Mexico*, for instance.) The anthology is out of print, but the compendium of primary documents translated into Spanish lives on in the citations of several publications, as well as captions in Facebook groups dedicated to Veracruz (both city and state) of yore. Tourists and locals alike can find the coffee-table book, *Veracruz y sus viajeros* (Veracruz and its travelers), in one of the two local bookstores in the downtown area. Then governor Miguel Alemán Velasco outlined the purpose of such a book in his remarks in the front matter. It served as a tribute to mark the hundred-year anniversary since the modernization of the Port. Alemán Velasco predicted it would become "required reading for all who love our history and traditions."¹⁶ The fact remains, though, that lovers of the Port need not read about it at all. As I detail in chapter 2, there is a plethora of cultural programming centered on the city's history and traditions. As these events highlight the past, they also explore what the jarocho is.

Mexicans throughout the republic know and understand the word *jarocho*. However, there is no consensus as to its referent. A working definition would have the jarocho as a person from Veracruz, Mexico, who self-identifies as such. This conflates origins with identity. Yet it is ambiguous as to from which Veracruz one hails—the city or the state? On the national scale, anyone from the state could be a jarocho. Within the state, however, regional identities carry more weight— particularly in the northern area. For example, a person from the state capital of Xalapa would more specifically be a *xalapeño*, rather than the jarocho as broadly defined. The jarocho, in contrast, is from the state's southern region, known as the *sotavento*.[17] To complicate the matter, the Port is varyingly included or excluded from the sotavento region. Therefore being "from Veracruz" may at first seem self-apparent but often requires a nuanced geographical approach.

Another criterion for defining the jarocho is the late twentieth-century best practice of self-identification. Censuses and rights-based policies, for example, rest on the foundation that individuals have the right to identify themselves as they see fit. Yet the categories among which one can choose are not of their choosing.[18] Despite this limitation, the individual is not passive in this situation. The "looping effect" generated between the classification and the classified creates a dynamism to collective identities.[19] However, it is worth noting that the looping effect occurs in instances beyond self-identification. This has been the case for the jarocho, especially as it has outlived the context of its creation and has adapted to the various societal changes that have taken place.

Finally, this definition has the word we are seeking to define within it. To say jarochos are those who identify as jarocho may be a true statement, but it lacks elucidation. When considering a word like *jarocho*, which has existed for centuries, you have the added complication that those who are self-identifying as jarocho may not themselves agree as to what the term means. The geographical dimension alone creates a segmentation effect in which the same person may define the group boundaries differently depending on whether their interlocutor is also from the state of Veracruz. However, because *jarocho* is the demonym for Veracruz, there is a large subset of the population who self-identify as jarocho based solely on where they were born. This ethnography, instead, focuses on jarocho publics. It thinks with those who contemplate their jarocho identity, what it means and how they can actively participate in its meaning making. It is about people like the poet and the academic who think about the jarocho type critically, or at least consciously.

Yet the poet and the academic's disagreement left us with more questions than answers. If defining the jarocho is such an ambiguous task, why is it that the typical jarocha/o is so clear? How can denotation be difficult but demonstration relatively less so? If we are destined to rely on its visuality or its performance, what do we do with the fact that both have shifted markedly over the centuries?

JAROCHO, ETYMOLOGICALLY SPEAKING

When I stopped looking for Black people and started attending to Blackness, my questions changed. I began to ask people: "What does *jarocho* mean?" In reply, people would turn to its etymology. At first, I found this odd. However, I have come to see this response as indicative of how jarocho publics make Blackness into a "useful past."[20] There are, in fact, various theories about the etymological origins of the word *jarocho*. Most allude to Blackness. That contemporary jarochos know and recite this information concretizes the idea that the Blackness of the jarocho has always already been present. Rather than distancing themselves from a "Black past," these recitations treat Blackness as foundational not just to their culture but also to the very name they choose to call themselves.

Interest in the word's origin is not a recent phenomenon.[21] In 1885 the Cuban exile and self-proclaimed "neoveracruzano" (new Veracruzan) José Miguel Macías dedicated his dictionary, *Diccionario cubana, etimológico, crítico, razonado y compresivo*, partly to the people of Veracruz as an offering and a testimony of gratitude, and partly to the Cuban people, his compatriots.[22] In his entry for the term *jarocho*, he defines it primarily as the rural folk of Veracruz's hinterland. Subsequent definitions name the jarocho as "an individual originating from the African race," as a "native of the state of Veracruz," and as that which is "related to the city, the state, or its inhabitants," in that order.[23] Therefore, late into the nineteenth century, the primary meaning of the term focused on the rural folks of the city. Its usage also signified African ancestry, origins in the state of Veracruz, or even a relationship to the city, the state, or its people.

Macías goes on to extensively document various hypotheses regarding the term's origins. After establishing that it does not derive from an indigenous language, he explains that the suffix *cho* signifies its pejorative nature. After that he offers that the first half of the word could derive from one of two Arabic terms: either *jara*, which is a shrub bush species, or *jaro*, which means a reddish color or piebald (dappled black and white) of the porcine family. Macías expresses a preference for the former theory but also sees the validity of the color theory. As he notes, at the beginning the word functioned only as "a generic denomination for those mulatos, chinos, zambos, or lobos, and the rest of the individuals of the Ethiopian and American races with a mixture of Blumenbach's Caucasian." Note how all the various categories—*mulatos, chinos, zambos,* or *lobos*—all applied to people with recognized African ancestry. Therefore, while the word itself might have ambiguous origins, its referent consistently was an Afro-descended person.

Historian Alfred H. Siemens has a variation on this theory. He argues the shrub theory could by extension refer to the *vara*, a herding tool made of such a material. He argues the *vara* tool was the southern counterpart to the uplander's *reata*. Therefore, *vara* would distinguish the person geographically, while also alluding to their occupation as a swineherd.[24] Furthermore, Siemens argues the belief that a jarocho was a repugnant person derived not only from their occupation as a swineherd but also from another Arabic word—*xara*—which means human excrement. While in the various retellings I heard about the word *jarocho*, I never heard about the association with tending pigs, one older person who disavowed the term did so because of her belief that the original jarochos handled human excrement. Instead, most people who mentioned the occupational beginnings of the jarocho focused on a different livestock—cattle.

One of the most repeated theories I heard argued that the *jara* was a herding tool used in the sotavento of the state. In fact, this is one of the theories the City Museum offers when answering the question "Where was 'the jarocho' born?" Cattle were and continue to be a dominant industry in the region. Historian Andrew Sluyter has explored how in the early days of Spanish colonization after the decimation of native populations, the Spanish repopulated the land not with people but rather with tens of thousands of heads of cattle.[25] Among the few thousand colonizers who populated the area in the first century of occupation, people of African descent predominated. According to Mexican scholar Hipólito Rodríguez, between 1640 and 1650, a century after the arrival of the Spanish, of the six thousand inhabitants on Veracruz's coast, some five thousand were of African descent, with about four thousand of them based in the Port.[26] Whereas those in the city primarily worked in port services, commerce, or the militia, those in the hinterland largely tended to the mostly feral cattle. The "dominance of livestock over people" would be the norm throughout the colonial period and into the nineteenth century and contributed to the long association of cowboy culture with Afro-descended populations.[27]

Sluyter argues the African legacy on herding practices in New Spain is undeniable, particularly related to lassoing cattle from horseback, a practice that did not exist in Spain or the Antilles. Cowboys developed this technological evolution in response to growing sanctions against the use of the *desjarretadera*, a sickled herding tool that was used to hamstring feral cattle to bring them to slaughter. With growing meat shortages, colonial authorities banned the fatal method, prompting cowboys to create alternative methods to capture the undomesticated animals. Although Sluyter argues the Afro-descended ranchers moved away from the *jara* and toward the lasso first, because they were the most punished under the new edicts, the relationship between the instrument and the vocation nevertheless suggests the jara-as-stick theory remains racialized in nature.

The museum also offers the theory that jarocho derives from the term *garrocha*, which is a spear. Occupational ties remain if the jara referenced in *jarocho* is not a herding tool but rather a militiaman's tool. Just as the ranch hands were predominantly Afro-descended, the militias of Veracruz and its hinterland boasted a significant percentage of Afro-descended peoples. Although white fighters were the predominant demographic of New Spain's early colonial defenses, people of African descent were a part of the forces since the mid-sixteenth century.[28] In fact, the presence of armed and unarmed Afro-descended auxiliaries dates to the conquest and pacification of the Americas.[29] Thus, for the entirety of the existence of New Spain, there were people of African descent who participated in its defensive forces, from the conquest to the War for Independence. According to scholar Juan Ortiz Escamilla, for most of the colonial period, those people of African descent involved in the militia were identified as "mulatos y negros," but with the Bourbon Reforms of the eighteenth century, they were classified as "morenos y pardos."[30]

Gonzalo Aguirre Beltrán argues the *mulato pardo* group was "without a doubt, the most numerous single group in New Spain" and included a wide spectrum of color descriptions from the color molasses to "color quebrado" (a broken color).[31] In the earliest decades of Spanish colonization, people of indigenous and African descent were labeled as *mulatos* rather than constituting a distinct *género*, or type of person. The historian Robert Schwaller maintains that Afro-Indigenous progeny most likely represented the plurality of the "mulato" population in the sixteenth century despite the current understanding of the term as being Afro-European.[32]

The jarocho was a subset of this broader term. Those who would cite to me theories of herding instruments, spears, and centuries-old disrespect were also quick to inform me of this fact. Jarocho publics of today know that their predecessors were labeled as such not just for their occupation but also—and primarily—for their ancestry. Its original purpose as a term of ascription for mixed-race individuals of primarily African and Indigenous descent is also well-known. While the casta term *zambo* refers to this type of people throughout Latin America, the locally used label was *jarocho*.[33] The eighteenth-century term was simultaneously racialized and regionalized. As Gonzalo Aguirre Beltrán explored, there were several locally distinct labels for this type of mixture: in Michoacán they were "cochos," while in Oaxaca, the preferred term was "cambujos." In Guerrero the word of choice was "zambos," but in Chiapas it was "loros." In Veracruz, they were named "jarochos."[34] As such, *jarocho* was always a hyperlocal term, while nevertheless emphasizing the fact that the terminology referred to the same types of Afro-Indigenous admixture.

While dictionaries offer interesting theorizations of the word's origins, it is important to remember dictionaries do not create terms for general usage; they collect those terms already in use. For that reason, it is worthwhile to consider also how people used *jarocho*, to whom they were referring, and in what contexts. This entails considering depictions of jarochos as well as self-presentations. Jarochos consume, reaffirm, and occasionally rebuff their long-established reputations. That which is jarocho in some ways may be objectified, but the jarochos themselves are also subjects aware of their own vocality.[35]

THE SHIFTING SIGNIFIERS OF THE JAROCHO

Jarochos have proclaimed their uniqueness since at least the nineteenth century, when *jarocho* was still an ethnoracial term for Afro-Indigenous peoples in the southern region of the state of Veracruz. For example, the French traveler Lucian Biart wrote in 1862, "The isolation of the jarochos have made them a people apart, with their own laws, customs, and traditions and they consider their compatriots from other parts of the Republic as strangers that only deserve contempt."[36] By the mid-nineteenth century, according the Mexican historian Ricardo Pérez Montfort, writers from that epoch even marked a distinction between "veracruzanos" and "jarochos," with the former referring to "those who had European blood" and the latter to those "who are a mix of Indian with Black, perhaps with a tiny pint of white blood."[37] This racialized distinction is noteworthy given the time in which the observation occurred, decades after the official abolition of the casta system and after generations of mixture. While a popular ethos holds that the Blackness "mixed out" of the general population, the jarocho as a type continued to give observers the impression otherwise.[38] Even as racialized distinctions fell further by the wayside with the homogenizing efforts of nation-(re)building after the Mexican Revolution, the jarocho retained its association with Blackness.

Pérez Montfort identifies the postrevolutionary moment as a turning point for the jarocho stereotype. In the 1920s and 1930s, many of the nation's regional types began to consolidate into their present-day representations. The folkloric image of jarochos as men in white guayaberas and women in white lacy dresses is a departure from the rural and peasant image of previous generations. The change was not merely sartorial and classist; there was also a shift in the ethnic image of the jarocho. This now classic image of the jarochos emphasized the Spanish—and specifically the Andalusian—root of the jarocho, which facilitated the broadening and flattening of the jarocho stereotype to apply to all veracruzanos from the perspective of outsiders.[39] Crucially, as Pérez Montfort argues, this attempt to whitewash the jarocho was more successful in erasing the Indigenous root. The Black component could not completely disappear and instead became a "distinctive trait."[40] To emphasize his point, Pérez Montfort turns to contemporaneous accounts that demonstrate the perduringness of the jarochos' Blackness. Pérez Montfort identifies mass media as a mechanism by which the stereotypical jarocho as dressed in white became more concrete. Film and radio were the primary outlets, but even then, the Blackness survived. I experienced mass media's impact firsthand one afternoon in the offices above the City Museum.

Although Ramón and I were seated looking at a computer screen in the fall of 2014, he was demonstrating his expertise as a public historian by taking me on a rapid-fire journey through time, spanning three centuries through different media in his personal archive. Ramón started the journey with transcriptions of census records from 1791, quickly ushered us through time to mid-nineteenth-century artwork, and concluded with mid-twentieth-century mass media. His popular history lesson culminated with two video clips he assured me captured postrevolutionary Veracruz. Ramón contextualized the clips as he cued them up from YouTube. The two sources presented two different facets of Veracruz—one from a movie portraying the port city as exotically Caribbean, and the other from a tourism video presenting it as romantically Spanish. As we watched the double feature, Ramón would point to the darker bodies present in the movie while their absence in the travel short spoke for itself.

The film he showed me was *Tierra Brava* (1938) from Mexico's golden age of cinema. Although predating the height of what were known as *cine de rumberas* (woman rumba dancer cinema), the scenes are similarly using what scholar Laura G. Gutiérrez calls "Afrodiasporic sounds and corporeal movements" to render Veracruz a Caribbean and exotic space to the protagonist from Mexico City.[41] Comedic actor Joaquin Pardavé's character, Benito, steps off the 7:40 train from Mexico City only for *pregoneros* (street criers) to immediately accost him as they hawk their wares of coconut, pineapple, limes, and other tropical goods, including rum. One man accompanies his own singing with a maraca as Benito walks away, smoking his cigar. In the following scene, Benito—still with his cigar—observes a group of musicians from his table in the famous *portales* of Veracruz, the outdoor arches alongside the main plaza that are filled with restaurants and bars. When a man from the crowd joins the song's refrain, "I'm going to dance," a woman interjects by singing that he does not know how to dance rumba. She then precedes to dance "the good rumba" with her silent compatriot. Everyone in the scene is fixated on the woman and her partner, but Benito stands up and moves closer for a better view of this impromptu display of local culture, even giving a little shimmy of his own near the end of the song. When she and the musicians begin to leave, Pardavé's character chats her up, only for her to dismiss him and scoff when he expresses ignorance about what a fandango is after she says he can find her and everyone else there.

The "everyone else" in the fandango scene is light-skinned until she and her partner—played by the famous Afro-Cuban rumba partners Rene and Estela (René Rivero Guillén and Ramona Ajón)—enter to perform a rumba in stark contrast to the son jarocho played and danced in the rest of the fandango scene. Their dress and dance style are not the only contrast—they, like the musicians in the earlier scene (including a not-yet-famous Compay Segundo of the legendary Buena Vista Social Club), are the only visibly Afro-Caribbean individuals present. Although Rene and Estela were famous Cuban dancers in the 1930s, their introduction and the musicians supporting their dancing work to naturalize their presence in Veracruz. Not only is the song they sing in the Portales "Rumba en Cubanacán," by the Veracruzan composer Emilio Cantarell, but Estela's remarks to Benito also make a clear insider-outsider distinction reminiscent of Biart's observation of the jarochos' singularity and tendency toward contempt. Benito, as an arrival from Mexico City, is an outsider despite being Mexican, while she and her partner are locals despite the ambiguity introduced by their real-life identity as Cubans. At the same time, however, this golden-age-of-cinema rendering of the jarocho culture also suggests the colonial distinction between the "fandango popular" of the mixed-ancestry "castas" and the "fandango real" that was exclusively for Spaniards and creole-born Spaniards through its stark racial segregation.[42] Nevertheless, it works to present both veracruzanos and jarochos as local to the port city. Moreover, the everyday life of the port city is presented as foreign, unique, and, to a degree, Caribbean.

In contrast, Ramón's second example, a 1946 "Travel Talks" short intended for a US audience, introduced the port city as "more Spanish than any other city in Mexico."[43] In the travel film "Visiting Veracruz," James A. "the Voice of the Globe" FitzPatrick enthusiastically compliments the "imperishable contributions" the "old Spanish conquistadors" brought to Mexico, including "architecture, music, and the spirit of romance." This voice-over accompanies images of blonde-haired women on tiled balconies overlooking roads that still have men on horseback traversing them while cars drive by in the background. With a transition calling locals "a people who know how to entertain visitors," the scene changes to a gaggle of women dressed in the traditional white jarocha costume dancing in two lines. The soundtrack of jaunty classical music clearly does not match the music to which they are dancing. As the camera pans across the scene, it eventually focuses on two young girls also dressed as jarochas. Over this image, FitzPatrick explains, "Folk dancing is an inherent tradition here, for even the children learn to dance as soon as they are able to stand on their feet." The shot of the two toddlers fades into one showing a "happy and carefree bevy of Veracruz maidens who find pleasure in the more simple [sic] diversions of life and take great pride in the preservation of the legends and traditions which they inherited from their ancestors." Unlike today, there was no mention of any of those ancestors being of African descent.

By the end of the twentieth century, the pendulum would swing away from emphasizing the Spanish traits of the jarocho toward focusing on the Afro-Caribbean and to a lesser extent the Afro-Indigenous characteristics. However, the legacy of the mid-twentieth century, when the jarocho became a broad regional type, persists. The jarocho is no longer the ethnoracial label of the colonial and postcolonial period. Neither is it a primarily Spanish type with a touch of African blood. Instead, it is a regional type within the wider republic that distinguishes itself from the other regional identities in part through its Blackness. In this way, the jarocho remains the relevant group identity, with Blackness serving as a feature delimiting the contours of that group. Because the jarocho identity can be quite expansive, not all who would call themselves jarocho know about or consider Blackness and its relationship to jarocho identity. Those who do, however, have learned to use Blackness in the service of their efforts to particularize Veracruz.

PERFORMING JAROCHO

Two months after his casting call for the "typical jarocha," El Vate posts another announcement for participants for a different commemorative video. While he cautions that participation would be uncompensated, he pitched it as an opportunity to "be a part of history." The film would be part of a collection of music videos celebrating the "Port identity," for the upcoming five hundredth anniversary. Unlike the typical jarocha, there were no somatic criteria listed, but the sartorial ones were quite specific. They were as follows.

Women: Long skirts or dresses of any color. Handkerchiefs of any color. Hooped earrings, long necklaces. Fans. Musical instruments that you need not know how to play. Curly hair preferred. Tank tops or swim top.

Men: Handkerchiefs of any color. Palm hats. Bright or vibrant colored clothes. Carnival shirts or sailor or pirate outfit. Musical instruments that you need not know how to play. Drums. Wooden boxes. Machetes. Nautical rope.

Banned from set were clothes showing commercial brands, caps, tennis shoes, and watches. Such markers would take away from the image he was trying to portray.

Below this dress code, El Vate helpfully attached a still image captured from one of his earlier staged scenes from a video filmed in the neighborhood of La Huaca. The whole group fills the frame of the photograph, but the viewer still gets the sense that the public space is sparsely populated otherwise. The image is the list of appropriate attire made visual. Every man is wearing a hat and every woman a dress. To the far right of the image, you see a man in a satin emerald shirt poised to strike his timbales. Beside him stands a man in printed teal shirt and white pants playing a set of bongos he has cradled under his arm. To his left and at the center of the photograph is a brown-skinned woman facing away from the camera and toward the timbalero. As with many in the photo, she has been captured mid-dance, and her skirt blurs with her movement. She is wearing a red halter top over a long skirt with printed blue flowers. Around her head is a red bandana, around her neck a long turquoise necklace. She clutches a fan in her right hand. Behind her is a smiling El Vate, dressed in a white straw hat, a carnival shirt of molten yellow and orange, and white pants. Half hidden by another dancer in a vibrant carnival shirt is a seated man playing a bright red conga drum. He is wearing a four-cornered hat, a black shirt with a loud print, and khaki pants rolled up to his knees. He is barefoot. In the foreground is a young child with her back to the camera looking down while wearing an orange dress printed with white flowers. She has a bandana tied around her neck and a maraca clutched in her right hand. Throughout the picture, one can see glimpses of the other participants. Here, a barefoot woman twirling her skirt and smiling; there a smiling man with his baby clutching his shirt. You can see a man in a blue shirt with matching blue hat, looking upward. Spot a sliver of a woman wearing an off-the-shoulder crocheted top typical of the region, with a string of pearls around her neck and a red flower in her hair.

In curating this Afro-Caribbean image, El Vate is treating race as local color. While his approach lacks subtlety, he is not alone in his aspirations. To treat Blackness as local color is to treat it as a particularity of a given place, a feature that is of a place and makes it distinct from others. Local colorists, which was the term for writers in the nineteenth-century literary tradition in the United States, held that place matters. They were committed to giving a sense of place through focusing on regional types and on the details of these people's everyday lives. Writers in this tradition focused on regionalisms such as speech, dress, and habits to observe how place impacts human nature.[44] The particularities of place and the events of daily life are the modes of ethnographic study—in every ethnographer, there is a bit of a local colorist. And while Clifford Geertz cautioned us that anthropologists study *in* villages rather than the villages themselves, where you study gives scope to the "complex specificness" and "circumstantiality" of your observations. As Geertz said, ethnography allows one to not only think about large, abstract concepts in a meaningful way, but also to think creatively and imaginatively with them.[45] Blackness in Veracruz forces one to think of it beyond the purview of Black identity.

Performance scholar Anita González put it best when she summarized: "Jarocho is a stereotype, an identifying marker, a label to be resisted, and an ideal to be incorporated into personal expressions of self. Jarocho is performance practice that sifts Mexican societal motifs through the sieve of individual experience."[46] The stereotypes of the jarocho are an inherited resource with which contemporary jarochos varyingly grapple or embrace. This is with or without an audience. While El Vate was creating videos for consumption and commemoration, locals were also engaging with the jarocho stereotype in their everyday lives. These, too, are performances. They may not call for instruments you need not know how to play, but they do help concretize what counts as "Port identity."

"Gracias a los chilangos, los hoteles se llenan!" Blanca declared as her fingers tensed around the cigarette she had angled away from her face. Her tattooed eyebrows had been creeping increasingly higher for the last five minutes as the *porteños* (people from the Port) around the table indulged in a favorite pastime—disparaging *chilangos* (people from Mexico City).[47] Her sharp tone cut through the relaxed and teasing atmosphere that had settled around the table. Blanca is no wallflower, and her indignant rejoinder that it was "thanks to the chilangos that the hotels fill" was both a defense and an accusation. After all, Veracruz is a major domestic tourism destination, with many of its millions of visitors hailing from Mexico City. For all the sins jarochos can—and do—lay at the feet of their brethren from Mexico City, the metropolitan visitors serve a very tangible good in Veracruz, at least financially speaking. They serve a less quantifiable function as well.

Neither the visitors' financial contributions nor their conspicuous consumption was the target of the table's well-worn complaints. The disparagement was about constituting their in-group as jarochos rather than villainizing chilangos as the out-group. In ribbing the defenseless—save, of course, Blanca, who herself is *chilanga*—the people around the table were performing just as surely as the group of musicians playing the son rhythms that served as our background music. They were performing their jarocho identity and all the essentialisms, stereotypes, and affectations associated with the label.

For decades, visitors have made note of the jarochos' uniqueness, and interested parties have curated that distinction. The state and cultural producers have been driving forces in using the third root concept to do this work. However, the everyday talk of jarochos makes each of them cultural reproducers of essentialized notions of self. Jarochos do not always explicitly articulate what is Black about these essentialisms in the table talk they engage in between sips of coffee or musical sets. Nevertheless, because the implantation of third root rhetoric rests on popular culture, such small moments of self- and group-making serve as scaffolding for these more abstracted understandings of something we may recognize or misrecognize as "race."

Perhaps not everyone knew Blanca originally hailed from Mexico City. She and her husband are prominent regulars at the various cultural events around Veracruz's historic center. Performers offer them salutations from on stage. Moderators pass them the microphone during forum discussions so that they can add anecdotes or corrections related to the topic at hand. If Blanca was not born a jarocha, she is at least a "jarocha de corazón," a "jarocha at heart" as people say in praise of those who, while not born in Veracruz, demonstrate an appreciation for or affinity with norms, traits, and characteristics associated with jarocho culture. Perhaps her familiarity allowed our table to slip into the commonplace conversation in which the figure of the chilango helped to crystallize that of the jarocho. In short, Blanca is not an outsider. She may have been *in* an audience enjoying live music, but she herself is not an audience for the more intimate performance happening tableside. At this interpersonal scale, jarochos engage in a performance and practice that does not cater to or expect an audience. Instead, they refer to their regional distinctiveness in everyday moments that do not require a schedule, budget, or public relations department. More than that, they are moments that do not rely on the occupancy status of the hotels.

People from the Port often engage in this type of talk where they manifest group identity through regional reputations. Chilangos from Mexico City and xalapeños from Veracruz's state capital of Xalapa are favorite foils. The contrast puts jarochos from the Port in a light they find favorable—one that paints them as *alegre*, fun-loving and rowdy, yet warm and open. The roots of this reputation date back centuries, back to when the jarocho was a casta term for Afro-indigenous rural folk from Veracruz. In the contemporary moment, these expectations manifest as authentic popular culture, something to be both demonstrable and tangible. The penchant for hospitality, irreverence, and exuberance—for *convivencia*, whether it be in a café, at a night of dancing, or a festival—are signature features of life in the Port.

Despite Veracruz's being the largest city in the state, with over six hundred thousand residents, the historic downtown area preserves a small-town feel. "Veracruz es un huevo" (Veracruz is an egg), a friend once remarked to me after we repeatedly ran into mutual acquaintances on the street.[48] While habits are slowly responding to increased narco-violence, people continue to live their lives in public, which contributes to the perceived intimacy of public space and the value placed on convivencia. In this environment, people from the Port often broach the growing precarity of their town through the lens of nostalgia. Music and festivals often instigate this turn to the past. Both music and a festival—the inaugural Festival de la Gorda y Picada—had prompted our gathering there in the renovated walkway in the middle of the Barrio de La Huaca.

This inaugural festival was a performance in medias res, with the event serving as the means toward two different ends—to celebrate both the food and the location. The festival worked to place local foodstuffs known as *antojitos* on a higher culinary and cultural plane. The organizers had taken as inspiration a recent food festival held in the *zócalo* (main plaza) celebrating another local snack food, the *volován*. This savory, handheld pastry is a French adaptation that ambulatory or bicycle vendors sell from baskets they carry throughout the city and on local beaches. The Gordas and Picadas Festival hoped to have a similar type of success while also celebrating La Huaca as a unique place in Veracruz. These two goals were complementary. Elevating everyday fare and attracting visitors to an ignored neighborhood near the historic center worked in tandem with efforts to revive popular culture in Veracruz, a process that at the turn of the twenty-first century necessitated engagement with Blackness as well. In fact, neighborhood organizers mimicked the tactic around Black heritage in general by bringing attention to something perceived as already there. Festivals like the one that brought us to La Huaca that evening seek to generate interest in preexisting places and objects, just as the third root concept worked to reframe popular and known practices and narratives as examples of Mexican Blackness.

Earlier that day, many of us had attended the academic forum hosted at IVEC, where experts discussed the celebrated antojitos—the puffed, fried, and filled with refried beans foodstuff called a *gordita* and the pinched-edged fried masa topped with salsa, onion, and cheese known as the *picada*. The experts declared them authentically *porteño* (from the Port), argued that they were healthy, somehow, and nearly recast them as haute cuisine. While there are similar dishes in other parts of the Mexican Republic, the gordita and the picada became loaded with local significance during this first festival and in the process became a way to celebrate the Barrio de La Huaca itself.

While the academic forum occurred at IVEC, the rest of the festivities occurred in La Huaca. The first night of festivities included a somewhat contrived "traditional" fandango where musicians gathered to play the folkloric musical tradition son jarocho. The night when Blanca intervened on behalf of her brethren involved a *baile tradicional* or traditional dance, in which local *son montuno* groups played the Afro-Cuban genre with brief interludes for danzón performances. This arrangement suited community members and their ongoing campaign to revitalize their neighborhood. Part of their narrative involves emphasizing that it is the oldest continuously existing neighborhood—although at its founding, it was originally right on the outskirts of the walled city. The extramural settlement was diverse and mainly consisted of Indians, Africans, and their descendants. As French sociologist Christian Rinaudo has succinctly described it, La Huaca is both "a Black neighborhood" and a "laboratory of mestizaje."[49] While having many Afro-descendants and having a reputation as a cradle of Mexican Blackness, it has always been a place of mixture. This reality is not contradictory. La Huaca as a "Black neighborhood" does not negate the ongoing mixture that has defined Mexico. In fact, La Huaca and its neighborhood association are eager to center it as the origin point of jarocho culture, not specifically Black culture. The relationship is similar to that of the jarocho and Blackness more broadly. The latter is critical to the former but also subsumed by it.

La Huaca became a part of the city once the port town outgrew both the need for its wall and the space delimited by it. When residents demolished the city's wall in the 1880s, the extramural communities like La Huaca experienced an influx of immigrants into their de vecindades, or tenement housing, where people lived in small rooms and shared a common area dedicated for cooking and bathing. While the living conditions were often poor despite high rents, it also created the conditions for social and cultural exchange among the new working class.[50] It was an environment where, as scholar Rafael Figueroa describes it, the built environment and the social fabric created the conditions for spontaneous conviviality and a festive community.[51] From this neighborhood came many of the iconic practices and famous personalities associated with Veracruz. The revitalized Carnival, which is now the largest cultural event in the port city and attracts thousands of tourists every year, started there. The danzón, the Afro-Cuban ballroom dance now part of everyday life in the Port, was first danced in La Huaca.[52] Son montuno also found its first home among the neighborhood's shared patios.

When I first arrived in Veracruz, many helpful people would direct me to La Huaca as a site of Blackness. They would also warn me away, worried about its perceived roughness. These reputations as Black and dangerous are likely related, though no one was impolite enough to explicitly make that connection. This also explains why a historian in Xalapa once assumed I was from that particular neighborhood based on how I look. Yet as Rinaudo has observed before me, there is little noticeable difference in appearance between residents of La Huaca and those from other lower-income neighborhoods in the city. Regardless, their historical and cultural difference is crucial and the basis from which they fight for distinction.

In that way, La Huaca is a microcosm of the broader phenomena occurring in Veracruz. They are the historical and the cultural lenses through which claims of distinction make sense. Those lenses in turn are avenues through which Blackness becomes both present and salient. However, as we have seen in this chapter, through the evolving significance of the jarocho, Blackness is indelible and irrefutable but not all-encompassing. It is foundational, undeniable, and reputational. It is regional and unique. It is also affected by broader trends and interests. It is always contextual.

It is not enough that the jarocho and Veracruz have a long history of being racialized as Mexico's Black aspect. That history and reputation must also be actualized. In what follows, we examine how that actualization manifests and what realities and possibilities it fosters. In the coming chapters, we will look at how Blackness manifests as historical, cultural, and traditional in contemporary Veracruz. The next chapter focuses on how local cultural producers transformed a national mission to recognize Mexican Blackness into a locally specific project.

Interlude

Tenacious Roots

By some appearances, the downtown area of Veracruz is dying. To the south, the twin city of Boca del Rio, with its ongoing construction, its big-box stores, and its shopping malls, provides a stark foil. In Veracruz, businesses struggle to stay afloat, and closed storefronts loom on both sides of the main drag—the old historical buildings with their peeling paint and rolled-down security shutters covering doors that once stayed open. The past glory of the city haunts the downtown area.

At the same time, the vestiges of the past give it strong roots. They give the city its charm. The old streetcar tracks peek through the asphalt. The tiled mosaics and crumbling Juliet balconies draw the eye upward. Spanish-era fortifications make for an imposing presence, and the *múcara* stone peeking from colonial structures reminds you the city is literally made by the sea.[1] Old buildings stand in various stages of disrepair, for they are protected from proactive destruction, but only just.

From this deterioration sprouts life. Strong trees grow through long-collapsed roofs, through windowless panes, through the very walls of buildings. Filament-like aerial roots hang from above you. These enterprising roots paint a picture of how the city has learned "the art of growing old."[2] This art is not always aesthetically pleasing, but it is striking. With enough care, that which has been abandoned can be repurposed, can support the new. Yet the repurposed always runs the risk of being abandoned anew. Tenacious roots, revitalization, and ruination keep company in the antique city.

2

The Living Past

The word *rescate* and its verb form *rescatar* ring out across the old port city—for those who care to listen. In listening, you will hear a variety of connotations behind the word. Sometimes *rescate* refers to a recovery. Other times it is a revitalization. Others still, it is a recuperation. All these words are shades of a common phenomenon—an intentional restoration of the past for an imagined future. It is the bridging of the two. In Veracruz, *rescate* dwells in the tension between preservation and renovation, between the impulse to freeze a moment in time as it is and a desire to recreate things as they were. In both instances, the presence of the past is palpable in the old city that has the dubious honor of being the oldest European town in mainland America. And while there are those who celebrate the European roots of the city above all else, it is its third root—its Blackness—that jarocho publics most readily work to recover, revitalize, and recuperate.

The built environment serves as a fitting backdrop and spatiotemporal ambiance for the presence of the past in the old city. It serves as a tangible reminder that the past is not some distant place. Through the city's materiality, the past is alive and affecting the present and the future. However, as archaeologist Shannon Dawdy has argued, while ruins and old buildings can trigger narration, it is not necessarily predictable.[1] So, while Veracruz embodies Michel-Rolph Trouillot's observation that "the bigger the material mass, the more easily it entraps us," the oldness of the cityscape alone does not guarantee the successful adaptation of third root discourse.[2]

While not a guarantee, the presence of the past does serve to reinforce the popular discourse that the city's Black past—which I will refer to as the *afrojarocho* past— is present as well. I use the term *afrojarocho* to signify the colonial and postcolonial

48

moment when the *jarocho* label applied to Afro-Indigenous peoples of Veracruz, as discussed in chapter 1. It is a recognition that the term *jarocho* has changed meaning through time and that it was always already a product of transculturation. The city's milieu creates the sense of pastness that Dawdy argues undergirds "social stratigraphy," or "the agency of things from the past in constituting our everyday lives in the present."[3] I find Dawdy's concept of social stratigraphy useful to think with because it combines both the tangible (such as landscapes, landmarks, and ruins) and the intangible (for example, music, dance, and language), creating the image of deep layers and grooves proper to a particular locality.[4]

Veracruz's built environment primes contemporary citizens to live with its past, but that alone would not lead to the current embrace of the afrojarocho discourse. It also requires concerted efforts to dictate what narrations would be salient and meaningful. Because of those efforts, jarocho publics recognize that their present reality is possible only through the contributions of Africans and their descendants. Today, this contribution is called the third root, and while the origins of the concept begin with Mexico's multiculturalist turn in the 1980s, the afrojarocho past is neither a multicultural creation nor a piece of invented tradition. Rather, the multicultural turn increased the attention given to that past. It became useful, noteworthy, and narratable because of the long association between race and region. Veracruz's particular history and reputation served as a reservoir of Mexican Blackness that helped naturalize the discursive shift toward what scholar Hettie Malcomson has called a "tripartite mestizaje," one that recognizes the African, Indigenous, and European roots of Mexico's mixture.[5] Rather than foreign, the idea of localized Blackness felt familiar to its audience because it is in a register they already valued and celebrated—jarocho identity. In this way, the third root resonated in the Port because it was less an invention or intervention and more a *rescate*.

The idea of rescuing Mexico's Blackness is not unique to Veracruz. For example, Laura Lewis describes how locals in San Nicolás, Guerrero, have grown accustomed to anthropologists coming into their village to study their African heritage. She writes evocatively of being brought to the outskirts of the town to its "African center," comprising a reconstructed round house and an overturned instrument belonging to an increasingly folklorized musical tradition, *sones de artesa*.[6] She starts her ethnography with this scene to emphasize the disconnect between what *la cultura* sees as Blackness and how residents think about the relationship between race and place.[7] While *la cultura* literally translates as "the culture," they use this label to refer to researchers and cultural promoters who come into the community to teach them about their culture and past.

This is a stark difference compared to Veracruz. There is no "African center" to the city, though some have attempted to market the neighborhood of La Huaca as something comparable. Rather than perennial interlopers, members of *la cultura* are a constant presence in the city. Not only do individual scholars engage with the public, the Veracruz Institute of Culture (IVEC) is such a protagonist in the cultural scene that it is more than a location for events; it is also an agentive and creative force and patron of or contributor to others' activities. Former employees of IVEC do not cease to be involved in the culture scene when leaving the organization, at times lending their expertise to IVEC events and other times creating new spaces for cultural programming. This constancy, I argue, is part of its success.

This chapter explores how people use history to ground and corroborate the importance of Blackness in contemporary Veracruz and the conditions that have made that process possible. It examines both how locals have re-membered Veracruz's past with Africans and their descendants and how they have internalized and interpreted that remembrance. This process has many sources—institutions, archives, popular culture, and nostalgia. This afrojarocho past comes to life both through the archive, with its preferential treatment of the written word, and the repertoire, with its reliance on embodied memories.[8] Contemporary jarochos rely on both the archive and the repertoire to argue for the localness and the liveness of their Blackness.

In Veracruz, the third root discourse outstrips the original intention to recognize the nation's African root in two ways. Firstly, cultural producers have shared a particularly local understanding of the concept. Rather than a broad narrative of how the African root has influenced all of Mexico, the focus is on how local culture has developed from Afro-Caribbean influences. Secondly, by making the root primarily Afro-Caribbean rather than African, cultural producers further particularize the narrative. As a result, the idea of a third root resonates most when attached to the jarocho figure and jarocho culture. In that way, the relevance of Blackness derives from its relationship to places, practices, and histories already known and revered. This unique approach is evident in how narratives of an afrojarocho past and culture circulate. It is that ongoing circulation that makes Blackness a presence in the everyday lives of people in Veracruz.

ROOTING CULTURE

We were in the administrative offices of the Veracruz Center for the Arts (Centro Veracruzano de las Artes "Hugo Argüelles," CEVART) surrounded by manila folders, half-packed bankers boxes, and off-kilter stacks of VHS tapes. My eyes tracked Javier as he moved around his soon-to-be-former office. It was the fall of 2014, and he was preparing to move several blocks away to the Centro Cultural Atarazanas, a former warehouse built in the eighteenth century that now functioned as a space dedicated to the instruction and diffusion of arts and culture. Javier was not changing jobs but merely locations within the vast constellation of buildings and organs that comprise the Veracruz Institute of Culture.

The relocation would give him more space as he continued to assemble an archive of IVEC events and programming—particularly the International

Afro-Caribbean Festival, colloquially known as el Afrocaribeño. While he would be assuming an expanded role in the organization, he had for years worked as the organizer for the festival's academic programming. The beloved festival simultaneously celebrates Afro-Caribbean cultures while making the case that Veracruz deserves inclusion in that cultural-geographic space. In addition to developing an archival project related to the festival, he would also support Atarazanas's community-oriented mission. In both capacities, Javier would contribute to IVEC's mission to "preserve, promote, and disseminate culture through the broad and plural participation of the citizenry in order to fortify the values and cultural heritage of Veracruzanos."[9]

That afternoon, his colleague Julia kept us company in the shared office space as I peppered him with questions about "the third root" in Veracruz and how well-known the concept was in the broader population. At one point, Javier told me the vast majority of people have no idea about slavery. At this claim, Julia interjected by asserting there was no slavery in the city. According to her, slavery was practiced in the hinterland of the city, yes, but not within the city itself. Javier picked up her thread but shifted his focus from contemporary Veracruzanos to historic ones. He recounted that *domésticos*, or domestic workers, may have lived in extramural communities like La Huaca, but they worked in the city and along the docks. The two of them recast urban slavery through the term *domestics* and argued that enslaved people were to be found on plantations and working in the mines.

At the time, Julia's interjection and Javier's tacit agreement struck me as odd because I assumed that they, more than most, would know that statement to be false.[10] After all, both have organized and presented at forums that work to educate the general population about the African presence in Veracruz. To narrate that presence without mention of slavery seemed impossible. Yet there is a decided lacuna regarding slavery within the city. In the time since Julia's interjection, the Port, along with Yanga, have earned official recognition as "sites of memory of slavery," as part of UNESCO's Route of Enslaved Peoples Project.[11] Many people worked for years to achieve this designation, chief among them academics working with the National Institute for Anthropology and History (Instituto Nacional de Antropología e Historia, INAH). Yet despite these efforts, the majority of people within the city—an internationally proclaimed site of memory—do not know about it. If those who are in charge of educating the populace think it a rural phenomenon, then this omission suggests the historical discourse of slavery is not as useful as other ones in contemporary Veracruz.

While this silence is crucial to understand the retrospective significance afforded to the peculiar institution and its impact in Mexico, it is equally worthwhile to consider what is mentioned, and to what ends. As historian Theodore Cohen has remarked, the history of Afro-Mexico "is still told in relation to what is presumed to be missing, not what is expressed."[12] To look instead at what people express and how it travels is to move away from the assumption that honoring a

Black past is a way to avoid recognizing a Black present or imagining Blackness into the future. People like Javier and Julia work hard in their pursuit to preserve, promote, and disseminate culture to the broader population. For the last decades of the twentieth century, the African presence and influence was critical to achieving that mission.

The Veracruz Institute of Culture is a key player in the cultural life of the Port. Founded in the 1980s, the whole of IVEC functions as the port city's *casa de la cultura* (cultural center). These cultural centers work to recompose "the social fabric through programs that stimulate creative and artistic sensitivity, promote the enjoyment of the arts and peaceful coexistence, and provoke the valuation and recreation of intangible cultural heritage."[13] Rather than one cultural center for workshops or art exhibitions, the port city has a network of sites dedicated to promoting its mission. The city of Veracruz is not the state capital, but it has the most IVEC sites, hosting seven of the thirteen locations found throughout the state. Five of them are under the arts and heritage division, while one is under artistic education and research. The seventh site is an eighteenth-century Bethlemite ex-convent that has served as the IVEC headquarters since the 1987 law that established the institute.[14]

IVEC is not just a constellation of places throughout the city; it is an actor in the Port's everyday life. It pursues its mission through various public programming offerings, such as festivals like the Afrocaribeño, through workshops that teach fine and plastic arts, with art exhibitions and academic forums. Because they are mission-driven to focus on local themes and topics, events that are historical in nature function to explain or contextualize local culture and traditions. In other words, the academic programming about historical topics serves to better understand cultural practices. What is more, the statewide division of this labor solidifies the locus of Blackness in the Port rather than other major cities with IVEC locations like Orizaba or Xalapa. Additionally, local actors like Javier, Julia, and their colleagues have faithfully promoted the belief that the African influence in the city of Veracruz is both present and significant. The Veracruz Institute of Culture has been integral to this dissemination from the beginning; in fact, IVEC predates the third root project by only two years. Because IVEC is by design focused on its immediate environment, it represented what was a national project through a local lens.

Both IVEC and the third root project are products of a long history of the Mexican government using culture as a means to their ends. According to sociologist Elodie Bordat, both the Mexican government and its citizens believe the state has not only the right but also the obligation to intervene in the cultural field. In fact, Mexico's cultural policy is such that the state is "the first producer and promoter of culture in Mexico."[15] There have been various governmental interventions in the cultural field since the founding of the nation. Since the beginning, culture has been a cohesive tool toward engendering nationalism and patriotism.

The pursuit of a national cultural identity led to the creation of the Secretariat for Public Education (SEP) in 1910. After the Mexican Revolution, when cultural nationalism became a concerted effort by elites and political leaders, many more federal institutions developed that would help support Mexico's cultural policy. The National Institute of Anthropology and History (INAH), founded in 1939, and the National Institute of Fine Arts and Literature (INBAL), founded in 1946, are two such legal entities, with the former charged with protecting and conserving the nation's tangible and intangible heritage and the latter created to promote the arts and arts education. Both would come under the auspices of the National Council for Culture and Arts (CONACULTA) as part of the institutionalization of culture in Mexico. CONACULTA was created by presidential decree in 1988 under the auspices of SEP. This structure would remain in effect until 2015, when CONACULTA became the Secretariat of Culture.

The "Our Third Root" (Nuestra Tercera Raíz) program, which started in 1989, was one of the first projects organized by CONACULTA. The program began under the direction of Mexican anthropologist Guillermo Bonfil Batalla, who was at the time in charge of CONACULTA's Cultural Studies Seminar.[16] Mexican academic Luz María Martínez Montiel, a scholar of colonial slavery in Mexico and its impact, served as the program's coordinator.[17] The program's goal was to study and appreciate the African presence in Mexico and to recognize it as a cultural root of the country's mestizaje alongside the European and Indigenous ones.[18] The research, expositions, symposiums, and workshops that stemmed from the program helped create the discourse that still exists today, both nationally and internationally. French sociologist Christian Rinaudo argues this aperture must be understood in its broader context. The late 1980s and 1990s were a time when UNESCO was actively supporting research focused on the cultural links between Latin America and Africa.[19] This support helped usher in the proliferation and circulation of research focused on the "Black presence" in Latin America. The "Our Third Root" program benefited from this groundswell of interest. As Theodore Cohen has noted, Bonfil Batalla's project was the first time in Mexican history there was a national organization dedicated to Afro-Mexican subject matters and helped create "a coherent interdisciplinary field."[20] Three years later, Mexico would declare itself a pluricultural country. While the indigenous question was at the forefront of this recognition, this multicultural shift benefited Afro-Mexican discourse as well.

The national "Our Third Root" program found resonance with a contemporaneous, local cultural politics in the Port. As Rinaudo has chronicled, local concerns with federal support facilitated the "entry of Veracruz in the Caribbean and the promotion of the third root."[21] However, unlike the broader focus on slavery, the local interest in Veracruz in 1989 and 1990 was coalescing around Veracruz's place in the Caribbean. These interests highlighted the cultural similarities fostered by close maritime connections within the region, rather than through the history of enslavement. This was not always the case. In fact, Martínez Montiel, prior to working with CONACULTA, helped establish IVEC in 1987 and served as its cultural heritage director. In that capacity, she spearheaded the renovation of the Veracruz City Museum. As part of that work, she commissioned the installation of the nation's first museum hall dedicated to slavery in Mexico.[22]

Christian Rinaudo argues there have been three competing orientations toward Mexico's Blackness in Veracruz. One, which he associates with the "Our Third Root" program and actors such as Martínez Montiel and CONACULTA, seeks to study the African cultural heritage of Latin America. They do so by focusing on the historical contributions of enslaved Africans and their descendants to Mexican culture. The second orientation he identifies as more political and encompasses those scholars and activists who are interested in the cultural and somatic specificity of the country's African presence. Their stance holds that Afro-descendants are a distinct ethnoracial group within Mexican society. The third approach, which he argues is highly influential in Veracruz, centers mestizaje as the essence of popular culture and holds that there are many cultural influences in what Antonio García de León has termed the Afro-Andalusian Caribbean. García de León coined the term *Afro-Andalusian Caribbean* in 1992 as an expansion on French historians Huguette and Pierre Chaunu's 1950s conception of the Andalusian Caribbean, which emphasized Andalusia's centrality in the Spanish colonization of the Americans. By adding the prefix *Afro-*, García de León sought to underscore the African influence in this process. The term Afro-Andalusian Caribbean brings attention not only to the role the transplanted, captured Africans played in the creation of Spanish America but also to the African influence in southern Spain and the fact that many of the technologies of colonization, including both the encomienda system and slavery, were first developed in the African Spanish colonies before their implementation in the Americas. The Afro-Andalusian Caribbean concept embodies this third approach in that it recognizes the importance of the African heritage within this process without treating it as a totality.[23]

In many ways, this third approach has become the dominant one, though the phrase *the third root* encompasses all three. Between 1989 and 1994, IVEC organized a number of events including the academic forum "Veracruz Is also Caribbean" in 1989 and 1990 and the forum "Veracruz: The Cultures of the Gulf and the Caribbean at 500 Years" in 1992.[24] The former aimed to concretize the idea that Veracruz is regionally and culturally oriented toward the Caribbean, and the latter was part of the events recognizing the quincentenary of the Spanish encounter with the Americas. While academic in nature, both events included musical, artistic, cinematographic, and folkloric performances.[25] This structure is also present in the crown jewel of Caribbean-focused programming, the International Afro-Caribbean Festival. For nearly thirty years, IVEC has organized this yearly festival with additional support from the state and municipal governments as well as through CONACULTA.[26]

Since its inauguration in 1994, the Afrocaribeño has been a reference in the city's cultural life. Scholar Mateo Pazos Cárdenas has conducted extensive research on the many public explanations for the festival. They have ranged from a simple statement that it helps reclaim the African contribution to their culture to an extensive one linking it to racial diversity and the revalorization of the third root in Veracruz's culture and more broadly national culture.[27] For its twenty-sixth edition, in 2022, IVEC described the festival as its way to "sensitize citizens about the value of Afro-Mexicanity" as well as to "strengthen the manifestation of creative diversity" and to "construct a culture of peace and non-discrimination."[28] IVEC seeks to accomplish this with a two-pronged approach. The festival, which is free and open to the public, has both an academic side and an artistic one. While the Festival lacks a permanent date, it is an anticipated event on the cultural calendar. Its absence is noteworthy.

CULTIVATING THE THIRD ROOT

"Can you believe they canceled the Afrocaribeño?!" he exclaimed, as we passed each other in the callejón. I cannot rightly say that I knew him, but our paths had crossed often in the historic downtown of Veracruz over the years. He was a denizen of the small plaza, La Plazuela de la Campana, where he was a member of the constant population that was always observing, never dancing. He was generally a quiet fellow, more apt to nod than to speak. The first time we ever spoke, he parroted to me what I was doing in the Port. This surveillance was a bit unsettling, but Veracruz is "an egg," after all—and I stood out. We eventually did know each other in that way that people who share common spaces know each other. We had that type of relationship where you always acknowledge each other's presence, but you would not go share an afternoon together in a café. Because we had seen each other at various events in IVEC, in Atarazanas, and in La Campana, perhaps he assumed I was the ideal interlocutor with whom to express his disgust. He railed at the injustice of it all before ending our impromptu meeting with a "¡Que asqueroso!" and going on his way. "How disgusting," indeed.

I remember vividly the first time I learned about the Afrocaribeño during my first visit to Veracruz, in 2011. The few marked bus stops along the *malecón*, or boardwalk, all boasted the poster for the festival's seventeenth edition (figure 2). Palm fronds provided a lush green background, and four figures in colorful clothing were in the foreground. The literally black silhouette figures were featureless save for the bright white smiles of the two male figures. Long dresses and gold jewelry, including the iconic stacked neck rings of the Ndebele people of South Africa, distinguished the two women. All four were playing instruments, which included bongos, a maraca, a guitar, and what looked to be a djembe. Although it admittedly did not look particularly Mexican to my eye, the kinetic image was arresting. Many people, particularly Christian Rinaudo, have remarked on how images like

FIGURE 2. Awaiting the start of an event taking place in the City Museum for the seventeenth International Afro-Caribbean Festival in 2011. Photo by the author.

these in actuality work to make Blackness foreign. All the signifiers point to an elsewhere—usually Africa or a non-Mexican Caribbean culture. A clear exception is the festival poster for the following year, in 2012.

That year's poster featured a woman, once again a pitch-black silhouette, against a yellow background. Her profile implies a kinky afro hairstyle, the only suggestion of her race. She is dressed as the typical jarocha. She extends her arms to better display the full white lace skirt she wears with the iconic black apron on top of it. She has a white lace shawl around her shoulders, with the lace patterned as folding hand fans splayed open. In the crook of her arms is a draped red stole, adding color and alluding to the typical red handkerchief of the regional garb. The image is simultaneously unmistakably a Black person and a jarocha. No poster since has been quite so unambiguous with its framing. Moreover, many critics of the festival argue that the publicity's visual grammar is less worrisome than the direction the festival has gone in since its inauguration.

Many interlocutors reminisced about how community-oriented the first festivals were. Like its current iteration, it was a form of "edutainment," being both educational and entertaining. Unlike more recent programming, earlier festivals also involved workshops in the zócalo and booths dedicated to religiosity, cuisine, and popular culture. Others complain that it has not generated a significant uptick in self-identification as Afro-Mexican because it continues to make Blackness foreign. The festival has always been international, and every year a different country is the invited guest. But this critique goes beyond the inclusion of others and instead emphasizes how the links are not sufficiently articulated for the general population. The festival is by no means perfect. It is a product of the state, and specifically the tourism department of the state. Yet it has certainly sensitized uninvested people to the idea that Veracruz is a Caribbean place. For example, in the early days of my fieldwork, a shoeshiner in the zócalo told me that Veracruz is Caribbean. When I asked him to expand on that sentiment, he told me, "Well, the Afrocaribeño!" as if the festival itself proved the point. This familiarity was also on display with the reactions people had to its absence.

In 2016 the scheduled twenty-first edition of the International Afro-Caribbean Festival was canceled with little fanfare, but a fair amount of outrage. My casual acquaintance in the callejón was not the only one upset at the sudden news. El Chivo, the street parker whose territory included the street perpendicular to the Plazuela, brought it up to me in one of my brief conversations as I traversed his street. My group chat of son jarocho enthusiasts on the social media platform WhatsApp mentioned it. Staff members of IVEC—members who had already planned the academic forum of the Afrocaribeño and were simply waiting for the funds to be released—mentioned it. I mentioned it. As my alleyway acquaintance had noticed in his short diatribe, organizers had attempted to downsize the Afrocaribeño to a single event hosted in another IVEC site, Teatro de la Reforma, but even that desperate move could not rescue the festival that year.

The nonoccurrence of the Afrocaribeño in 2016 was an event in and of itself. This festival was legitimately missed by locals, and not purely for the potential tourism revenue. The hotels did not fill with visitors like during Carnival season, but more urgently, the public spaces did not fill with foreign and local musicians playing for an oversized audience. Of course, there were still local musicians playing and people dancing—it was, after all, Veracruz. Nevertheless, the specialness of the Afrocaribeño became even more apparent with its cancellation. As my acquaintance implied, even a drastically downsized event, limited to one day—and indoors!—would have been better than nothing at all. For those who are even remotely connected to the cultural scene in Veracruz, it was "disgusting" that one of the oldest, most successful festivals was so unceremoniously canceled without a by-your-leave. Yet its cancellation did not immediately imply that the Afro-Caribbeanness of Veracruz needed revitalization. The festival fomented it, but it has a life outside of the multiday celebration that generally happens in August.

The abruptness of the cancellation was partly due to the chronic disorganization surrounding it. From outside of IVEC, many interlocutors I spoke to argued that the fault lay with the governor. To their mind, he was not interested enough in the arts, and, since the arts in general and the festival in particular were the purview of the state, his disinterest was reflected in the planning. In fact, the news at the time reported that the reason the festival was cancelled was financial—there were over half a million pesos promised but undelivered for financing the major event. While the drastic decision to cancel the festival was only in 2016, for the last decade, there had been a certain degree of uncertainty around the festival, regarding both its dates and its scope. This was not the first time it had been suspended, which is why the twentieth edition of the festival fell in 2015 rather than 2014. During the years I conducted research, there was always a suddenness to the festival, where everyone seems to anticipate its arrival, but remain uncertain of the actual dates. Whereas it was originally a late summer festival, it has also occurred in the spring and since 2019 has shifted to the fall.[29]

Locals are the intended audience. Because dates are impossible to know for certain, there is readiness among them as well, a "should be around this time" mood in the midsummer weeks. Even though the academic forum does not enjoy the same attendance as the musical side of the event, nonacademics regularly attend. It remains one of the primary disseminators of knowledge regarding the Caribbean-ness of Veracruz. The festival is often the first piece of evidence everyday people cite when defending the claim that Veracruz is Caribbean. Rather than merely exploring the cultural ties Veracruz has with the rest of the region, the festival itself has slowly come to stand in as justification for the sentiment. At the same time, those involved since its inception have critiqued the ways in which the spectacular aspects of the festival—including its nightly free music events—have overtaken the didactic aspects, arguing that it has evolved into a vehicle predominantly for entertainment purposes.

With that shift, the festival has faced criticisms from a variety of fronts. For hoteliers, the uncertainty around its dates has made it hard for the hospitality industry to capitalize on the free music concerts. For academics, the vision of the festival seems to have been subsumed by the political boons local government reaps by providing free entertainment to a population that oftentimes does not even realize there are daylong forums in IVEC that precede the nights of open-air concerts. Cultural promoters also have felt the shift as their roles in the festival have been downsized. The fact that the staff at IVEC had to plan for an event they could only hope would transpire speaks to the ways in which finances have negatively impacted cultural events. In the beginning, finances could bolster the revitalization of events, as they did with Carnival; now, there is a worry that funds or the lack thereof could have an outsized influence on what parts of popular culture remain viable, regardless of how popular they are among jarochos.

Because IVEC is protected by law, there is little worry the institution is in danger of dissolution. However, staff are aware that political interests may shift and that they are subject to the austerity measures that the state is facing due to the corruption and budgetary crises it has weathered. For that reason, staff decided to house a new project on the local iteration of music in the Fonoteca Nacional,

FIGURE 3. Members of the son music group Pregoneros del Recuerdo playing onstage in the Plazuela de la Campana as part of the Festival to the Traditional Veracruzan Son with a Cuban Root. Photo by the author.

the national sound archive. The staff used blatantly protectionist terms during the project's inauguration in 2015. They argued that by putting jarochos' local patrimony in the national archive, it would be better preserved for posterity and would make it forever available to jarochos and researchers. With this move, they preemptively rescued their local patrimony for an imagined future where the original compositions may no longer exist, but the interest would remain. It is at once hopeful and disillusioned, pragmatic and—since the room was filled with the participating musicians—personal.

The festival was dedicated to celebrating the musicians who gave life to what IVEC branded as son tradicional veracruzano de raíz cubana (traditional Veracruzan *son* with a Cuban root). IVEC had been organizing festivals dedicated to the music that they describe as traditionally of Veracruz, while acknowledging its Cuban root, for a few years, though even earlier, there had been different festivals that celebrated the same genre of music, more commonly known simply as *son*. Because of the changing of the guard, this release party would be the last event this iteration of IVEC would organize. Coupled with the cancellation of the Afrocaribeño, the festival cycle had been broken temporarily. Although massive spectacles that work toward the *rescate* of local Blackness are subject to the vagaries of politics and budget balancing, the dedication to revitalizing jarocho culture—and in consequence a localized Blackness—is already a shared

investment among various practitioners and enthusiasts of quintessentially jarocho culture (figure 3).

THE THIRD ROOT'S LOCAL FRUIT

The overworked air-conditioning unit made a not-so-low hum of white noise
as the professor read her lecture about Cuban culture from the stage. We in the
audience were a modest crowd, spreading ourselves across the auditorium of
the Veracruz Institute of Culture. Given that it was an all-day affair in the middle of the workweek, however, it was an impressive showing. The symposium
on Cuban history would be a way to learn about Cuba but also about Veracruz,
given the intimate relationship the Port has had with the island. When they
announced the coffee break, we unfolded ourselves from the red cushioned seats
and stepped out into Veracruz's humid, midday air.

As people mingled throughout the courtyard, I approached the scholar with
a question. Why is it, I mused, that Veracruz is committed to the term *Afro-
Caribbean*? "Is it not redundant?" I asked. She agreed. While the heterogeneity
of the Caribbean is its hallmark, it is difficult to think of the region without considering the *Afro*. The unmarked term *Caribbean* is not one in which the African
element has been or can be ignored. Yet *Afro-Caribbean* continued to slip through
her lips and from the tip of my pen during the afternoon session. Regardless of our
courtyard consensus that the prefix was not necessary, it is a useful term. *Redundant* perhaps has too negative a connotation. *Emphatic* better captures it.

This is all the more evident given that people still allude to Blackness through
the term *Caribbean* even without the prefix. To say that Veracruz is part of the
Caribbean is to make an argument toward Veracruz's Blackness. Keep in mind,
Veracruz is nestled within the Gulf of Mexico and is not geographically part of the
Caribbean. If you were to search "Mexican Caribbean," tourism websites would
dominate your results and point you to the Riviera Maya in the Yucatán Peninsula.
Few spring breakers or newlyweds turn their gazes to Veracruz with its brown
sand and turbid water when the image of the Caribbean is white sand and clear
blue waters. Fortunately, the tourism industry is not the authority on the matter.

Veracruz is historically and culturally part of the Caribbean.[30] As one of the
great ports of the circum-Caribbean where peoples and practices intermingled,
they have created new ways of being along similar grammars. Not only was Veracruz a key node in the colonial era circum-Caribbean both politically and com-
mercially, the continued migrations in the nineteenth century directly impacted
the development of jarocho culture, including its music, dance, architecture, and
gastronomy.[31] The deep, horizontal ties Benedict Anderson credited as essential
to imagined communities tether the city made by the sea to the rest of the Caribbean even though the body of water it neighbors is not the Caribbean Sea like
its compatriots to the south.[32] As Stuart Hall has argued, "the culture of a people

is at root—and the question of roots is very much at issue—a question of the fundamentals of a culture. Histories come and go, peoples come and go, situations change, but somewhere down there is throbbing the culture to which we all belong."[33] Speaking specifically of Caribbean identity, Hall paints the search for one as problematic because it is "impossible to locate in the Caribbean an origin for its peoples."[34] Moreover, the immense diversity within the region from language to traditions to phenotype troubles the attempt. Indeed, as scholar Ralph Premdas has argued, the Caribbean is, in many ways, an arbitrarily appointed imaginary region.[35] Many scholars have theorized about the common threads that help constitute the disparate locales into a region, arbitrarily imagined though it may be. One such scholar is anthropologist Michel-Rolph Trouillot, who reflected that the region is "inescapably historical, in the sense that some of their distant past is not only known, but known to be different from their present, and yet relevant to both the observers' and the natives' understanding of that present."[36]

This relationship with historicity compels jarocho publics to go to festivals and midweek talks, but exposure to the past is not limited to occasions when people seek it out. It also occurs in the everyday rhythm of life. Because the past is so present in the city's cultural politics, people often learn about the third root as part of partaking in common pastimes—pastimes like going to free concerts or simply existing in public spaces.

THE PRESENTATION OF THE PAST

The main plaza was hosting a free concert series as part of the 2015 International Festival of the Desert of the Lions. In a calendar filled with such events, the group of us from our son jarocho *taller* (workshop) did not know the particulars of this new festival, but we showed up en masse, commandeering a row of seats to ourselves. Later, I would learn this festival is part of a project that "generates spaces for coexistence free of violence where the inhabitants have the opportunity to appreciate cultural spectacles to which they generally do not have access."[37] This mission was not what brought us to the zócalo that Saturday evening in February, however. We were there to see Mono Blanco perform. The son jarocho ensemble is one of the leading musical groups in the son jarocho community, a forerunner in the genre's revitalization, and a vocal member of the *movimiento jaranero* (jaranero movement), which, according to the Mexican scholar Rafael Figueroa, is largely an intellectual affair with tight interpersonal connections and overlap between the musicians, academics, and IVEC.[38] What is more, Mono Blanco is a pillar in the port city of Veracruz's son jarocho scene—hosting free monthly fandangos where enthusiasts can come together and convivially play musical pieces called *sones*.

Like our group, many other members of the son jarocho community sat among the plaza's crowd, though perhaps the crowd in the zócalo did not do justice to the group's international acclaim. Nevertheless, the crowd featured a mix of onlookers and passersby, both locals and tourists. Distinct from the more theatrical or commercial version of son jarocho as seen in ballet folklórico and promoted since Mexico's golden age of cinema, Mono Blanco, like other traditionalists, often take the opportunity to offer lessons alongside their musical stylings.[39] The ethos of such presentations holds that one should not merely be entertained; one must also be informed.

For this performance, Gilberto "El Mono" Gutiérrez Silva has set a rhythm of introducing an aspect of the genre before beginning the next musical piece. After performing the slower-paced "La Guacamaya," El Mono transitions into his explanation of the next son, "El Chuchumbé." He explains for the crowd that this piece is "original to the group Mono Blanco but now very much so in the traditional repertoire." In his miniature history lesson, Gutiérrez recounts how Mono Blanco added music and expanded upon the verses found in the National Archives. El Mono informs his audience that no one knows how the music originally sounded before transitioning into the melody that is now known and taught the world over as "El Chuchumbé."

"El Chuchumbé," with its preservation in the mid-eighteenth century and its subsequent restoration in the mid-twentieth century, is an ideal case study for the relationship between the archive and the repertoire. As anthropologist Diana Taylor has theorized, the archive and the repertoire are systems of transmission that work in tandem and in a constant state of interaction.[40] When Mono Blanco rescued the son from the archives by attaching a C-chord progression to archival material, they cemented it in the son jarocho repertoire. However, its entrance into the archive is important as well. According to Cuban musicologist Alejo Carpentier, the dance known as el chuchumbé first arrived in New Spain in 1776 when immigrants from Cuba "of irregular color" disembarked in the port city.[41] Carpentier argues that, in the early days of colonization, many dances in the Americas were quite similar despite their different names. Based on contemporaneous descriptions of the dance and its "choreographed pursuit of the female by the male," Carpentier argues it qualifies as a type of rumba.[42] Many of the descriptions came from Inquisition records for while the new dance was immensely popular among inhabitants of the city, it was as equally concerning for the powers that be.

The lyrics were irreverent and audacious, with some even pointing out the hypocrisy of promiscuous clergymen. El chuchumbé, for example, cheekily refers to the area five inches below a man's belly button.[43] The dancing was also salacious, with one observer describing it as "alien to propriety" as "dancers thus entwined paw one another from step to step."[44] Said dancers themselves were mulattos and people of the aforementioned "irregular color," which is to say people of mixed ancestry. The scandalous nature of the music, the dance, and the people earned el chuchumbé its longevity. As Eleana Deanda Camacho has highlighted, by documenting the object of their disdain with such meticulous care, the Inquisition censors ultimately protected the practice from obsolescence.[45] However, it is not just the work of the censor or the archivist, it is also the work of Gutiérrez and his desire to recuperate an artifact and restore its importance to the son jarocho tradition. Without his actions, "El Chuchumbé" would not have reached its current vivacity. "El Chuchumbé" literally comes from centuries past while only really being created within living—and playing—memory. In many ways, "El Chuchumbé" is an ideal representation of the trajectory of both son jarocho and Blackness in general—its transcultural past, its revitalized present, and, perhaps, its canonized future.

Within academic circles, "El Chuchumbé" serves as an exemplar for how to read the archive for marginalized voices. By interpreting its lascivious lyrics in the inquisitorial record as a critique of the clergy (for example, its most famous verse references a clergyman engaging in indecent exposure), historians and musicians have called it a protest song. In total, the historical records of the lascivious dance includes thirty-nine couplets recorded across five complaints issued between 1766 and 1772.[46] These complaints preserved the lyrics, the corporeal movements, and the demographics of the enthusiasts, with all of which contemporary enthusiasts are aware.

Other sones condemned by the Inquisition follow similar trajectories. One of the most common and frequently played sones, "El Toro Zacamandú," is a *son de pareja*, or a paired dance, in which the dancers' fast-paced stomping accompanies their pantomiming of a bull and a matador.[47] The male dancer, with his fingers crooked to represent horns and his foot scraping back, reminiscent of a charging bull, dances toward the female dancer as she repeatedly teases him with a handkerchief before finally catching the cloth around his neck (figure 4).

This "torea," or teasing, performed by the woman is considered offensive in some regions of Veracruz.[48] "El Toro" in fact has a long history of offense. As the scholar and jaranero Álvaro Alcántara López recounts, the dance called *zacamandú* first came to the attention of the Inquisition in 1779, when a Black Cuban introduced it to Veracruz.[49] Years later, in 1803, the Inquisition notes a dance that accompanies a son varyingly called "El Torito," "Toro Viejo," or "Toro Nuevo." The recorded choreography is remarkably similar to the contemporary "Toro Zacamandú," with the man making horns and charging the woman, who plays the role of the bullfighter, teasing and irritating him. This pantomime, according to the nineteenth-century Inquisition informants, was impolite and vulgar in that it appeared similar to "the ludic dynamics that precede the sexual act."[50] However, as Alcántara notes, no one knows how the zacamandú—the dance first registered in the Inquisition records—was danced or accompanied by music. As he highlights, "What we can see is that 'curiously,' the description made two hundred years ago of the Torito coincides with the way in which the son 'Toro Zacamandú' is danced today in the jarocho fandangos."[51] The way in which these two dances became one is unknown. Regardless, "El Toro Zacamandú" is one of the most popular sones played and danced. It is also one of the first songs jaraneros reference when acknowledging the third root in their musical tradition.

FIGURE 4. Taller members practicing the son jarocho song "El Toro Zacamandú." On the tarima, the pair of dancers perform the traditional dance moves, with the male dancer mimicking a bull while the female dancer flourishes her handkerchief. Members surround them while playing instruments and observing the scene. Photo by the author.

In the performance in the zócalo, El Mono's—and by extension, Mono Blanco's— politics were certainly on display with the son with which they decided to follow "El Chuchumbé." In his interlude, El Mono discussed how previously the government denied "la presencia de la cultura africana en nuestra cultura"—the presence of the African culture in our culture. As one of the early staff members of IVEC in the 1990s, Gutierrez has a unique perspective having worked with and outside of the state. It is fortunate, he continues, that the "Our Third Root" program began thirty years ago, before explaining what the program is for the audience members who may not be familiar with it. Speaking personally of Mono Blanco's experience, Gutierrez recounts how they have interacted with Caribbean and African musicians and with them have found "a natural amalgam through the rhythmic, through that African rhythm that is also ours. Because our rhythms are also Afro."[52]

He used this statement to segue into their next piece, "El Camotal," which means "the sweet potato field." Although Mono Blanco has recorded this son on their albums, is not a very common piece and is played infrequently and only in certain regions.[53] Mono Blanco reinforces the allusion to Blackness already present in the association sweet potatoes have with afromestiza cuisine and culture through their performance choices. They put down the stringed instruments associated with son jarocho in favor of the percussive ones.

Through this performance style, Mono Blanco continues their revivalist tendencies by demonstrating for the masses an art form they proclaim to be both theirs and "afro" while standing in the symbolic heart of Veracruz. The percussive dancing on the *tarima* (wooden platform) blended with the *pandero jarocho* (an octagonal tambourine), the *quijada* (donkey jawbone), and a small *güiro* (notched gourd), whose rasp of the stick against its ridges was all but drowned out by the more assertive instruments. Once the son was finished, they picked up their stringed instruments—the eight-stringed *jarana*, the *arpa* (harp), the melodic *requinto*, and the bass instrument known as the *leona*—and continued their set.

Mono Blanco's authority derives from the group's role in son jarocho's revitalization since the 1970s—a moment in time when autochthonous forms of knowledge coalesced into a genre, something to be objectified and therefore authenticated. The jaranero movement was created largely in response to the folklorization of son jarocho music, which many of my interlocutors derisively called "for show." The all-white ensembles of the jarocho regional garb, and the trio of musicians who go from café to café hoping for a tourist to tip them for their troubles, are considered a world apart from those who go to fandangos, the *fandangueros*, who know more than folkloric steps and mainstream verses associated with stylized versions of the tradition. They also know narrative themes, traditions, and the rituals of the tarima such as the proper moments to get on and off it, when to dance forcefully or simply mark time, and the parts of the sones that require certain steps. The ten-line poems known as *décimas* are recited, composed, and improvised in fandango spaces. The genealogies of the most famous jaraneros and decimistas as well as current gossip are common knowledge. History itself is also requisite knowledge for those involved in the jaranero movement.

This history entails at least a vague familiarity with the discourse of the third root, often with generic assignation of aspects of the music to specific "roots." This leads to common assumptions that the naturalistic themes are indigenous, the strings Spanish, and the percussion the third root. However, unlike El Mono's lived experience with cultural fusion, the theories I have heard bandied about are far ranging—from the lack of drums being a result of them being taken away due to their communicative power in the flatlands of the sotavento's *llanuras costeras* (coastal plains) to the close position of the feet while dancing being a carryover from when the enslaved danced while shackled. The neat assignment of qualities to roots and the stereotypes that bolster them exist despite the fact that the movimiento jaranero was at its origin an intellectual affair, as the scholar Rafael Figueroa recounted to me.

The rescue of the genre was not only in the face of its diminishment but also against the strength of the folkloric son jarocho. This created a space for the academic within the culture as well as a tendency to authenticate. The tight connection between the academic and the popular continues today. Most of the prominent scholars of son jarocho are also jaraneros. However, it is not simply the ethnographer's participant-observation. It is not mere method. It is, as scholar Martha Gonzalez has theorized about *convivencia*, a "deliberate act of being with and present for each other as community."[54] Many scholars *convivir* (share life) in the fandango space, socializing with the very same people who may recount their research as a history lesson during a workshop, or whom they may quote in a new ethnographic piece of literature. The scholars and the practitioners know each other, live with each other. In literal ways, they are each other.

It was the first fandango in the cultural center el caSon in months. The monthly schedule in 2015 had been interrupted for a variety of reasons, including the touring schedule of Mono Blanco, who spearheaded the center's cultural efforts. This mini inauguration of the space was on a hot, humid night. From my place in the audience, I spot Álvaro Alcántara among the tight semicircle of musicians ringing the tarima at the fandango's center. Earlier in the day, he had sat behind a table, speaking into a microphone as he played his role as an academic. Tonight, he needed no microphone as he participated in the call-and-response of the son that had been playing for the past twenty minutes. When the "una!" had been called—the signal to let everyone know that it was the final cycle of the chord progression—he wiped the sweat from his brow and joined a different semicircle, one comprising academics drinking their Indio beers and catching up. As he had told us in his conference panel, he is an academic, a rumbero, and a jaranero.[55]

We were in the final stretch of the XX Afrocaribeño Festival, which, as Álvaro had mentioned earlier in the day, was where a lot of those participating musicians and academics had "grown up together" as both scholars and people. This new semicircle included a visiting scholar from Colombia, the aforementioned Rafael Figueroa; Jessica Gottfried, who has written extensively about son jarocho and who is an active and present personality in the port's jaranero *flota*, or crew; and another scholar of the third root from Mexico City. Despite having attended a full day of talks and presentations as part of the festival, they were lively and reminiscing in the garden of el caSon, right by the recently cut, formerly majestic coconut tree. They were in their own world within the convivencia of the fandango, yet not set apart from it.

I saw the same clique the next day in the zócalo during the closing concert for the festival, which that year, contrary to claims of distancing through international music, ended with son jarocho. A group from Oaxaca was onstage performing a rather rousing and entertaining version of the son "La Iguana" complete with the dance moves imitating the animal. When another local academic of the sotavento and his friend from the region of Los Tuxtlas came to greet me, we had our own conversation about son jarocho. We were academics, but this same conversation could have been had with a group of enthusiasts. In fact, it is hard to say which "hat" people were wearing that night—that of the practitioner or the investigator.

The lines blur, and the positionalities overlap. The footings seem to follow the same paths.

A FLOURISHING THIRD ROOT

Alfredo and I agreed to meet in the Plazuela de la Campana one afternoon before the space came to life, but late enough for the shadows of the old and new buildings to stretch into the small plaza and make it comfortable enough to pass the time. He is a constant presence in the zócalo as well as the Plazuela. His regular attendance at the nights of public dancing in those two locations made him recognizable to me before we even officially met, an unacquainted acquaintance as is so common in the intimacy wrought by the public spaces of Veracruz that moonlight as dance floors.

For many nights, our paths had run parallel, but they never crossed until one evening Alfredo noticed my attempts to capture a song for my archive. The famous local band Pregoneros del Recuerdo were playing a song I had never heard before but whose lyrics immediately captured my attention—"El Esclavo." With time, I would learn that local sonero groups played the song with enough regularity for it to be considered a standard even if the ballad about a slave's lament and nostalgia for home did not have the same rotation as some of the more upbeat numbers. The song was written by the local composer and railroad worker Félix Barragan and made famous by Pedro "Moscovita" Dominguez Castillo, also from the port city. When it comes to Afro-Antillean music, local artists and composers remain featured in the near nightly performances of live dance music. "El Esclavo" is no different. For this reason, my archive is filled with truncated recordings of this plaintive song. The first full recording, however, was courtesy of Alfredo and the occasion that found us together on a cast iron bench in the Plazuela.

I watched his eyes slip closed as he drew on the pathos required to do justice to a song about a protagonist's journey from being enchained in a caravan somewhere in Africa to being brought to a faraway land [America] "where our color is an affront to other people." Voicing this lamenting enslaved person, Alfredo asks the "white man's god" to one day take him back to the distant jungle where he was born so that he could die among "dark-skinned people" whom he now refers to as his "sister race." In my recollection, Alfredo's a cappella version was sung into the silence of the Plazuela, but that is not quite true. Along with his voice, clear but wavering from strain and passion, on the recording are the sounds of people doing construction nearby, the murmur of people, and the clinking of glasses from the abutting restaurant. However, in the moment, it all fell away, laid bare, as this light-skinned Mexican sang a song about being enslaved.

After thanking him for his rendition, I asked about his childhood recollections of his father playing the song. Instead, he offered a deeper, more expansive historical memory:

There arrived a moment when indigenous people joined together with black people like brothers. Why? Because Spaniards had Indigenous peoples enslaved just as they had Black people. They became like brothers and then shared their suffering, their music. For example, it is said that after intense days of work during slavery, in the afternoon they would get together to sing, they would get together to dance. And this that you see here—that they come, and they get together to dance—comes from centuries past.

Not only did Alfredo explain the phenomenon, but he also explains this transhistorical need to come together to sing and to dance. As he puts it:

[T]his is what is left to poor people. Rich people do not come here. The rich are counting their money in their house. And all these people [here] have no money. So how do they face life? They shake off anguish; they shake off poverty and take a cynical view of life. [. . .] So people come here to . . . they enjoy. They enjoy and they forget about their poverty. They forget about their problems. It's like . . . it's like a drug.

When I asked him if he were speaking about the here and now in the Plazuela or the referenced time of the enslaved workers, he replied, "No, before and still today. Now it's still the same."

It comes from centuries past, and it comes from mere decades ago. It comes from last week, and it will come in the next. It comes from within the blood of the jarocho, and it comes from the cooperation of the community. It comes despite the state's absence, just as it comes scheduled on the events calendar posted by the municipal tourism office. It even comes when the sky turns a burnt sienna, a sure sign that rain is imminent. It comes when tourists descend like locusts, and it comes when even the ambulatory vendors do not bother to show up for want of clients. It comes from all these things and more.

Intentionally or not, Alfredo captured the way in which multiple times are gathered in the antique city he called home. The temporal slippage exemplified by Alfredo's reflection manifests constantly in the quotidian experiences in the historic center. It is made audible by the strains of old music played from permanent, open-air stages. It is made visible by the multigenerational use of public space. It is made tangible by the close company kept by buildings spanning centuries in varying states of disrepair. The different tempos that dictate the everyday lives of jarochos create, among other things, an aural, corporeal, and theoretical connection to a jarocho type, rendering it ever timely and timeless. Time signatures abound in the public spaces of the old port city, not merely in the iconic genres beloved by locals.

Linearity succumbs to the cyclicity like the repetitive motifs that characterize son jarocho, the danzón, and son veracruzano. It forms a throbbing bass line above which the improvisation and the call and response of everyday life are laid.

It courts the dreaded ethnographic present for "this thing you see here" is ever contemporary as it came, comes, and will continue to come from centuries past. It was not mere hyperbole when Alfredo connected the present customs of gathering together with an unspecified anterior time. He made his claim confidently, not carelessly. As we sat in the early twenty-first century, he used a mid-twentieth-century song to make a direct connection with the colonial period. He took a common practice, this coming together to sing and to dance, and identified it as a cultural retention borne of the circumstances found in Veracruz, not grounded in an elsewhere.

In a time when people and practice are objectified as representative of the third root, Alfredo instead placed both people and practice at the root of Veracruz itself. In his retelling, the habit, the tradition, and in some ways, the *need* to gather together and dance becomes constitutive of Veracruz itself. This, what you see here, comes from centuries past. In this chronotope known as Veracruz, the past and future are dance partners, and the present keeps time. Such temporal slippages treat the past as a cultural resource from which the present is contextualized and the future is imagined.

Over the last three decades, locals have come to acknowledge and celebrate the Blackness of this past that slips into the present and shapes the future. Alfredo's narration, for example, echoes Mexican scholars' contention that the ordinal "third" makes the third root a misnomer by implying a ranked importance. In many places, such as Veracruz, it was not third at all. Europeans were just as absent from his colonial fandango as he claimed the rich are from the contemporary gatherings in the Plazuela. The fictive kin ties between the oppressed were binding. The historical record proves that those kin ties were not fictive at all. The oppressed faced life together and made lives in the process. The local term *jarocho* was originally a casta term for persons of African and indigenous ancestry.

Today, *jarocho* functions more as an ethnoregional term than an ethnoracial one. Nevertheless, the concerted dissemination of historical research to the local populations has made Blackness if not an identity then a critical aspect of one's identity as a local. As Michel-Rolph Trouillot noted, while "The Past" needs to be someone's past, it does not belong to its narrators alone. It also belongs to those who take it in their own hands.[56] Alfredo's commentary is an example of this possessive and localized treatment of Blackness that is so often expressed in those communities I call jarocho publics. Within these publics, discursive moves interpreted as acts of racial distancing, such as emphasizing the pastness of Blackness, take on a different significance. Rather than situating Blackness in the past to imply its absence in the presence, jarocho publics instead treat their Black past as a cultural resource upon which to draw when positioning their practices as locally specific and generative of identity. When one is concerned with whether someone identifies as *negro*, or Black, redirecting the conversation to the past may sound like a denial. However, if one were to consider how someone identifies with

Blackness, the proprietary and localized understanding of Blackness does not sound like denial at all.

That afternoon in the Plazuela, I had expected to record Alfredo singing a song for my archive. When he then interpreted the song not as a personal recollection but rather as a truth about jarochos' past and present need to come together to dance as a way to shake off their despair, he became a singer of Veracruz's tale. A singer of tales, as Albert B. Lord argues, is singer, performer, composer, and poet simultaneously. Rather than merely preserving, they are constantly re-creating tradition. The ultimate purpose, he maintains, is "a true story well and truly retold."[57] For Alfredo, singing "El Esclavo," the lyrics of which have no mention of music, dancing, or community formation, was an opportunity to fluidly tell a true story about Veracruz that centrally included Afro-descendants and, by collapsing both time and scale, connected people who are otherwise thought of as in denial as to their cultural forebears.

Alfredo as a singer of tales demonstrates how Blackness has become useful for a population living in a location that has been spatialized as Black and has historically been associated with Mexico's Blackness. The whitening of Mexico and the erasure of Blackness on a national scale were not wholly successful in Veracruz even as the ideology of mestizaje was. In that way, jarochos have learned to embed Blackness within an ideology that has traditionally not made room for it. Locating Blackness not in "The Past" but in *their* Past not only acknowledges what cannot be denied, it capitalizes on the multiple tempos and temporalities at play in the old city. As cultural practices iconic to the city increasingly get revitalized, the past, populated with Black bodies, becomes increasing important in jarochos' place- and future-making. This is how public dancing, which is not a practice unique to Veracruz, becomes for them a through line connecting that which you see here to centuries past. This is how Afro-Indigenous conviviality as a way to "face life" happened "before and still today."

The Black Past, which is not an unclaimed third root but "Our Third Root," functions as a cultural resource, in the sense outlined by Stuart Hall. For Hall, cultural identity comes from "those historical experiences, those cultural traditions, those lost and marginal languages, those marginalized experiences, those peoples and histories which remain unwritten."[58] These cultural resources are not to be rediscovered but rather are to be used in the construction of future identities. More than just resources, they are a gift. As Elizabeth Povinelli observes, "gifts of memory move along specific routes, raveling and unraveling worlds in the process. Memory does or doesn't transfer across space (as organized kinds of places) and time (in the sense of generational logics), and it is here that we can see, perhaps most clearly, that gifts can be given long after the spherical world in which they make sense has collapsed."[59] That spherical world has not quite collapsed though it has evolved through the centuries to fit its present condition.

What you see here, facing life and striving to be happy together through music and dance, is a cultural resource in the construction of the jarocho's present and future. It is a gift from enslaved Africans and subjugated indigenous peoples coming together at the end of the day to make music and make it through life. None of these practices are unique to Veracruz, Mexico, and yet it is through practicing and valuing them that jarochos create a group identity, an identity that, while not Black, takes its Blackness as foundational.

In this chapter, we have examined how and why the state has disseminated a localized understanding of the third root discourse. By focusing on jarocho publics of the festival and forum scenes, we have also seen how private individuals have taken up that message and have used it to make sense of their practices and preferences. In the next chapter, we will explore two other jarocho publics, enthusiasts of music-dance complexes organized around two different genres: son jarocho and the danzón. Whereas this chapter focused on lessons on the jarocho's Blackness received from stages or through microphones, the next chapter explores embodied lessons, lessons learned through practice and practicing.

Interlude
———

Mother and Child

In the corner of the Plazuela, there is a rental space where many a business has tried to make it work. Once, there was a well-lit dance studio where you could go to learn Afro-Cuban salsa. The owner-instructor—who was actually Peruvian—filled the space with photographs and images of Afro-Cuban people and was a patient teacher as you danced to recorded music. Most nights, these recordings would have to compete with the live music coming from the speakers on the Plazuela's stage a few feet away. In the end, the recordings and the studio lost that struggle. Many short-lived ventures have come and gone since the dance studio closed, but sometimes I wonder about a young couple I observed there once. I wonder if they ever debuted what they learned in the studio among the dancing bodies a few short steps away in the Plazuela. While it is not formal training, there is something to be said about learning on the dance floor.

Years later, I think of this couple as I stand in the back of the Plazuela, observing the scene. After a long break, deep into their three-hour set list, the Pregoneros del Recuerdo are ready to give the people some more son music to dance to. By the end of the opening measure, a young mother and child have made their way to the center of the Plazuela, which serves as an open-air dance floor during these nights of free music. The little girl clings closely to her mother as dusk settles into night. The pair are smiling at each other as they share an intimate moment in the public space. As I stand in the back of the square observing them, I am struck by what this small slice of everyday (night) life represents.

They are at play, swinging arms and moving legs to the live music coming from the stage. Yet the woman is also leading her daughter to the rhythms the young child will grow up hearing simply because she is from Veracruz. I imagine this night and many like it as part of the development of what someone may later mis-recognize as innateness—what in some future time can serve as further evidence that Veracruzanos are Caribbean folk who carry rhythm in their blood and joy in their spirit.

At the end of the song, I catch sight of the mother and child once again as the crowd thins. The little girl, who seems to have only recently mastered walking unassisted, is learning a new way of being in and moving through the world. She is learning a new world in itself—a world where the clave rhythm really is the key to life and the repetition of a chord progression never truly feels repetitive. The mother and child return to their shared table, mimicking the other couples' exo-dus away from the floor in the interlude. Another lesson: the steps you take to and from the dance floor are just as important as the ones you take while on it.

3

Practicing Innateness

Confronting relatively positive stereotypes that you as a Black person can sing or dance is an easier cross to bear when you come from a home country where whether Black lives matter is a contested question. Presumed musical and dance talents, joy, and sensuality are preferable to assumptions of inherent criminality. They are nevertheless stereotypes and authenticating scripts that adhere to Blackness and, by extension, to jarochos. The essentialisms speak to the enduring association of Blackness and jarocho identity. However, as Stuart Hall has argued, the essentializing moment is "weak because it naturalizes difference, mistaking what is historical and cultural for what is natural, biological, and genetic."[1] The curious thing about the essentialism in Veracruz is that they consider Blackness to be historical and cultural while using it to naturalize, biologize, and make genetic their jarocho identity. The valorization of the historical and cultural Blackness works in the service of performing their regional identity. Yet this regionalism by way of racialized logics carries with it expectations more typically associated with race rather than region.

In his 1993 piece "What Is This 'Black' in Black Popular Culture?" Stuart Hall outlines how the popular carries the perception of being simultaneously authentic and appropriable. The "popular" implies a rootedness in its originating communities through its particularities to its subculture, but it also lends itself to homogenization when the control passes from the creators to cultural producers and promoters.[2] Among jarochos, this tension between authenticity and appropriation exists in the transition from the jarocho as an ethnoracial type to an ethnoregional one. Yet, just as Hall argues, despite the flattening of forms in the expropriation from specific to generic popular culture, the original repertoires and the experiences undergirding them remain distinguishable. He calls this "style" and points to the body as a way to make oneself a "canvas of representation."[3] The Black community remains signified by its popular culture. Veracruz and its jarochos trouble the wholesale application of Hall's theory about Black popular culture, but the question remains: what is this "Black" in Veracruz's Black popular culture?

To name something "Black" in the absence of Black people demands nuance. You must avoid the trap of appropriation—the accusation and the action. Likewise, you must avoid expropriation. Both presume a proprietary stance to Blackness, Black art, and Black popular culture. To call the *Afro-Cuban* ballroom dance the danzón a "Black art" or "Black popular culture" is an easier argument to make than to say the *Mexican* folkloric tradition son jarocho is a Black art form. Although people may deny it, there is still an assumption that Blackness supersedes all other aspects. It is as if naming something a Black art precludes it from also being transculturated and the product of Indigenous and European legacies as well. At the risk of being misunderstood, let me state that both the danzón and son jarocho are Black arts and that many jarochos access them with Blackness in mind.

Whereas previous chapters outlined the jarocho type and contextualized how popular culture and the discursive past have become access points to Veracruz's Blackness, this chapter looks at style and bodily comportment. I reiterate: members of jarocho publics are not "playing at being Black," or even interested in forging diasporic links that go beyond Cuba. Instead, Blackness is a found object they use on the way to being more themselves—to being more jarocho. The third root discourse is integrated in sites where people learn how to execute the danzón and son jarocho, both of which are iconic jarocho practices.

The writer Toni Morrison once said Black art must look cool and easy. Yet she cautions that there is effort in the effortless. You must *look* like you have never touched it, but you also must put in the work and discipline to be able to improvise with found objects. If it makes you sweat, she said, you have not done the work.[4] This framing resonates with my experience in Veracruz and my attempts to learn alongside others how to access our inherited Blackness. We collaborated on this endeavor; we workshopped it.

This chapter is about innateness and its misrecognition; the process and consequence of revitalized traditions; and the lessons learned through leisure. It is about scenarios in which common, if not essentialized, notions of Blackness become enmeshed with one's actions and where one can practice the performance of their belonging to Veracruz. It is about the effort in the effortless and focuses on how— rather than making perfect—practice makes the practitioner. Unlike the mother and child who precede this chapter, most of the protagonists of this story pay for the pleasure of learning their local culture. Like the pair, however, the endeavor is still leisurely and is the pursuit of happiness and self. As interest in local popular culture increases, so too does the number of jarochos who enroll in *talleres*, or pedagogical workshop spaces dedicated to those practices. The workshop structure has become the prevailing method of learning art forms performed and interpreted collectively. These spaces are where embodiment, discursivity, and sociality converge. They are the vehicles by which jarocho publics learn simultaneously about regionalized cultural practices and about the Black heritage integral to those art forms. As workshop spaces anchor the revitalization of local traditions, these social scenes become spaces where third root discourse disseminates, and individuals learn to articulate their relationship to their Black heritage. Talleres, in short, are where jarochos construct alternative forms of embodying Mexican Blackness, not as Black people but rather as jarochos.

TALLERES AND THE REVITALIZATION OF TRADITION

For around three hundred pesos a month, one can join an intergenerational group of enthusiasts as they learn local dance and music forms.[5] Two communities in particular stand out—the *fandangueros* who practice the folkloric tradition *son jarocho*, and the *danzoneros*, who dance the Afro-Cuban ballroom complex the *danzón*. They are part of a broader subpopulation of Veracruzanos, the *jarocho publics*, which encompasses residents in the city who actively seek out opportunities, encounters, and scenarios where they engage with what they consider local culture and jarocho identity. In a city of over half a million residents, jarocho publics represent those who practice and support cultural activities iconic to the port city. Through their actions, these participants constantly reinvest in the jarochos' regional distinction. Ever since the official investment in celebrating the Black heritage—that is, the third root—of the jarocho, these publics have worked both passively and actively to rescue Blackness from disappearing within the ideology of *mestizaje*. Jarocho publics deploy the power of repetition, be it physical or narrative, to make real and present the idea that they as jarochos possess an African—or more accurately, an Afro-Caribbean—heritage. Among the broader jarocho publics, workshops function as spaces where individuals collectively engage in repetition in both its discursive and its embodied manifestations. In the process, these spaces bring to the fore Blackness for participants.

Although the third root is not a daily conversation or prerequisite mention in these regularly scheduled gatherings, talleres introduce, reference, allude to, and cultivate understandings of Black heritage among parties who do not necessarily seek it out. These interactions are the types of spaces where lessons and their significance become instantiated through the actions of people. In Veracruz, it is where the lofty idea that Mexico has a "third root"—and that that root is Black—becomes a social fact and useful to group- and place-making. The workshop is both physically and conceptually portable. The people—not the place—make the workshop.

These spaces are part of the cottage industry of revitalized tradition that has flourished under the benign hand of the state's cultural policy. As chapter 2 outlined, the Mexican state, through institutionalization, plays an active role as the producer and promoter of culture in Mexico.[6] Citizens expect the state's involvement in the arts, but private interests often work in tandem with state projects. This has been the case in Veracruz and its revitalization of music and dance practices. Workshops are a key social space through which cultural practices remain alive and relevant. They also become the mechanism through which cultural policy propagates to and through everyday people. As a result, they have played a critical role in the broad embrace of the third root concept.

While academics and activists have worked to educate the public on how Afro-Caribbean heritage is at the root of what it means to be jarocho through books, articles, and presentations, the narrativization and dissemination of this information within the intimate workshop setting has also circulated the idea of a Black past in an ambiguously Black present. Moreover, the corporeality and embodied nature of these workshops on danceable genres of music foster a different relationship to the transmitted information than that developed from a seat in a forum's audience. Put plainly, the lessons learned in class go beyond chord progressions and choreography. And while some of the information shared is not entirely faithful to the scholarship, such a scenario nevertheless transmits a taken-for-grantedness to the idea of African ancestry being integral to popular culture as it currently exists and is practiced.

This, in part, is why Veracruz and its implantation of the third root differs so starkly from the situation anthropologist Laura Lewis found in the Costa Chica of Guerrero. As briefly mentioned in chapter 2, Lewis described a scenario where the third root manifested as an alienated imposition brought about by "la cultura," which collectively refers to scholars, politicians, and other culturemongers.[7] Although "la cultura" identified local African retentions, it did little to convince the community members to invest in these artifacts. In Veracruz, the third root became a lens through which to view practices already associated with local jarocho culture rather than rescuing objects and practices that have little resonance today. This is in part an issue of timing.

The revitalization of local cultural practices such as son jarocho and the danzón coincided with the strongest investment in third root discourse. Workshops dedicated to the music and dance genres have become the social space where the multiculturalist third root narrative spreads. According to the scholar Rafael Figueroa Hernández, for example, the *movimiento jaranero* (jaranero movement) has been indispensable to the genre's revitalization and has had an academic bent from the beginning. Workshop spaces as a result simultaneously disseminate instructional and educational information.[8] The movement was synergistic with the multicultural politics of the 1980s that worked to localize the national-level interest in the African root in Mexico. Thus, the revival of son jarocho interfaced with academic research and presentations in the city and created an association between enthusiasts and cultural promoters. Ad hoc son jarocho workshops concurrently proliferated throughout the city to accommodate the growing interest in the musical tradition. The integration and dissemination of son jarocho revitalization and state-level third root discourse was both intentional, in the alliance between cultural producers and jaranero community leaders, and organic, in the word-of-mouth exchange of information among the community's social networks. Together, this resulted in a widespread yet undisciplined incorporation of information about the African influence in such a quintessentially Mexican folk genre.

Several scholars of son jarocho are also practitioners, and they slip between these positionalities fluidly. The familiarity inherent in this dual role constructs an informality between enthusiasts and academics. Fandangueros often flock to academic talks with instruments in hand and in anticipation of the fandango to follow. Likewise, many son jarocho groups take time during their performances to educate listeners about the history of the genre—a history that necessarily includes Africans and their descendants. By attending both events clearly marked as educational and those as entertainment, enthusiasts repeatedly receive information about the third root and its relationship to son jarocho. Uptake may vary across audiences, but the repetition has created an unquestioned association between son jarocho and the third root.

Because the danzón is from Cuba, locals understand its link to Blackness to be simultaneously more apparent and less noteworthy. It is more apparent because Cuba looms as a Black space in the local imaginary. As a more obvious link, it also requires less mention. Danzón enthusiasts know the dance is Afro-Cuban but also laud how integrated it has become to local culture. Its localness rather than its origin receives the lion's share of attention. This occurs in its workshop culture as well. Unlike son jarocho, for which roots are part of the revitalization efforts, the danzón's revitalization primarily relies on the opportunity to dance in the public squares of Veracruz. This is not to say that the roots are not important. They are drilled into the consciousness of practitioners just as choreography and bodily comportment are. However, the emphasis is on the practice of the dance rather than its historical significance and trajectory.

Compared to son jarocho, a stronger division also exists between practitioners who engage in workshops and those who do not. Fandangueros often join workshops to gain the skills needed to better participate in son jarocho culture. There are those who then form their own groups, who then perform locally and even cut an album if they have the resources. These groups are not as proficient or popular as the professional jaraneros such as the internationally renowned group Mono Blanco, but they do often name themselves and perform as openers for monthly fandangos or other local gigs.[9] However, workshop collectivities do not form with the intention of creating a performing group. The same cannot be said for danzonera groups. Danzonero talleres often function as feeder groups for performance groups who commission matching attire and travel the country competing in the danzón. This orientation toward performance undergirds the divide between people who dance the danzón and people who are members of danzonero workshops.

There is little social interaction between the danzoneros and the fandangueros. Their workshop cultures have important ideological differences, but also striking similarities. Both, for example, leave space for learning aids like a sheet of choreography or a book of lyrics. Yet such aids are not the primary mode of learning. Instead, you learn by repetitive corporeal action. The workshop is a social setting with common characteristics. It has a teacher—often male—who is the primary demonstrator of a new skill. This is the person who decides what we are to do and for how long. This is the person you pay. The teacher has authority and respect, but they are not the sole purveyor of knowledge. Your fellow workshop-goers share the burden of demonstrating already learned skills or sharing context for the activity at hand. For danzoneros, this may mean working through a particular step of choreography in between practicing as a group to the music. For jaraneros, this can mean looking to each other to figure out which note comes next in the piece. Because workshops attract people with a wide range of experience in the genre and people often grow and stay in the workshop community, the teacher is not necessarily the only expert. In other words, the workshop structure allows for spoke-and-wheel transmission of specialized knowledge alongside a more dispersed network of exchange.

Although a teacher-student relationship exists, these talleres are not classrooms or traditional classes. Instead, they function more like social clubs where a significant portion of the time together is spent in convivial interaction rather than learning chords or choreography. Fellow workshop-goers are keystones in new spaces and members of group chats. The group lives on word-of-mouth information about the chosen genre, social events, and more. They are places where rumors are peddled and secrets kept. They are also where the third root rhetoric has found its most fertile soil. This shared responsibility helps to build the strong conviviality of the workshop space. Talleres, while organized with the intention to teach a cultural practice, often have a lot of "down time" when people are gossiping, flirting, consoling, bragging, teasing, or a myriad of other interpersonal interactions that do not relate to the task at hand. In the process, the third root looks less like a top-down cultural policy and an instrument of neoliberal multiculturalism, and more like a vouched and vetted lens to better understand oneself.[10]

In each of the following sections, I juxtapose two ethnographic vignettes—one from a son jarocho workshop and one for the danzón. Comparing the two social scenes reveals the commonalities between the two types of jarocho publics, the way Blackness appears and recedes in such social spaces, and what the workshop space makes possible for practitioners. I argue that the sociality of the spaces makes ideas like Mexican Blackness both thinkable and tangible. These are not workshops or lessons in how to be Black. Nevertheless, expectations, essentialisms, and invocations of Blackness permeate the narratives and embodied practices that exist in these communal spaces.

By looking closely at popular cultural workshops, the chapter argues that through such activities, participants do not just repeat and rehearse local traditions. They iterate and reiterate Blackness itself. In taking the third root frame and integrating it with local culture, *talleristas* (workshop-goers) embody lessons about the third root beyond what would be possible in a classroom. Instead, they are working over the idea of an Afro-Caribbean root in their hands, their feet, their understanding of their past. The chapter raises questions concerning the relationship between innateness and proficiency and the power of leisurely practices to covertly and thoroughly spread the radical recognition that Mexico—the famously mestizo nation—has a strong and critical African root.

INNATENESS AND ITS MISRECOGNITION

Jarochos carry rhythm in their blood, or so the argument goes. Metaphors of blood are further unpacked in chapter 5, but the presumption of innate rhythmic abilities comes to a head when considered against the work and effort in finding and maintaining rhythm within talleres. As ethnomusicologist Hettie Malcomson has outlined, the danzón is one of the crucial avenues through which Veracruzanos relate to their Blackness, which they equate with "being good at dancing, sexually 'hot,' happy, rhythmically adept and so forth."[11] These reputations affix to the jarocho type, leading to expectations that they themselves feel compelled to meet. Despite the failures to access or maintain this sanguine rhythm, the expectation of innateness persists.

Rhythm becomes a demonstrable trait in the project of belonging to jarocho collective identity. People believe that innate rhythmic ability explains why the Afro-Cuban genres of the danzón and son music have "stuck" in Veracruz and serves as proof positive that Veracruzanos are also Caribbean. The poets among the residents sometimes look to metaphors beyond the blood, finding inspiration in the incessant and constant tide that continues to shape the city and its future. Others turn to the seasons' rhythms, marked by the high winds from the north called *nortes*, which lore says ends the third of May every year. Nowadays, the festival cycle celebrating the regionalisms of Veracruz creates its own rhythm, so well known that cancellations like that of the Afro-Caribbean Festival discussed in the previous chapter create a stutter step in everyday life—an *engaño*, or trick, to use a term from the danzón community.

Regardless of which analogies interlocutors use, there is little if any resistance to valuing the possession and demonstration of one's rhythm. Nevertheless, the workshops are spaces where innateness butts against the narrative and compulsion toward proficiency. Practitioners of both the danzón and son jarocho regularly acknowledge that the genres have a learning curve and that the rhythm is a significant barrier to overcome. This is as true for the danzoneros as for the jarane-ros, as will be seen in the next two scenes, respectively. The cast of actors and the genre of choice change, but the script stays uncannily the same.

The group of us were facing our dance instructor Pablo as we waited for him to speak. We had been meeting twice a week on the stage of the Plazuela since the start of the new year. Although not a resolution, many of us nevertheless viewed this foray into the danzón as a longtime goal. Most of the group were the stereo-typical women of a certain age, but each had taken their own path toward this stage.[12] There was Luna, a widow who wanted a hobby—something just for her. She would, on occasion, bring her granddaughter when she was the designated caretaker on the Tuesdays or Thursdays we had class. Fran and Lino were an older couple who were dating. Each had previously danced the danzón years before, but this was their first time dancing as a couple. Flor—who would also bring her granddaughter sometimes—was the newest addition to the group. She tended to have a hesitation in her step and a hunch to her shoulders despite Pablo's emphasis on holding a proper frame. Elena found her way to the group through her friend-ship with Esme, who was a more advanced dancer and a member of Pablo's com-petitive group. For Elena, the danzón was a way out of her shell, out of her house, and onto the stage. Rounding out our community was Jorge, who would come to the beginner class to help Pablo and serve as a floating dance partner. Like Pablo, Jorge came from the ballet folklórico world. Not only was he a great dancer, he always had a ready smile and a wealth of patience for our beginner group.

Our group had been dancing together for weeks before Pablo decided to approach class time differently. After gathering us together near the back of the stage, Pablo declared we needed to learn how to count before we could properly dance the danzón. Our task was to count aloud as a group. Once we mastered that, we would clap. The claps were to correspond with the downbeat counts of the basic steps we had already learned. After explaining our task, Pablo cued up the music on his boombox. Flor flashed a nervous smile around the semicircle. Some shifted their weight in a way that was decidedly not a ball change. The exercise was new, but the melody was familiar. It was one of the first songs for which Pablo taught us his choreography.

After the pickup notes that started the introduction, Pablo began to count aloud the bars: "Uno . . . dos . . . tres . . ." and so on until we reached the eighth measure. He held his hands in the air to show his fingers as he kept track of the numbers. Once the introduction's melody repeated, he gestured for us to start counting as well. Pablo had taught us to stand placidly during the first eight measures, gently waving our fans. Not everyone honors this convention, but we were not to shift from our position until the fifth bar of the second pass. However, since most of us had not been counting bars and beats prior to this class, we mainly relied on Pablo's verbal and nonverbal cues to know when to open and start the choreography. A pointed nod and raised voice proved sufficient indication of when to stop methodically fanning ourselves and start dancing. Even though we were not dancing during this counting exercise, we continued to perform these nonverbal cues and leading intonations. Most of us followed. When he dropped out, things fell apart.

Without Pablo's voice rising above the recording, many of us missed the all-important entrance at the fifth measure. We practiced this for several rewinds since the entrance is of tantamount importance. Eventually, Pablo decided we were ready for the clapping exercise. Once the first melody began after the two refrains, Pablo switched his counting pattern. Rather than counting each full measure, he began to count the slow-quick-quick rhythm of the steps: *Uno, dos tres. Cuatro, cinco seis. Siete, ocho nueve. Diez, once (doce).* The eleven—sometimes twelve—beats he counted spread across four measures. The rhythm requires a hesitation in your glide as you continuously step tougher in different figures. After the first melody, the introduction returns and with it the counting of measures rather than steps. That day we never managed to complete Pablo's counting and clapping exercises for the whole song. Our group could not count out the rhythm. Eventually, Pablo rewound the track, and we danced instead. In my time with the group, we never attempted to count and clap again.

The group of us were out in the garden where we met twice a week to practice. Half under the metal carport roof and half under the scant shade of the large coconut tree, we sat together in a circle of green plastic chairs with our bodies turned slightly toward our instructor, Nico. On any given Tuesday or Thursday, there would be a different configuration of the core group of participants, with new people coming and going. The most consistent attendees were the retirees—Don Justo, who used to work for the national oil company Pemex, and Chucho, a former school superintendent. Alberto, the dental technician, was not retired, but he rarely if ever missed a class. Manuel, the school principal, and Enrique, who worked in the nuclear plant north of Veracruz, were also reliable, though often tardy, participants.

Over the years, others had passed through the group. There was Gabriel, a young teenager whose mother would drop him off at the ornate gate to the garden. Doña Alicia would come on Thursdays just to dance the zapateado. Rosita both danced and played, but her new real estate job was encroaching increasingly on her time in the taller. Two brothers, Carlos and Angel, an architect and an engineer, would come as their schedules permitted, making their presence a pleasant surprise rather than a sure thing. Guillermo and Lena, a young hippie couple, would bring their positive energy along with their instruments, whereas Juana and Pablo, a pair of friends from the ballet folklórico world, would bring their white

FIGURE 5. Son jarocho members practicing a son on their jaranas while other members practice the accompanying dance, the zapateado, on the tarima. Photo by the author.

heeled shoes. At the center of this multigenerational motley crew was Nico, whose
silver-capped tooth flashed when he laughed (figure 5).

As we would play in our circle, our eyes would flit to each other's nondominant
hands along our jaranas' fretboards to make sure we were each at the same point in
the song's cycle between the C-chord and G-chord. Lost in concentration, I did not
keep track as people trickled in to join the group. When we were in the middle of a
son, latecomers either joined in or waited patiently until we stopped before going
around the circle to greet everyone with an individual handshake. That afternoon,
we were playing "El Zapateado," a quicker number for which those two notes were
the only ones we would need to play on our eight-stringed instruments. Normally,
we would have followed Nico as we strummed percussively. This day, though, Nico
has left us on our own. There is no *guitarra de son* to follow for the melody, no
leona or *marimbol* to provide the bass line, no dancer on the low, wooden *tarima*
to follow for the beat. We just had each other.

In a fandango setting, "El Zapateado" tends to be one of the longer pieces, as
various couples mount and dismount the tarima to show off their dancing skills. In
a performance setting, it often serves as the background music over which a *deci-
mista* recites the ten-line poetry common in son jarocho culture. In our workshop,
it would last until Nico told us to stop by waving his hand and offering a smile
that did not always reach his eyes. He offered that smile to us as he waved us off,

stopping the cacophony that was emerging. As Nico began to tune a latecomer's instrument, he asked us what went wrong.

Don Justo, the eldest and longest-attending member of Nico's taller, offered an assessment: we were not playing forcefully enough so we got lost. Without Nico's assertive playing, we had tried and failed to reach a consensus on who to follow through raised eyebrows and lifted shoulders. Nico further proved the point when he swung his jarana from his back to his front and began to play once again. He elicited a sound from his instrument with an ease and forcefulness that was missing from our combined jaranas minutes ago. When we started to drift after joining in, he accented his playing to get us back in sync and gesticulated without lifting his hands from his cedar instrument.

This is how Nico liked to teach—by doing something the correct way with gusto. There was no sheet music, no counting, no metronome, just Nico leading us through sones for three hours. Some participants would bring books with printed lyrics or notebooks to jot down new verses or chord progressions. However, at heart, this was our son jarocho workshop. You learned by doing. Sometimes you failed to do it right, to change chords at the right time, to stay on tempo. So you did it again.

LESSONS THROUGH LEISURE

"What does *gurumbé* mean anyway?" I asked as we took a break from playing "Los Negritos." Having practiced the son regularly over the past few weeks, we had sung the word countless times. Not knowing the exact meaning of the word that made up the bulk of the refrain had not compromised our understanding of the piece in its broad strokes, so the unfamiliar word had not given the group much pause. Usually, when our class came across something uncommon, our teacher, Nico, would defer to one of the educators, either Chucho or Manuel, for their ability to impart knowledge on our community. To this question, however, neither had a definitive answer.

"Los Negritos" is not part of the most played canon in the fandangos, where jaraneros collectively and improvisationally interpret the music. It is an old son with a mixture of old and new lyrics. Several groups have recorded it for their albums, and it is known enough to be recognizable in a fandango, but many casual enthusiasts do not know offhand how to play it. It is, as Erandi García Cabrera has argued, an amalgamation of recovery and innovation.[13] Nico had chosen to practice the piece partly in deference to my ongoing investigation and partly to break up the monotony of son selection in the city's fandango scene. In that way, it served both our purposes—adding variety and an opportunity to broach the question of Blackness and the third root. However, when I asked my question about gurumbé, the group turned contemplative. In the face of Chucho and Manuel's uncertainty, another member, Juana, took out her phone to search the internet. The answer remained elusive, yet the class still came to a consensus.

The first idea became the prevailing one—that it is an African word of unspecified meaning, probably of Bantu or Guinean origin, as some suggested. As participants reasoned aloud, the group argued that the word sounds "African" and is part of a son that valorizes Blackness and Black features. Therefore, the word itself became an example of "the third root." As enthusiasts of the folkloric genre, we knew son jarocho to be one of the most illustrative manifestations of Mexico's third root. By deeming the word as the third root, the group placed the unfamiliar word within an intelligible narrative, freeing us to let go of the mystery and return to perfecting our finger positions on the instrument's neck and taking turns initiating the call-and-response pattern of the genre. For our class, gurumbé became evidence of the African influence in son jarocho. Our chat over, we went back to playing.

This conversation is illustrative of how the third root discourse presents itself in workshop scenes. The shared burden of authoritative voicing and the striving to align the unknown to the known frameworks facilitate the dissemination of expertise. The third root discourse does not stay in the ivory tower. People do not articulate it through amplified microphones or behind lecterns alone. It is shared in circles of confidence where the term *third root* is not necessarily nuanced but is effective. Because the workshop-goers are audience members invited into the ivory tower and attentive at fora and festivals organized to teach them about themselves, they take that knowledge back into the circle of the workshop space. This movement has helped integrate the third root discourse into the revitalization of the genre. The third root in the danzón functions differently. Rather than teasing apart the African footprints on local practice, danzoneros know Blackness to be at the root of their dance, even if it has undergone important evolutions that make it as jarocho as son jarocho.

Pablo called us together once again to have a chat. "Does anyone know the history of the danzón?" he asked. The more advanced deferred this lesson to the beginners, who were fairly confident in their response: it came from Cuba. This is true, but incomplete, according to Pablo. Asking Esme to fill in the blanks, she offered that the danzón came from Matanzas, Cuba, but it was an adaptation of the contredanse, which she believed came from Haiti. This was the beginning of the narrative that Pablo wanted to make sure we all knew. The danzón, which evolved from the contradanza in Cuba, came from the contredanse that Haitian migrants had brought to Cuba. But the contredanse was itself a French dance that was an adaptation of the English country dance! Country dance. Contredanse. Contradanza. Danzón. It was not the first time I had heard this genealogical report; in fact, nearly every danzonero in the port city has this story in their repertoire.

Pablo's impromptu lesson offered me an explanation as to why. Before we went back to dancing, Pablo insisted that we know this history, "in case a tourist asked." Although we were enthusiasts learning for our own personal edification, we had to be at the ready—willing and able to share the story connecting Veracruz to Cuba, to Haiti, to France, and, ultimately, England. An answer I never got, though, was where the other side of the family tree would lead, for the distance between Mexican danzón and an English country dance is more than just an evolution in vocabulary.

In two different conversations, cultural practices uniquely formed in the Americas—products of the transculturation that created a new cultural form from the interaction of the old—are atomized into disparate parts as if the African or the English (!) can be precipitated out of the cultural forms practiced today. This is also a story about two different paths taken at a fork in the road wherein the danzoneros chose to follow the dance's evolution back through the European side and the jaraneros chose the path toward Africa. At this point, both narrative tracks are well entrenched, with academics recording these narratives only for practitioners to take up academic texts to further authorize these stories.

The question becomes, Why? What is the usefulness of taking the chosen path in each case, and what assumptions and values does each group's choice reveal about the story the genre now tells itself and others about itself? The danzonera community, which is primarily dancers, focuses on the English side of their family tree partly for the prestige associated with Europeanness, but also because of a relative disinterest in the musical qualities of the dance complex they practice. As mentioned, the evolution from the English country dance to the danzón is not merely linguistic. The African cinquillo rhythm is fundamental to the danzón and the reason the dance is heralded as rhythmically complex. Moreover, this musical inclusion was not a cooptation by displaced French refugees in Matanzas, Cuba, but rather a development among Afro-Americans imitating European dances. Danzoneros need to know the history of their practice in case a tourist asks, but how that history is told also reveals the practice's present. The Cuban origin of the dance complex is deemed sufficient mention of the genre's Black roots.

Sufficient mention exists in the son jarocho community as well. Among jaraneros, Blackness enjoys equal billing with the other roots of son jarocho, but understanding remains nearly as shallow as it is among the danzoneros. While many academics and leaders of the community disseminate detailed knowledge, in the workshop space, this information becomes simplified, mentioned, and little more than that.

DISCIPLINE AND FLOURISH

By March, our danzón class had advanced quite a bit. Pablo had added the danzón "Cecilia" to our repertoire, and I had developed enough to participate with,

FIGURE 6. A group of danzón enthusiasts practicing choreography onstage in the Plazuela de la Campana in preparation for a competition and performance. Photo by the author.

and not just observe, the more advanced group that immediately followed the beginners. The more accomplished group would run through four or five different pieces of choreography a session and had their own touring schedule (figure 6). Yet back in my beginners' group, Pablo had begun to add details to our dancing beyond the basics. By now, we almost always opened on the fifth bar of the introduction without fail. Now and again, he would yell "Face!" to remind us to discipline our faces as much as we did the rest of our bodies. Besides the odd tourist passing by, the idlers in the Plazuela proved to be an indifferent audience. Nevertheless, we would school our faces to be an approachable smile as we made sure not to wave our fans too aggressively. In fact, Pablo had noticed the progress and invited us to come join his performance group on Fridays in the zócalo where they met to dance publicly but not performatively. It felt a little bit like being invited to sit at the cool kids' table.

It was around this time when Pablo once again called us together as a group for a rare mini lecture. "To dance danzón," he intoned, "you must listen to the music. It tells you what to do." At this lofty statement, Flor glanced down at the printed piece of paper with Pablo's choreography on it that she had grasped in her hand before training her eyes back on him. We have never danced without choreography. Up to this point, *he* has been the one telling us what to do, not the music. A list of steps choreographed the beginners and advanced groups alike. In fact, I had gone with Flor around the corner to make the very same copy she now had in her hands from a book borrowed from Celia, Pablo's dance partner. Knowing and learning the choreography was how we spent our many Tuesdays and Thursdays together. Suddenly, Pablo wanted us to dance freely. It did not go as well as he may have anticipated. Echoes of the counting exercise came to mind. To this day, I cannot dance the danzón well unless I have a strong leader as a partner. But I can pick up choreography.

Because danzonero workshops emphasize dancing while jaranero workshops primarily focus on playing the music, thinking through the choreographic lends itself more easily to the former rather than the latter. Nevertheless, choreography occasionally enters the son jarocho spaces. Although not the end goal of the group, there are occasionally performances either for audiences or for fellow son jarocho practitioners. For these, the dancers make sure to know certain passes and when to deploy them in a given son.

Juana suddenly paused in the middle of her zapateado to listen to Nico stomp the pattern on the tarima. They had been practicing "El Conejo," an old son that Nico wanted the group to perform for the upcoming Encuentro of Jaraneros in the town of Tlacotalpan. Nico, having announced that it was to be his last performance at the annual event, wanted to make sure his group did something worthwhile, as opposed to the popular sones like "La Bamba" or "Colas." "El Conejo," which is rarely performed, fit that bill. It is also probably why Juana had been momentarily stumped with the new pattern Nico wanted her to perform at the end of the month. As soon as he was done, though, she stomped in her burnt orange suede shoes twice before affirming that she got it. With her outer skirt raised in her hands, exposing her crochet-hemmed underskirt, she proceeded to mimic Nico's pattern perfectly. Satisfied, Nico left the tarima and returned to playing the jarana. He would not dance during "El Conejo" because it was a *son de montón*, meaning it is a women's dance. Instead, Juana would dance this with Rosita.

Earlier in the day, Juana had performed with La Palmera, the workshop's off-shoot performance group, which is why she is dressed up. On a normal class day, she wears workout clothes instead of today's outfit of a crochet-shouldered white linen top with the two-sided wrap skirt over her slip skirt. While this look is supposedly more traditional compared to the all-white ensemble of ballet folklórico, Juana had bought the outer skirt from a market stall dedicated to selling clothes from India. There is also something contrived in the performative.

Prior to joining the group, Juana's performance attire consisted of the all-white regional jarocha costume with its usual accoutrements—a black apron, a hanging fan and hanging golden necklaces, a ribbon tied in a bow on her hair, which is also adorned with flowers and an elaborate hair comb, and a handkerchief tucked in the waistband. You see, she is trained in ballet folklórico, the stylized dancing to son jarocho music that my workshop members derisively referred to as "those in white," in distinction to those who learned the tradition along with the dance. When Rosita joins the class in the third hour, she dons her white zapateado shoes—a vestige of her own past in a ballet group—before learning with her feet the new steps Juana has just mastered. Both Juana and Rosita could be considered crossovers—opting to learning how to dance on the tarima in the traditional way, as opposed to the choreographed display of the ballet folklórico.

These two distinct snapshots point to choreography's uses and limits. Both Pablo, in belatedly introducing the idea of listening to the music instead of the choreographed steps, and Nico, in relying on Juana's formal training in order to quickly reorient her dancing to be more traditional, are working within a framework of both liveness and sincerity.[14] The inertness of the page Flor clutched in her hand or—at least according to the traditionalists—the stiffness of the stylized dancing in ballet folklórico suggest an authenticity orientation that is trying to ossify the lived experience of folkloric culture. However, the liveness of embodied practice disallows any such ossification.

Choreography, or at least experience with choreography, was a means to an end, a means to give the language necessary to make legible meanings that may otherwise be invisible through one's bodily comportment. In *Choreographing Mexico*, scholar Manuel R. Cuellar focuses on the role embodiment and kinesthesia play in the process of nation formation and its aesthetics. He argues that the dancing body, which both "operates as an archive and as a means of archiving," is a key practice through which *lo mexicano*, or that which is Mexican, is both produced and consumed.[15] As he puts it, "embodied cultural expressions allow people to transmit knowledge, create communities, and question power."[16] This is particularly true in the pedagogically oriented *taller* space. Students are forming community, learning about their Afro-Caribbean heritage, and remapping what their Mexican identity means and looks like through both performing choreography and learning to move through it.

Therefore, the body in motion is necessarily re-creating and reanimating whatever design is intended through the choreography. Anthropologist Aimee Cox's rumination on choreography is useful to think with in considering how Pablo and Nico were using choreography to move beyond inertness. Cox argues that choreography is "embodied meaning making, physical storytelling, affective physicality, and an intellectualized response to how movement might narrate texts that are not otherwise legible." She uses the idea of "staying in [one's] body" to argue that the imperative asks the dancer to "move from a place of intuitive knowing that allows movement to both feel and look organic."[17] This organic, intuitive movement was what both teachers were trying to draw out of the groups.

Both instructors are also attempting to imbue liveness into the repertoire that their students have at their disposal. Or rather, both instructors engage the archive and the repertoire. Diana Taylor contrasts the liveness of the repertoire to the inert archive.[18] However, she also notes that they work in tandem. More than that, the archive in many ways allows the repertoire to remain alive. For example, the salvaging of son jarocho, its revitalization, created an archive of sones that are photocopied, sold, posted online, made into liner notes, et cetera, that are integral to the rescate project. Think of the notes Nico and others allow us to take—notes that students take home and use to practice. These pages of notes were once learned by immersion. Now they are made tangible by the written word, just as they continue to be transmitted live. In Nico's class, for example, only the most beginner of beginners reads the lyrics. Most others learn new lyrics by being the responder in the call-and-response interchange. You start to learn individuals' preferences by their go-to lyric on specific sones.

This feedback loop exists in the danzón as well, but to a different degree. The danzón experienced its boom in the 1990s, nearly two decades after son jarocho began its resurgence. In the twenty years since that boom, there has been a somewhat ad hoc pedagogy in place. For instance, while Pablo may have his notebook of choreography for his students, the terms he uses for certain moves may not be intelligible in other groups, even as the embodied movement is the same. The terms you use to describe moves held in common tell a story of your journey through groups, just as your style of dance does.

Despite its role as a foil in the workshop culture, ballet folklórico has played a key role in the revitalization of both son jarocho and the danzón.[19] Crossover practitioners like Juana and Rosita in the former tradition and Pablo and Jorge in the latter bind the two modes of learning and dancing. Many young people pass through ballet folklórico and are disciplined by it. The crossover practitioners insert this discipline into the workshop structure. According to original members of Pablo's competitive group, for instance, their group was the first to exercise uniformity in competition—including their dress and choreography. Before Pablo's group demonstrated the elegance of choreographed presentations, most danzonero groups presented couples dancing at the same time but with individual steps. While some groups continue this practice, the trend tends toward the disciplined form of dancing for an audience. Therefore, while the workshop culture distinguishes itself from the ballet, partly through language of authenticity and partly through the importance placed on history, the boundaries are soft and malleable.

IN PERFORMANCE, NOT PRACTICE

Seeing something done well amplifies your ability to detect when it is not. For this reason, I do not mount the tarima unless under duress. I was under duress. Manuel had invited the group to perform at his middle school, and we had eagerly agreed. It was an easy decision—not only is Manuel one of the more affable and outgoing members of the group, the performance represents an opportunity to connect with young people and in turn help them connect with their culture. I had been eager to join, for ethnographic purposes, of course. I had replaced my jeans with a long, patterned skirt that I informally dubbed my "fandango skirt," in deference to the tradition of women wearing skirts. I had even worn my wooden heeled boots—the only shoes that made a noise, even though I had no intention of mounting the tarima. After all, Juana was going, too. She could do the dancing. I was content to play my jarana somewhere on the outskirts, preferably away from a microphone. That last wish was not granted, but I do not mind overly much. I was decent at playing the jarana after summers of coming to the workshop. The zapateado? Not so much.

Nevertheless, somehow, group members urged me to join Juana for the son "La Guacamaya." This son is one of the most ubiquitous sones; it would be highly improbable for me to not know how to dance to it. It is a son de montón, which means that the basic rhythm known as "café con pan"—which when said aloud mimics the rhythm and stressed beats—can get you through the whole song. I even knew that when the refrain begins to tell the imagined guacamaya to fly, I should elegantly raise and lower my arms, imitating a parrot in flight. I had even danced it in one or two classes. But being compelled to dance it in front of a large crowd of middle schoolers was not in my plans for the day. I knew how to dance "La Guacamaya," both in theory and in practice—but in performance? I would have much preferred to play the jarana that was now slung across my back and clutched in my right hand, one of the many outward signs displaying my discomfort, I am sure. Practicing local culture, it became clear, was affectively different from modeling it.

Pablo invited me to join the advanced group for a performance at a local nursing home. I had been interacting with the group for several practices, and Pablo was always eager to help me with my ethnographic research. However, he was not inviting me to merely observe—he wanted me to dance. The timing of the event meant that the whole group would not be able to attend, and since I knew the choreography to the numbers they were going to perform, it was to be a mutually beneficial excursion. The snag in the plan was that whenever the group performs, they wear one of their customized outfits—Esme would often comment that she had a closet of dresses from the danzón, not all of them flattering to her figure and coloring. Naturally, I had no such closet full of performance outfits. I had just barely gotten a white dress and shoes to look the part when I danced in the zócalo for special occasion events. Luckily, the shoes would suffice, but I was still in need of a dress. Celia, Pablo's dance partner, volunteered to lend me one of her performance dresses, a soft white number with a layer of chiffon over the backing and rosettes at the collar. It was not at all the ruched, emerald green dress with silver accents they had already decided to wear. To try to make my dress blend in, Pablo asked one or two people to switch to their white dresses to make the two different styles appear to be by design.

After quickly changing in the nursing home's bathroom, I somewhat looked the part before joining the group in what would be my first and only performance. We danced our choreographed numbers for our elderly audience before inviting several of them to dance with us. Despite the one or two curmudgeons in the audience, many of them looked transported back to a time when the danzón was danced in salons and on every street corner during Carnival. Due to their ages, they predated both the workshop culture and the public dancing culture that now takes place in the zócalo and the Plazuela. Nevertheless, many of them gamely followed where they were led as we danced the danzón to Memo Salamanca's classic "Lindo Veracruz."

The preceding ethnographic scenes are entry points to Diana Taylor's idea of a scenario as portable framework of transmission, using performance as a form of community service and one of information transmission. Whereas the nursing home scene relied heavily on nostalgia, the middle school scene assumed it would be introducing kids to a perspective on the music that is robust, but not quite as visible as the ballet folklórico image. Each group also invited their own audience members to join in the dancing. At the school, this involved the more extroverted students trying their hand at the tarima but was followed by teachers who surprised their students by knowing how to *zapatear*, though their technique suggested a ballet folklórico training behind their dancing feet. The danzón example, in contrast, involved group members selecting and cajoling members of the audience to dance with them to a song that is not technically written as a danzón, but nevertheless facilitates its dancing. The "not quite, nevertheless" quality of the danzón echoes throughout the genre, especially when dealing with older people who have not learned the dance through the structured engagement of the workshop. Nostalgia can be authenticated up to a point.

In this chapter, I have focused on these workshop scenes to better understand how recreational spaces become spaces to practice and embody traditional forms in an untraditional way. The workshop space emphasizes collaboration and therefore recruits participants to be both recipients and disseminators of knowledge, including third root logic. For them, Blackness is a found object on the way to being more jarocho. However, it becomes entangled with the bodily enactment of regional identity. The iterative nature of practice spaces consolidates the idea that jarochos have a third root and makes it a social fact. Workshop spaces become occasions where narratives attach to practice. It is another manifestation of Blackness as a concomitant trait of jarocho identity.

In many ways, this chapter is about Blackness and the body. It is about sweat, muscle memory, rhythm, and innateness. It is work done together and done in the body. It is somatic but not phenotypic. In the next chapter, we explore how jarochos work at fulfilling the racial scripts of the jarocho—primarily the type's association with happiness. Whereas this chapter looks at the need to practice cultural forms associated with the jarocho, the next chapter looks at discontent and the work involved in keeping such a feeling at bay.

Day and Night

Mr. Danzón has seen better days. Then again, he has seen many days just like this one, too. He is disheveled in the harshness of broad daylight. His glassy eye looks cloudy, and one shirttail is loose. He is slouching languidly on the city bench with an empty bottle of Tonayán nearby. Drink in moderation, reads the label of the famously cheap and potent liquor. People mostly ignore him. He is not the first drunk person to find respite here in this public square, nor is he nearly the drunkest. Though unkempt, he is also clearly not an indigent. Mr. Danzón, after all, has a place he calls home. Perhaps that is where he goes when he eventually rallies. Few watch him as he firmly plants his feet shorn in dove gray and cream saddle shoes on the almost matching tiled floor and ambles out of the small plaza. You barely watch as he turns the corner, knowing you will see him again.

It is night, and Mr. Danzón is in his element. There is a pep in his step, a woman on his arm, and a drink in his hand. His shirttails are tucked into sharply creased pants. His saddle shoes seem to catch the light the government finally installed. When the band is playing, he is in the middle of the action, earning his nickname. There is a magnetism to his style of dance. He always escorts his dance partner to the cast iron bench at the end of the song. When the band takes its longer break, he will make his rounds around the plaza, greeting the people he knows and a few he does not yet. When the music starts, he takes his companion out to dance; he is quite the dancer, expertly leading his partner through the steps. When the number ends, he escorts her back to their spot and makes the rounds again. He has seen many nights like this.

He is the same man in the same plaza as before. It might be a different shirt, but those are the same shoes. He occupies the same bench—the one that held him up when he was down. It may even be the same brand of liquor he had consumed in the harshness of day. But in the smoothness of night, partaking is not so bad. It is not so out of place. Eyes track him rather than slide away. He seems happy, and he does not need to go home. He is home. He is Mr. Danzón.

4

Affectations

In Veracruz, being happy is both a point of pride and an obligation for jarochos. As the previous chapters argue, the jarochos' group identity is bound up in narratives of race, roots, and reputation. Chief among the reputation of people from the Port, sometimes known simply as *porteños*, is their happiness—and to lesser, though related, degrees their sensuality, irreverence, and laziness. Although now regionalized characteristics, these personality traits originate from a time when the jarocho was a racialized type. Even in the contemporary moment, jarochos associate these affective behaviors with their "third root," which is to say their Blackness. The conflation of race, roots, and reputation facilitates the local tendency to abstract Blackness beyond the individual and treat it as a collective—and, in their case, regionalized—possession. Happiness, then, although not unique to jarochos, takes on an added significance in Veracruz. It is an expectation jarochos strive to meet as a demonstration of their belonging to their collective identity.

The porteños' (people from the Port) reputation for being fun-loving dates back decades, and it is part of their branding. Their carnival, for example, is the self-appointed "happiest in the world," even as many locals are decidedly unhappy about the havoc Mexico's largest carnival celebration wreaks on their daily lives and home. If it is the happiest in the world, it is certainly not locals' happiness carrying the lion's share. Nevertheless, the expectation of liveliness and fun is a boon for the port city. Especially during Carnival, but throughout the year, individuals, the community, and the state invest in happiness and treat it as a performance of self. Cognizant of their reputation for being happy, jarochos in ways large and small work to make their happiness demonstrable and tangible both for others and for themselves.

The penchant for talking loudly, for *convivencia* (harmonious socializing), whether it be in a café, during a night of dancing, or at a festival, is a signature feature of life in the port city. While tourists are invited to engage in these activities with them, those in the Port are not waiting for—nor are they particularly interested in—the tourist gaze. Despite its importance as a domestic tourism site, Veracruz functions as a city for its own people. The city is not wont to "turn itself inside out for any of these ephemeral visitors," as the travel writer Frederick Turner wrote of his impressions of the city.[1] Once one gets a "sense of the place" called Veracruz and dwells in the port city for any length of time, thereby growing attached, the contradiction and tension underlying this happiness become apparent.[2] This is not to say that jarochos' happiness is false. Instead, it is to show how they strive for something that is said to come naturally.

This chapter aims to impart a sense of place and the tension surrounding happiness through an analysis of popular culture and public space. Through an emphasis on music, Carnival, and public dancing, the chapter traces how jarochos encounter the expectation for happiness and how they respond to that expectation. These cultural practices are integral to everyday life in the Port. They also serve as proof of Veracruz's third root. Dancing bodies become the evidence for Veracruz's inclusion in what they call the Afro-Andalusian Caribbean. The dancing becomes an expression of their happiness to outsiders while simultaneously being the participants' effort toward achieving it. They dance not because they are happy, but rather to be happy. There is work involved, but for jarochos, that work does not have to be laborious; it can be through leisure.

But how is happiness both coded as Blackness and used as a cultural resource for local belonging? This chapter offers a rumination on happiness alongside Blackness. It flirts with the stereotype of the "happy Negro," partly because the jarochos also flirt with the stereotype. The expectation of *alegría*—which I have translated as "happiness" rather than "joy"—is a burden, but also a driving force. Think of the common expression "ánimo!" often used to rally someone, to cheer them up. To enliven them. The call to liveliness—another translation for the jarocho's *alegría*—only makes sense if one is down. It is an encouragement, a willing, a striving. Ánimo! This moment where one needs to be cheered up, and hopefully rises to that occasion, captures Veracruz and her jarochos. So while jarochos have naturalized happiness as part of what it means to be jarocho, it, like identity, is always processual. It is not an inert state of happiness. It has verve. And often, it works in the "nevertheless." It is like Mr. Danzón in the preceding interlude. The image of a person succumbed to public drunkenness is not the image of happiness—except, perhaps, in the state of exception known as Carnival. Mr. Danzón captures something important about the relationship of affect and affectation. He reflects Alfredo's theory about coming together as a way to "face life." Happiness is work, and the commitment to it can be both a balm and a burden. For some, it is the inverse of the Christian psalm: weeping may endure for a day, but joy cometh in the night.

REGIONALIZED BLACKNESS

As we have seen, Blackness is part of the regionalized reputation with which jarochos contend as they fashion themselves as distinct within the nation. They emphasize it to shore up their claim that Veracruz is also Caribbean. As Kwame Appiah argues, "We make up ourselves from a tool kit of options made available by our culture and society. We do make choices, but we do not determine the options among which we choose."[3] For jarochos, Blackness is a tool they have that is not part of the general Mexican tool kit. Therefore, it serves as an ideal differentiator vis-à-vis the rest of the nation and as a common tie with the rest of the circum-Caribbean.

At the same time, their embrace of Blackness is a response to the long-standing association between race, roots, and reputation and the expectations created by that interaction. That is to say, Blackness can only serve as a tool for jarochos in Veracruz because multicultural politics in Mexico have made it one. People of African descent exist throughout the republic, and their impact is crucial to the ethnogenesis of Mexicans as a whole. Yet the consolidation of the third root discourse effectively correlates its presence with the nation's two coasts. Mexican Blackness is primarily spatialized along the Costa Chica of Guerrero and Oaxaca on the Pacific Coast and in the state of Veracruz on the Gulf Coast.[4] This discursive charge manifests differently on the two coasts: whereas the popular imaginary assumes Costa Chicans primarily express their Blackness somatically, for jarochos, affective expression is its main manifestation.[5] In this process, jarochos' reputation for happiness and liveliness takes on a new significance. It becomes a racialized and strategic essentialism they must constantly work to enact. It becomes a difference that must be performed to be seen.[6] As a result, happiness becomes one of the many expectations associated with Blackness and against which individuals measure themselves.

Because it is a collectively shared trait, an individual in Veracruz does not need to be Black to have Blackness. This unmooring of Blackness from Black people is not necessarily unique to jarochos. Moritz Heck, for example, has described how in Bolivia, one can productively understand Afrobolivianity along the axes of feeling and being. One can feel Black ("me siento negro") and be Afro-Bolivian ("yo soy afroboliviano"), but those two states are not interchangeable.[7] The decoupling is different among the jarochos. It is not a question of feeling or being; rather, it is one of accessing. The pertinent verb is *tener*, "to have." Blackness is something they have as jarochos. "To feel" or "to be" come into play through affective qualities like happiness. You can be or feel happy. But more to the point, jarochos feel compelled to demonstrate that state of being.

There are echoes here of what Livio Sansone observed in the youth culture in Brazil, a "Blackness without ethnicity."[8] By this, Sansone refers to a desire to "act like a Black person" rather than identifying as Black. Yet most jarochos are not trying to "act Black." Instead, they are trying to act in accordance with the expectations jarochos collectively bear. French ethnographer Christian Rinaudo has characterized this performance in Veracruz as an "elective Africanity."[9] In his research at the intersection of youth and popular culture, Rinaudo analyzes the tendency to opt in to Africanity through symbolic and corporeal gestures that signal Blackness and specifically Afro-Caribbeanness for locals. As he emphasizes, it is not about defining oneself as "Black," but rather performing an affectation recognized as such.

This turn to affectation and corporeal gestures is reminiscent of Antonio Benítez-Rojo's description of two Black women in Havana walking "in a certain kind of way" that reassured him that the Cuban missile crisis would not end apocalyptically.[10] Despite the succor their ambulation provided him, he confesses he cannot describe this "certain kind of way." Elective Africanity also carries this inability to be articulated definitively and the subsequent resignation to mere allusion. Perhaps it is because in Veracruz, Africanity, Blackness, or what it is more often called—the third root—all signify an Afro-Caribbeanness. If, as Benítez-Rojo writes, the Caribbean is a repeating island, then Veracruz with its elective Africanity is one of those repetitions. Perhaps he would recognize that "certain way" not in walking women but in dancing bodies—the same bodies in which Rinaudo sees the choice to engage with presumptions of Black culture. Perhaps Benítez-Rojo would see the manifestations of the ethos he calls Caribbean culture: "Here I am, fucked but happy."[11]

There is a laudable resilience in this worldview of being presently fucked but happy. This condition speaks to a willfulness and an effort. Even if one does not say the quiet part aloud, the message reaches its mark: "Here I am . . . happy." It is in the resignation of both the declarative opening and the punctuating period. It is not a question or an exclamation. It is not even a statement of fact. It is a statement of will. You can hear it in the stories jarochos tell about themselves. You can feel it when they move a certain way.

LYRICALLY SPEAKING

Andrés and I broke away from the crowd and joined the few people who were in the garden of IVEC. It was quieter out there along the defunct tiled fountain and mature foliage. Truth be told, the half-length black netting hanging from the archways of the old building did little to impede the sounds coming from the walkways surrounding the garden. It was the inauguration of the twentieth edition of the Afro-Caribbean Festival and the sonero group Juventud Sonera was performing.

The sounds and the din of people enjoying the music, each other, and the open bar served as background noise as Andrés and I discussed the recurring allusions to Black and mixed-race figures in the songs played throughout the city. Veracruz's sonic landscape owes much to Cuba and other parts of the Caribbean, but as IVEC has also made clear, this is a traditional Veracruzan sound, though its roots may be Cuban. After all, many songs were written or made popular by people from the state of Veracruz. The genre may have been imported, but many of the songs were not. For example, a native son wrote "El Esclavo," and its popularity does not reach far beyond the city itself. Yet it is a beloved standard to jarochos in the Port. While most songs are not as explicitly about Blackness in the same way, a significant number of songs in the city have allusions to Blackness, from being the thrust of the song to a throwaway line. Andrés and I were discussing the impact this aural education may have made on the general population's understanding of their Blackness.

Andrés maintained that you must consider the lyrics within their contexts, both temporally and regionally. He hypothesized that the constant allusions to Black figures was an outgrowth of the negritude movements in the Caribbean and the trendiness of Blackness at that time.[12] It was fashionable to celebrate the Black aspect of Veracruz. One could argue that when we were having our chat, it was once again fashionable. But the songs did not go away in the intervening years. Instead, they were part of life's soundtrack for generations and generations of jarochos. In formal and informal ways, these types of songs have remained part of the everyday lives of jarochos across different audiences and across a range of interests. Andrés and I may have been having a pedantic conversation in the heart of the city's cultural center, surrounded by the types of people—the jarocho publics—who spend their Thursday nights at festival inaugurations. But like the sounds of Juventud Sonera into the night, these interactions with Black allusions escape such bastions of culture. You hear them on the radio; you dance to them in the streets.

Jarochos receive a steady influx of music proclaiming their uniqueness, Blackness, or Caribbean character. Often, the three are interchangeable. Stuart Hall argues that questions about identity are necessarily questions about representation. Representation, he says, involves selective memory and invention, which requires silencing some things for others to speak.[13] Song lyrics are key sites for representations, invention, and selective memory. It is as Lila Ellen Gray wrote of the Portuguese genre fado and music in general: knowledge is transmitted by and through music. The affective power of music lies in its ability to "make sense" to the listener, partly through its "capacity to point to diverse memories, places, and histories while saturating these memories, places, these histories, with feeling and with sound."[14] Like Alfredo's relationship with "El Esclavo" (see chapter 2), songs speak to both the time of their creation and their recitation. As both primary and secondary sources, the lyrics about Veracruz tell a story that transcends time. They are also modes of transmission that are more subtle, more personal, and more pervasive. It is one thing to go to an Afro-Caribbean Festival or IVEC talk; it is another to grow up listening to popular songs about your hometown.

In 2005 the state of Veracruz established by law the hymn of Veracruz.[15] Polish composer Ryszard Siwy Machalica created a tune reminiscent of what Thomas Turino calls the "musical nationalism in the early republics," which aspired to cosmopolitan nationalistic legitimacy rather than cultural uniqueness.[16] In other words, sonically, it sounds of a kind with the Mexican national anthem, which predates it by more than a century and a half. The first time I encountered the Veracruz anthem, I could not quite believe it came from this century. Then I listened to the lyrics.

The lyrics, particularly the last verse, resonate with the cultural politics of its time. In the song, the lyricist alternately refers to Veracruz as songs, joy, fandango, danzón jarana, and son music, among other things. The anthem names musical complexes associated with the state—the fandango of son jarocho, the huapango of son huasteca, and the Afro-Cuban ballroom dance, the danzón. Likewise, the jarana, a small stringed instrument, the harp, and Afro-Antillean son music conjure Veracruz. All these things exceed the bounds of Veracruz—the cradles of both son jarocho and son huasteca extend beyond Veracruz into neighboring states. The danzón and son are importations from the broader Caribbean. Yet when listed together, they evoke Veracruz. This anthem could not refer to any other state in the Republic. As the legal state anthem, this turn-of-the-century artifact of musical regionalism has made songs and joy official characteristics of the state. From a regionalist standpoint, Veracruz is joy. Yet this song from 2005 that sounds both old and timeless is not the first anthem to bespeak Veracruz. Nor is it the most popular.

The ballad "Veracruz" is arguably the anthemic song of the city.[17] Written by famed Veracruzan composer Agustín Lara, the song is instantly recognizable, be it played from the zócalo's stage by the danzonera, pounded out on the wooden marimba keys by an ambulatory marimba band, or sung at an open-mic event at the Gran Café de la Parroquia. Just the three notes played in the cadence of the final "Veracruz" are enough to evoke nostalgia in the listener. The famous Café de la Parroquia hosts karaoke nights organized around the piece. There is a museum dedicated to Lara that emphasizes both "Veracruz" and another, more upbeat song by him, "La Cumbancha."[18] The song's title is an Afro-Cubanism for a lively party, but the song is really about such a party's ending. The protagonist asks the last laugh of the party to take away their sorrows and songs. It juxtaposes laughing and crying, as well as sorrows and songs. Although the message is universal, one gets the impression that Lara was thinking of a fellow jarocho. At the end of a lively party, there is laughter, but a laughter that is still striving to be happy. It speaks to the happiness in Veracruz and the effort to achieve it. Here I am, fucked but happy.

THE HAPPIEST CARNIVAL IN THE WORLD

The woman I rented from locks up her home and heads out of town to avoid Carnival. Her home is right along a major thoroughfare that leads downtown and is a block off the parade route. In other words, she is in a prime tourism zone. While the state and business proprietors may look toward the pre-Lenten festival with anticipation, she contemplates it with anxiety. During one of the peak tourism moments in a domestic tourism town, the hotels are at capacity. However, it does not stop there. The streets and callejones, the zócalo, the malecón, the restaurant, the aquarium, any and all public spaces are at capacity too. The broken sidewalks fill with bodies, trash, and piss. The event's tagline, "The happiest Carnival in the World," is aspirational at best. The power of positive thinking can only get you so far.

During the four-day affair during which thousands of Mexicans flock to the city, many locals who live closest to the downtown area are inconvenienced. Not only is the thoroughfare boulevard connecting Veracruz to its twin city Boca del Rio severely constricted by stands before being closed for the parade route, the smaller side streets are also obstructed by motorbuses filled with tourists who cannot afford the many hotels in the area, both chain and informal alike. Houses near the parade route put out makeshift signs advertising access to their bathrooms for five to fifteen pesos. The homeowners' advertisements emphasizing the cleanliness or ready supply of toilet paper may limit but do not eliminate the number of people who opt to urinate in the streets. As a rule, people expect petty crime will increase while insisting that it is only the foreign elements taking advantage of the anonymity of the dense crowds.

The marines, tourist police, transit police, and other law enforcement agencies parade themselves about, their presence even more conspicuous than usual. They do not impede the public drunkenness that is so regular a sight that it is unremarkable. The parade, which invariably will start late, feels later still for the people in the middle or the alternating end of the route, those who came in time to get a good seat and in their boredom, excitement, or combination of the two prove why the beer company Sol, a sponsor, boasts an excellent return on investment. Even as Carnival organizers vow to make it more family-friendly and eliminate the flow of beer within the stands, there are plenty of nearby convenience stores—Oxxo, Modelorama, Six—that are stocked and ready to provide a service for those who wish to imbibe. The festivities last four days with the happiest—if happiness is a euphemism for bacchanalia—being the first two days and the last ones being almost lazy, hometown affairs. A quieter, more tired, and yet more intimate Carnival.

The local economy, both the informal and the formal sides of it, benefits from the influx of millions of pesos. However, all of this comes at a cost—that cost being the natural "alegría" of the porteños, and in some ways the naturalness of the "natural hospitality and friendliness of the locals," that a 1930 editorial in *El Dictamen* argued would undoubtedly shine through.[19] Since its revival in 1925 after years of official nonobservance, Veracruz's Carnival has become the second largest popular festival in Latin America behind the one in Rio de Janeiro.

Through an analysis of clippings from the local newspaper *El Dictamen*, Andrew Grant Wood traces how an event that organizers originally imagined as a local affair became such a large phenomenon.[20] By 1928 an editorial already expressed a vision of Carnival as an "event that can bring to the city one of the most important economic activities of the present age: tourism."[21] A year later, in 1929, American tourists favorably compared the festival to Coney Island's Mardi Gras, citing that Carnival in Veracruz was "más alegre" because the local event was more "vehemente y contagiosa," more passionate and contagious. In fact, that assessment is codified in the festival's nickname: "El Más Alegre del Mundo," the happiest in the world. However, that happiness is not quite as "vehemente y contagiosa" as before, and a different sort of contagion, known as exasperation, has taken a toll on the "natural" happiness and hospitality that was touted in the 1920s.

Visitors fill the hotels, and the streets, and the private residences that hang their homemade signs advertising space for rent. Billboards leading out from the airport begin the inundation of advertisements, as if the visitors do not know why they are there. One 2013 advertisement sponsored by the beer company Sol riffs off the classic Las Vegas slogan: "What happens at Carnival, stays at Carnival!" In fact, Sol inundates the scene with signs hanging from each streetlamp post on the parade route from Veracruz to the neighboring municipality of Boca del Rio. Licensed, privately owned stands flank both sides of the six-lane boulevard, the modern location for the parade route that already feels too small. Another ad campaign reads, "Find out how your Carnival ends . . ." Little did I know at the time that mine would end with me absolutely exasperated with that year's international pop earworm and seeking respite in the familiar, less spectacularly happy place— the Plazuela where the same local son band played at the same time, despite the competition put up by the international star Miguel Bosé, blocks away on the Macroplaza. This is a sameness that soothes rather than grates. It is a sameness the state harnesses as popular culture on display for the tourists that have somehow made happiness in Veracruz a zero-sum game.

This speaks to the way in which the fissures caused by Carnival are not wholly antagonistic. Even as many locals negatively comment on the crowds Carnival brings, few wish the tourists would go away completely. Carnival is a moment of interaction between the port city and the rest of the country; it is a moment shot through with intimacy and performance. It is the commingling of regionalism and nationalism—and increasingly internationalism. As the port authority continues to section off the actual port from the city, Veracruz increasingly becomes less a port of entry for foreigners into Mexico, but rather one for Mexicans into a Caribbean culture. The friction, however, that foments the unhappiness during the "Happiest Carnival in the World" has more to do with the delocalization of the festival than anything else.

For this reason, even the modern-day Carnival needs rescuing, according to the new president of the Carnival Committee, Lic. Luis Antonio Pérez Fraga. This time, however, instead of being rescued from obscurity, it needs to be rescued from itself and the ways in which it has become unfamiliar from what it once was. Including the 2017 slogan of "Devolviendo al Pueblo Su Carnaval" (Returning to the People Their Carnival), Pérez Fraga has made public statements about his desire to reign in the alienation some have felt with regard to the festival. Mary Rumbas and Juan Carnaval—allegorical figures who were most recently represented by a Cuban and a Brazilian model, respectively—have been reimagined and will now be portrayed by porteños rather than foreigners. Juan Carnaval will now be the gentleman with the longest time in the Carnival; Mary Rumbas has been changed to Mamá Rumba and will also be the woman with the longest participation.

Part of the Carnival committee's mission to return the festival to the people included a survey of fifteen questions soliciting the public's opinion on a range of issues, from the number of parades to have to the musical acts to invite. Pérez Fraga and the committee pledged to bring Carnival back to the heights it had in the 1980s, including the revival of popular dances. Not only would the plan include a large Carnival mask stating "Welcome to the world capital of happiness," he also promised that they would have a wooden platform for dancing, called a tarima, on every street from Ocampo to the zócalo, with local salsa groups.[22]

Happiness remains a selling point of the festival, and the monetary success suggests that people are still buying it. Organizers are trying to manufacture what was once considered as natural a resource as the warm welcome that attracted domestic tourists. The recent additions of the Diosas de la Alegría (the goddesses of happiness) and the newest addition, the Guardián de la Alegría (the guardian of happiness, who in his lamé briefs serves as the male counterpart to the small group of women in bedazzled bikini sets and parade tights), are part of that effort. In other words, even though porteños living in the downtown area may be ambivalent or even unhappy when Carnival comes around, the four-day party is not going anywhere.

For my first Carnival—and in the spirit of "doing ethnography"—I adopted a grueling schedule of happiness and having fun. It was 2013, and Korean vocalist Psy's earworm of a megahit "Gangnam Style" seemed to blast from every other float that made the North–South route between the twin cities of Boca del Rio and Veracruz. I endeavored to go to each parade, but with the same floats, the same local *comparsas* (parade troupe) and *batucada* groups, and the same hired models, it got old. Perhaps this makes me a bad ethnographer, but there is only so much happiness in relentless succession a person can take. Though both holidays are in February, Carnival is not intended to be Groundhog Day. I needed a reprieve. Living close to the parade route, a reprieve was not to be found in my room, but rather further downtown. I went to the small square downtown called the Plazuela.

It was, of course, brimming with people. As much as people enjoy complaining about Carnival and the tourists it attracts, there are many who benefit from its windfall. Despite the uptick in dancing bodies, though, everything else was the same. The same musical group was on the stage; the same waitstaff serviced the tables, paying special attention to the regulars; the same catalog of songs—none of them K-pop one-hit wonders—were played after long breaks between numbers. A musical oasis in a desert of more music. A few blocks away, in the Macroplaza—a space much larger and more open than the Plazuela—an internationally famous musician was doing a sound check. That space would soon fill with the same bodies that had been dancing in the stands along the Boulevard. Yet eventually those rented stands, those wasted bodies, those international stars would go away and leave the port's residents alone. The Plazuela would remain the same. During the happiest Carnival in the world, the Plazuela would be my happy place. It is, in fact, the happy place for many people interested in pursuing the joy they are supposed to already have. If, in Veracruz, being happy is both a point of pride and an obligation for jarochos, the strivings to meet this expectation are an effort to belong to their collective identity as jarocho. Consequently, public dancing, a practice that is in no way unique to Veracruz, has nevertheless become an iconic image of Veracruz.

ALL WE NEED IS MUSIC

Public dancing to Afro-Antillean music like the danzón and son music strengthen Veracruz's reputation as a Black space within a mestizo nation. Therefore, the municipal government financially supports this image in a variety of ways. While nearly every public space has hosted its share of dancing, there are two places that stand out—the zócalo, or main plaza, and a smaller square a few blocks away called the Plazuela de la Campana. The local tourism board invests heavily in the zócalo by contracting musicians and providing free seating for audience members. In the Plazuela, the state is less present, and a local business owner is the main force behind maintaining the space as an open-air dance hall. Nevertheless, the tourism office directs visitors there as a site of authenticity. Despite these disparate levels of state investment, both spaces attract people whose leisure practices the state can then present as unscripted evidence of Veracruz's Afro-Caribbean nature, of its living third root.

Even though danzón in the zócalo is a main tourist attraction, the practice did not start for their entertainment. In the documentary *Danzonero*, a dancer recounts that in 1982 people did not come to the zócalo to dance, at least not until Sigfrido Alcántara and his wife began to dance in front of city hall, just the two of them, for the sheer joy of it.[23] One would wonder what the Alcántaras would think now. Four nights out of the week couples dance for the love it. They may smile for the tourists, but they dance for themselves. The state may have harnessed the energy for their own ends, but the practice survives because of jarochos' enjoyment of the music.

Multiple activities occur in the large main plaza. Many genres of music rend the air, from ambulatory groups playing requests from those drinking and eating snacks in the Portales to folkloric dancers playing recordings of son jarocho music as they dance in their white costumes on personal-size tarimas. Clowns draw their own circle of observers, and some people just want to sit a spell under the trees and foliage and take in the views. Light-up toys shoot up in the sky and float back down. Vendors play a cat-and-mouse game with the tourism police as they try to sell embroidered shirts or shawls without licenses. There is laughter and scream-ing and traffic noise. There is also the danzón. Amid all this busyness, there is a ring of observers watching people young and old dance the danzón. There are sentimental partners dressed up or down. There are social dance club members who on occasion wear their matching performance attire. Sometimes they prac-tice their group's choreography, and other times they dance freestyle. Regardless, out of all the dancers in the square, they are the ones most attuned to the tourist's gaze (figure 7).

They often dance alongside their club members but pay visits to other dancers in the wider danzonero community. Teens in school uniforms sometimes dance a number or two, and even younger children dance if their parents are also danc-ers. A city employee serves as mistress of ceremonies. There is amplification for the musicians who played on the stage before it was torn down to put in a water feature—a new administration's beautification project.

Like the Sundays of danzón in the Plazuela, there is a fixed and known sched-ule for danzón in the zócalo. In addition to Alma de Veracruz's Friday and Saturday performances, the city band also performs danzón in the main plaza on Tuesdays and Thursdays. These weekly events perennially take a hiatus when the band is on vacation, which is never really announced, yet somehow most people know. One time I showed up, ready to participate and observe, only to find the bandstand empty and the chairs put away. There were a couple of other people who had also been caught unawares. Sensing an opportunity, a three-piece marimba band swooped in and started banging out a danzón. Good enough. The people danced.

FIGURE 7. Members of a danzonera club wear matching outfits and dance freestyle in the zócalo among other enthusiasts while tourists look on. Photo by the author.

A similar story belongs to the Plazuela. It is not a space created or maintained with tourists in mind. With that said, enthusiasts who go to enjoy Afro-Antillean music do not mind the presence of visitors—especially if they can dance. In the following vignettes, I describe the Plazuela and its denizens, hoping to impart a sense of the place and what *alegría a la veracruzana*, or Veracruz-style happiness, looks like.

Before the hum of anticipation from the crowd and the hum generated by audio equipment feedback, you will hear the classic sounds of downtown Veracruz float into the insular space. At dusk—that time between the slowness of daytime and the movement of night—an aluminum door clanks as it unrolls down to cover the entrance to the fishing tackle store facing the public square. You will hear the cling-cling-cling of the pedicart vendor announcing that he, with his wares of refreshingly cold dessert called *nieve*, is near. The musical strains of whatever scene the University of Veracruz's ballet folklórico group is practicing that day will carry on the wind, as will the impatience of commuters on the main drags, both a block away in either direction, Independencia leading people further downtown and Zaragoza leading them away. There is a chance you will hear the scraping of in-line skates on tiled walkways as groups of young people take the shortcut through the square, avoiding said thoroughfares. Their scraping sound is smooth,

FIGURE 8. The early stages of setting up the tables in the Plazuela de la Campana in preparation for a night of free live music and dancing. Photo by the author.

more of a whir compared to the scratchy scraping of the big brooms that the sanitation workers use to push debris onto shovels and from there into trash cans. The two sweepers, who had only recently found this little corner of Veracruz through their work assignment, now take their lunch break on one of the benches on the shady side as the waiter Jesus from the restaurant offers them a Coke and a smile (figure 8).

Some days you will hear the foghorn of a boat either coming into or leaving port, reminding you that the ocean is ever near even though no horizon is to be found in this negative space made from buildings butting against each other. Tuesdays and Thursdays, a danzón number will be playing on repeat from the boom box nestled under the old bell that gives the Plazuela its name. Above the music, you will hear novices counting more or less on beat, the murmur of feet sliding along the ground as they make box steps, and the firm voice of a young man giving directions to his dance students. Later there will be more variety to the danzones played, less counting and directing, and more nitpicking in between repetitions— this is the advanced group. Later still, as the sun dips lower in the sky and the heat lifts a fraction, you will hear heavy chains sliding to the ground and lightweight plastic tables being placed along diagonals in preparation for one of the four nights of live music this little square hosts. Even before the rhythm section steps onto the stage, the Plazuela has its own cadence, its own vibration.

The back wall is a palimpsest of peeling layers of paint and graffiti tags, its expanse broken up by crumbling Juliet balconies on which pigeons perch and a tenacious tree in the corner growing directly out of the wall from the second story. On what becomes the dance floor, the broken remains of a since removed water fountain feature create a hazard. Twelve cast iron benches flank the small square with mature trees in between. These are the most coveted of places during the nights of music for they are free to occupy. Two sides of the square house storefronts and apartments, with the side opposite the back wall having more established businesses. The fourth side is the restaurant bar where the waiter Jesus works. Those in the know disparage the restaurant owner for placing chairs and tables in front of his business whenever there will be live music. Those in the know do this because the de facto proprietor of this public space is not the public or the state, but rather Don Miguel. He is the one who contracts the musicians who play. He is the one asked to cut ribbons on anniversaries and appear at musical festivals organized by the Veracruz Institute of Culture.

Don Miguel is an older gentleman who came to Veracruz from the city of Córdoba many years ago. For several years, he has owned a cafeteria right at the joint where the Plazuela narrows into a callejón, or alleyway. In the beginning, he would sell coffee beans in bulk, but now it would be more accurate to call his place a beverage counter. You will find him perched on a stool, often with a cigarette in hand. During the day, he has the odd customer stop by for a cold beverage, but his moneymaking hours are at night, when there is music playing, when there are bodies dancing. He stores the sound equipment for those events in his back room and has a black letter board announcing the schedule of acts for the week. It rarely changes from week to week and is not consulted by the attendees, but it is there all the same. It is to Don Miguel that the state has given permission and ceded authority to host these nighttime activities. Beyond that, the state does little more than print the events on their monthly and weekly tourism calendars. A bit like the restaurateur, they take advantage of the events with minimal effort on their part. Don Miguel is an institution and an integral part of what you see in the Plazuela. But he did not start it. It started with a group of friends and the introduction of a girl.

I met Don Óscar through mutual friends—ironically, some of my oldest friends in Veracruz were some of his, my years to his decades. I had met this group of men through my participation in the son jarocho community. We were classmates. Don Óscar knew them from having lived a long and full life. They had an old, easy friendship, the details of their meeting never fully materialized. It was the type of friendship that involved serenades at birthday parties and Thursday night meetups in the Plazuela. Don Óscar—when he came—always sat at the lone cast iron table. He rarely danced and instead received visitors to his table. It was as if he knew everybody, or rather, that everybody knew him. Sitting at his table felt different, and women never paid. He held court there.

In fact, Óscar could be considered a founder of the Plazuela as a social scene. He, along with our mutual friends, were once middle-aged fellows cast out of their regular haunt, the Café La Merced, and in need of a new place to spend time together. They settled on the Plazuela. At the time, according to Óscar's retelling, the Plazuela had recently been a contested space between the prostitutes and youth. In the end, both groups were forced out. Óscar and his group of friends filled the void. The Plazuela's bad reputation meant they did not have their own battles to fight.

Óscar had done many things in his life. He had been a photographer, a laborer in the port, a technician, and an amateur musician. Soon, he and his relocated group of friends added a bohemian night to their long chats over coffee in their new domain. Óscar and others would bring instruments to sing and play among themselves. According to another member of that old crew, it went downhill when the first friend brought a female companion—no one remembers exactly who it was to break the ice. No longer a boy's night out, the space became increasingly coed and eventually began to feature dancing music. In that way, the creation of the Plazuela was not a savvy business plan, but rather an organic and happenstance development. Its revitalization from an abandoned former red-light district to what it is today can be traced to key figures but no overarching strategy. What if a man from Córdoba had not been selling coffee precisely when a group of friends were in search of a new place to chat while enjoying the beverage? What if Óscar had not had a talent for music and the gumption to start a bohemian night? What if so-and-so had not "ruined" it by bringing a girl?

The Plazuela existed this way for over twenty years. During the celebration of its twentieth anniversary, Don Miguel was rightfully feted, but no mention was made of the exiled coffee drinkers. Don Óscar probably would not have made it to the celebration if it had been, anyway, due to his declining health. Without him anchoring his special table, his friend group dispersed as well. Our mutual friends barely go anymore. The space, though, is as lively as ever. The state has invested in new light fixtures, new paint, and new trash cans. It is a place transformed, yet still the same. It may have survived its founders, but will it survive Don Miguel? Chucho, the mutual friend who introduced me to Óscar, thinks so.[24]

Although he is in his late fifties, Chucho was one of the originators of the Plazuela scene as well. He had, in that sense, grown old with the Plazuela. When I expressed my concern about the future of son music and dancing in Veracruz's public spaces, he firmly disagreed:

Look. The music is not ever going to disappear. It will always find a corner. Because the young people of today who are dancing salsa, when they get old, won't be able to dance salsa and they are going to keep on dancing. So, it nourishes itself. You say right now in the Plazuela the old people dance son. There will always be old people. They won't be the same old people; they won't be the same ones . . .

There will always be old people even if they will not be the same ones; of this, he has no doubt. He is equally confident that there will always be dancing bodies. They may not be dancing salsa—which generally has more energetic movements than son dancing—but they will not stop dancing, merely slow down. They may not be in the Plazuela, but they will find a place, somewhere, to dance at whatever tempo they can.

At the time of my research, the Plazuela is that place. It has a regular crowd like Óscar and Chucho and constantly welcomes new people. When I met her, Carla belonged to this latter group. It was her first night there, so she did not know yet that Rita the tamalera would offer to add salsa to your *tamal de masa* or *de elote* and return to discard the trash when you were done—a full-service operation she and her husband had been doing for over seven years. Carla did not yet have a preference between the two cheese vendors—the young man with sleepy eyes and enough hair product to have his mane defy both gravity and reason or the middle-aged man who was already training his young daughter in the art of the business. Carla had not had a chance to discover that the peanut vendors sell the same nuts and seeds so the closest one would do. Maybe she had noticed that the vendors who target tourists do not come to the Plazuela, but the shoeshiners and cigarette and candy sellers do. Since she and I were squeezed together on the bench, I knew she had already realized that those were the free spots, the coveted spots. As she told me, the best things in life are free.

She had also already adopted the trust that seems implicit in the space. Because seats are prime, and because numbers must be danced, people leave all manner of personal effects as placeholders. Purses, shopping bags, handkerchiefs, you name it. The calculated risk seemed to suggest it was far riskier to lose your seat than your belongings. So, when Carla would go out to the dance floor with her partner—an older man who more regularly attended the space—her things kept me company. When the song ended and the dancing partners returned to their places, our conversation resumed.

Carla worked in the port, as her family had done for generations, though she was the first woman in her family to do so. On the weeks when there were many ships, she would work a double shift for up to fifteen hours a day. For her efforts of checking inventory for merchandise that would make its way across the Republic, she was compensated 2,300 to 2,500 pesos. At that time, the daily minimum wage for general labor was lower than the current wage of 73.04 pesos. When there were no boats, she was not paid at all. Despite the feast or famine cycle, Carla had what would be considered a good paying job. Her dance partner had a better one. He also worked in the port but had a higher salary in his unionized position.

His economic security, however, did not translate to largesse on date night. Rather than pay the ten peso a seat cover charge and the fifty-peso drink minimum per table, he stiffly escorted Carla to the space beside me on the free public bench and stood to the side. At one point, he sauntered down the callejón, passing Don Miguel on the way out and back again with a bag filled with Caribe wine coolers from the corner convenience store. If he saved money in this way, it was not a significant amount. Perhaps it was the principle of the thing. Why take away the enjoyment of a slow drag with your date by paying for the evening? After all, as Carla said, free things are more enjoyable.

Be that as it may, the "free" music we were enjoying comes at a cost—though it is euphemistically called a *cooperación* rather than a cover. Throughout the night, the musicians remind everyone present that what they are providing is free entertainment without support from the government. The evening events, which the state advertises but does not materially support, are made possible through the audience's contribution. This cooperative act could take many forms, from paying for a seat and a drink, to buying one of the sonero group's CDs for 100 pesos, to dropping money in the open end of the güiro as the musician scrapes the ridged instrument in your direction. Contribution may sound mild, but it takes on a different connotation as the conga player sings a slow, sing-song ditty that taunts, "Please cooperate; don't play the fool," as the güiro player and saxophonist methodically go up and down all sides of the plaza. The Sunday danzonera group has a different method of extracting payment. Carla and her date would certainly not go there. Not only is it a genre more associated with "old people," men must pay to dance.

Every Sunday when I would visit the Plazuela for danzón Sundays, I would dance with my dance partner, El Caballo Viejo. I never remembered his real name, only this first name he gave me. El Caballo Viejo was a talker, both a poet and a flirt. He was not much of a dancer. Although the Afro-Cuban ballroom dance the danzón is not the type of dance one talks through, I would ask him questions to derail his off-color remarks about my color. In one of our dance conversations, I learned of his mother-in-law's poor health. This was not a passing cold, but rather a new normal. She stayed with him and his wife, and he shared in the caretaker duties. Sundays were his escape from the house. He would come to the Plazuela to not be at home. He would come to dance, and somehow, I became his dance partner. After paying the 25 pesos in exchange for a ribbon that worked much the same way as a club stamp or wristlet, he could enjoy as much of the three hours of the danzón as he dared. El Caballo Viejo rarely stayed the whole evening, but while he was there, he danced every number.

FIGURE 9. Regulars enjoy a Sunday afternoon in the Plazuela de la Campana as the danzonera plays onstage. Photo by the author.

Despite his innuendos—his nickname, for example, was one that missed my ken until someone recommended that I listen to the popular song where he got his moniker from—he was quite content to be a dance partner and nothing more. Doña Luna, a member of my danzón class, also made clear the distinction between an intimate partner and a dance partner. A widow, she had a permanent dance partner whom she barely interacted with outside of their time on the dance floor. Of course, there were several couples during danzón Sundays who were sentimental partners as well. One pair stands out. They always sat on the restaurant side of the Plazuela, at a blue wooden table instead of the typical plastic ones. As she was visually impaired, the husband would lead her out to dance and back again with such care. When they danced, they would hold each other close, closer than the norm with such a formal dance like the danzón. There was a constant smile on her face.

Another older couple sat on Don Miguel's side of the Plazuela. They always came in matching outfits and brought their own food. They danced as close to the musicians as possible and even danced during the musicians' break, when son and salsa music were played through the speakers. They held hands during the *descanso*, the moment in the danzón piece where dancers would stand side by side, facing the musicians until the next melody began. In class, we were taught to rhythmically wave our fans in unison, to not let the smiles slip from our faces. But danzón Sundays in the Plazuela were not the imagined venue for this sort of corporeal discipline. In fact, there was little overlap between those who took danzón classes and those who danced for three hours every Sunday in the Plazuela (figure 9).

El Caballo Viejo certainly had not taken classes. Though he claimed to have danced the danzón for nearly his whole life, someone with formal training would determine that he did not know how to dance it properly. He stepped instead of glided; his feet never quite came together. He kept trying to dance through the descanso. Maybe he felt he had no time to waste. This was his break; why take a break from it simply due to custom?

The fact is, there were many styles of dance represented in the Plazuela those afternoons. Some dancers were very theatrical, as they had learned the genre in Mexico City. Others were disciplined, as if they had taken a class or been a part of the social dance clubs that populate the city. Many more simply danced how they were moved to dance. One cattle rancher from a nearby town outside of Veracruz would dance only to the numbers he liked, and he liked only about two pieces. Though he did not dance, he still spent hours in that square, enjoying the ambiance. The dancing, in some ways, seemed like an excuse for these people to come together and simply be. Many came explicitly for Danzonera Manzanita, the performers onstage.

Danzonera Manzanita used to perform in the bandstand in the middle of Parque Zamora, where dancers used to go on Sundays to dance. The group has a loyal following and drew a regular crowd to the park until the municipal government forced them to find a new location. Like Óscar and Chucho, their exile led them to the Plazuela. Their loyal followers adjusted to the location, but nearly everything else stayed the same. That is why they can charge 25 pesos to dance when no other group would be able to make such a request. The money goes to the musicians; the danzonera does not receive financial support from the state despite the tradition they keep alive. Several of the musicians receive money from the municipal government, but as members of the state-sponsored danzonera group, Alma de Veracruz, that plays in the zócalo, or main plaza, on Fridays and Saturdays.

When I asked Don Miguel why there were three solid hours of the danzón, he explained that people were accustomed to it. On Sundays, he recounted, people from the towns nearby would traditionally come into Veracruz to shop and pass the afternoon. Because this was the one time they would come into the city, the Danzonera Manzanita would play long sets so that people could take full advantage of the trip. When the danzonera moved to the Plazuela, he agreed that they should keep the extended schedule. So, from six until nine at night, there is the danzón. Once Danzonera Manzanita leaves, a salsa group takes the stage until the end of the night.

Danzón Sundays are not nearly the only night of open-air danzón in the port city. In addition to Alma de Veracruz's Friday and Saturday performances in the zócalo, the city band also performs danzón in the main plaza on Tuesdays and Thursdays. In the zócalo, the municipal government puts out chairs for the dancers, and the tourists make a ring behind them. Most dancers face the band as is custom, but others feel compelled to face their audience. Some who dance in the zócalo would never dance in the Plazuela, but other people attend whenever and wherever there is a danzón piece being played and room enough to glide in box formations. For them, even a marimba band will do if the full danzonera is on vacation. But there are others who dance only in the Plazuela, whether it is because it is the only time they can escape familial duties; a convenient time to come into town; or a standing engagement to visit with friends and dance to the band they prefer above others. Sundays in the Plazuela feel different; they feel like coming home.

What you see there in the Plazuela has a very recent history. A group of men found a place to chat and play music together. A danzonera group found a place to relocate and keep a weekend tradition alive. Don Miguel facilitated both things in a place the state has barely touched, despite the Plazuela having been identified as a priority site for revitalization. But how do you revitalize a place that is so alive? They have painted and repainted; they have added lights. But people do not come for the paint or the light. They come for the music and the atmosphere. They come to face life together. As Alfredo says, they have been coming for centuries. There is always a need to face life, and this is what is left to them. As Chucho says, they will continue to come. For there will always be a *rinconcito* somewhere, and there will always be old people dancing to the tempo that they can. People like them may intellectualize these habits, whereas people like Carla want to enjoy a night out for free, or people like El Caballo Viejo want a moment of freedom. All these attitudes coexist in the Plazuela and in Veracruz more broadly.

To say that happiness and dancing are the hallmark of Blackness is to propagate common racial scripts. Isar Godreau describes racial scripts as a variant of essentialism, stereotypes, and stigmas. Their defining difference, however, is their close association with celebratory notions and attributes seen as positive and exceptional.[25] Godreau argues that scripts are verbalized, collective, and ideological instruments. As we have seen in this chapter, the fact that the jarocho is happy is a dominant story that compels individual jarochos to seek their own happiness. This association dates back to the time when the jarocho type was racialized and has survived the deracination of the jarocho. As a result, people are not trying to be "Black" or even trying to be "jarocho." Instead, they are, in the words of Alfredo, trying to face life by engaging in leisure activities purported to make people happy. It is effort toward happiness, not the state of being, that characterizes the jarochos.

In the following chapter, we will see another method by which people attempt to conform to racial scripts assigned to jarochos: ancestry. Because the collective jarocho is understood to be an Afro-descendant, there are different techniques people use to write their personal narrative along similar lines. Sometimes it is the presumption of a Black ancestor; other times it is attributing traits to one such predecessor. Sometimes ancestry is forward looking and imagined as manifesting in future generations. These ancestral imaginings do not necessarily translate to personal self-identification, however. This, I argue in the next chapter, is a consequence of the project of belonging to a local collective identity rather than a diasporic one. Regardless of personal ancestry, one has access to Blackness by virtue of being jarocho. Nevertheless, some work to individualize that connection.

Interlude

A Hand to Hold

My new acquaintance Robert and I have been in the Italian Coffee for too long. The cool air-conditioning, once welcoming, has veered into a downright chill. With the dregs of coffee turned cold and the crumbs of our cookies picked over, in my head I am rehearsing how to take my leave gracefully from this encounter. I have grown increasingly discomfited by the personal—and, to my mind, not at all relevant—information he is oversharing. In contrast, Robert only gets more comfortable. Robert, the former merchant marine, evidently has nothing better to do than to while away the better part of his afternoon with me, explaining how he, unlike his brother, is Black.

We had met at a daytime event about the third root hosted by the Veracruz Institute of Culture. After explaining to him my presence at the forum and in the city more generally, Robert volunteered to have a conversation with me. He insisted I would want to talk to him. I was intrigued. He was, after all, one of the few people I had met who called himself *negro* outright.

In fact, Robert wishes he were Blacker. He tells me so. When I push to understand how he reckons with the fault line of Blackness that cleaves him from his brother, he instead begins his lament. Although he considers himself Black, he complains he is not Black enough. Interestingly, it is his palms, not his skin or hair, that tell the tale. They should be whiter. For Robert, the slight ruddiness of his palms is undeniable proof that he is not "pure" but instead mixed. He demands to see my hands. Confused and intrigued, I surrender myself to this unorthodox palm reading. I wonder what he will find as he looks to my past instead of my future. Disappointment, it turns out. Upon inspection of my not-white-enough palms, Robert wishes I were Blacker, too.

After our conversation in the café, I would run into Robert a few more times on the streets of Veracruz. More than once, Robert would show me pictures saved on his phone of African women, admiring their Blackness among other things. I never knew how to react to these encounters, never knew what exactly he wanted from me. I am not sure he knew what he wanted from me, either. Long before I met him, he was self-identifying as Black. But maybe he wanted to identify with another Black person. Maybe he was lonely in his not-Black-enough Blackness, with his reddish palms and non-Black siblings. Maybe he wanted to talk with a Black woman rather than merely admire them on his phone.

I was always uncomfortable in these interactions, but as I sit here now, I think that Robert, the former merchant marine with his palm readings and his longings, wanted a hand to hold as he navigated what Blackness meant to him and whether he was truly in possession of it.

5

Sanguine Blackness

The association between the jarocho and Blackness is long and multifaceted. In recent years, cultural producers and their audiences have rendered Blackness as a concomitant trait of the jarocho archetype. This is Blackness abstracted to the group level. However, it also at times is personal. This personal connection does not necessarily manifest as self-identification. It can also take the form of Black ancestry. Not everyone has, can, or wants to identify their Black ancestry. Christina Sue has compellingly argued for a more nuanced interpretation of "the downplaying of African ancestry" beyond denial or avoidance. Instead, she offers that many Veracruzanos may be ignorant of, rather than embarrassed by, their ancestry. The "absence of generational transfer of ancestral information" could explain why African heritage is often assumed but unexamined. Moreover, she observes that claims of identity do not follow from claims of ancestry.[1] Like Sue, I observed how many people who did not know their ancestry would assume they had African heritage but did not necessarily fixate on it.

When I searched for Black people, the responses aligned with that of other scholars—denial, avoidance, downplaying, ignorance. Note how negatively connoted these terms are. I posit that they reveal more about the questions asked than the answers received. These are questions intended to "discover" something "principally knowable."[2] They also take as a starting premise the erasure and invisibility of Afro-descendants in Mexico. In this context, equivocations about Black ancestry can reveal much about the racial hierarchy in the mestizo nation and the place of Afro-descendants therein. However, as Stephan Palmié has maintained, ethnographic objects lead double lives; not only do they change, but our contextual vantage point also changes. It is why, as he vividly puts it, "one can imagine generational cohorts of ethnographers marching across the same geographically or thematically defined terrain and seeing different things—not just because of substantial changes that have factually occurred, but because they have come to ask different questions."[3] While my questions—especially at first—were not much different from the ethnographers of Afro-Mexico whose paths I retread and paralleled, my attention arrested on different things. I asked different questions of similar data. Instead of focusing on lack, absence, or denied expectation, I ruminated on what was volunteered, mentioned, speculated aloud.

I am not ignorant of the fact that my perceived Black identity may have influenced what people chose to share and the manner in which they chose to share it. As often as not, my conversation partner bodily wrested me into their example or explanation. I became part of their story or a reason to remember a story at all. In these encounters, I found that in Veracruz, there are avenues to identify with Blackness irrespective of one's identity as Black or not. Ancestry is one such avenue. In speaking with jarochos from various backgrounds, I noticed a tendency for people to leave space for Black ancestry regardless of their self-identification. Many people I spoke to were quick to label a known or unknown ancestor as Black.[4] Some projected this ancestry forward to real or imagined progeny. Black ancestry was something many could have—and, in fact, were eager to have—but it did not align with how the state was coming to define Blackness.

The conventional reading assumes these people are in denial or that this non-identification is an expression of the anti-Blackness embedded in mestizaje. This reading flattens the nuance and complexity at play. Instead of trying to rationalize why someone does not identify as Afro-descendant, it is more interesting to understand what the identification of ancestors as Black does in the contemporary moment. I argue that this is another iteration of Blackness in the service of jarocho identity. It scales down the third root discourse to the individual level. Whereas traditionally, mestizaje could introduce plausible deniability regarding one's proximity to Blackness, many people who are cognizant of the third root do the reverse. Black heritage becomes something one "should have" and becomes linked to demonstrable traits such as phenotype, penchants, or talent. Memories, rumors, and even nicknames about great-grandparents and great-great-grandparents one has never met become the link to these ancestral Afro-descendants of Veracruz. The genealogies of many participants in jarocho publics are littered with such figures, varyingly identified as Cuban, *chino*, or simply remarkably tall and strong.[5]

In this chapter, I attend to moments when people referenced a Black ancestor to understand what Black ancestry does for contemporary jarochos on the personal level. I argue that ancestry does impact identity, just not identity as Afro-Mexican. Instead, Black ancestry becomes a linchpin in a project of belonging, not to the broader African diaspora, but rather to jarocho culture. From structured interviews to happenstance encounters, I present instances when people are grappling with and reconciling how Black ancestry does or does not result in their self-conception as Afro-descendant. In these theorizations, suppositions, and reckonings, individuals are situating their personal stories vis-à-vis the broader narratives of how the jarochos are, as one interlocutor told me with affection, *negritos mexicanos* (little Black Mexicans).

ON SEEING WELL

I met Ellery through some US expat friends who were eager to help me find Black people—back when I was still looking. Ellery was a jack-of-all-trades sort of handyman in his thirties. An earnest type. He was also, I would learn from one of his anecdotes, a father. His son had recently been bullied at school, and Ellery was recounting to me how he helped address his son's hurt at being called *negro*. With pride, Ellery shared with me that he told his son that they were not *negro*, but rather *cafecitos*, or "brown." He explained to his son that his classmate was mistaken because he did not see well. Ellery insisted to his son that *negro* was an adjective best suited to describing the color of their shoes, perhaps, but not their skin.

It would be easy to read both the bullying and the cajoling as manifestations of anti-Blackness. Not only was "black" used as an insult; Ellery denied the "black" description and replaced it with that of brown, which itself was tempered with its diminutive form. Moreover, Ellery taught his son that *negro* was not even a term applicable to skin, but rather more suited to an inanimate object. In soothing his son, Ellery worked to "soften the taken-for-granted negative connotation of *negro*" that exists across Latin America.[6]

Avoidance of the term *negro* or the turn toward a euphemism like *gente de color* do not shelter darker-skinned Latin Americans from the material consequences of a pigmentocracy. Coined by Chilean anthropologist Alejandro Lipschutz, the term captures how inequalities fall along a color and ethnoracial continuum where darker-skinned people, often Indigenous or Black, face higher rates of discrimination. Recent scholarship by the Project on Ethnicity and Race in Latin America (PERLA) has found that skin color is a stronger indicator than social categorization.[7] So while Ellery interpreted *negro* as purely a color label rather than a racial category, some scholars of race in Mexico have argued that such a distinction is untenable in practice. For example, sociologist Christina Sue, who also worked in Veracruz, has demonstrated how mestizo Mexicans grapple with questions of color as they consider a myriad of social interactions including not only racial identity, group boundaries, and racial discrimination and inequality but also family dynamics and romantic preferences and entanglements.[8] Sue argues that because there is the belief that neither race nor racism exists in Mexico, which she calls "nonracism," color has become even more salient and therefore serves as a proxy for racialized poles and a manifestation of race.[9] This aligns with the belief that Latin American nations are functionally pigmentocracies, wherein "skin color is a central axis of social stratification."[10] Not only that, race and skin tone have both subjective and material consequences in the lived experiences of Mexicans— in the perceived discrimination suffered based on one's appearance and in access to public goods and services, respectively.[11]

Nevertheless, Ellery and his story do not align as neatly with this discourse as it may appear at first blush. Though his rejection of the term *negro* may speak to broader manifestations of mestizaje's ideology and lived reality, he does in fact "see well," unlike his child's bully. What he sees is not just physical complexions but also what legacies they may represent. While he rejects the color label *negro* for him and his *cafecito* son, he quite forthrightly described himself as having *piel oscura*, or "dark skin." When describing his ancestors, he uses skin tone and other descriptors such as hair texture or facial features to best describe them. When mentioning his great-great-grandfather, Ellery recounted that the man "looked very African," according to family lore.[12] His grandfather was a very brown-skinned person with curly hair—his exact words were that he was "una persona morena-morena." In Veracruz, as in other parts of Mexico, the doubling of the descriptor is a common discursive device to emphasize the intensity of the feature.[13] Ellery admitted he did not know the exact ancestral roots of his grandfather, but he volunteered that I could pass for a granddaughter. In contrast, his grandmother from the nearby town of Medellín was white with blue eyes, which explained why his father was light brown with a narrow face and fine features. Nevertheless, in describing his family, Ellery said his grandfather's genes had a stronger influence because, while some of his aunts and uncles are light-skinned, no one is white with blue eyes like his grandmother's family.

With this recollection of his family tree, Ellery was also making broader claims to his local roots. If color was helping him draw a boundary, it was a regionalized one rather than a racial one. He connected his complexion with his status as a native-born Veracruzano when he told me that people who are really from the city—especially in comparison to more recent transplants—are *morenos*.[14] In his family tree, it was his "very African"-looking ancestor who not only lived in but also fought in defense of the city. In contrast, his paternal family's white ancestry was the transplanted root. His Black ancestry ran deep in the Port.

THE PRINGA

Fidel is not Black. Rather, he was not Black when we sat together in a garden, feeling our way through a conversation about Blackness and race in early 2015. Fidel was not Black, but he is brown. He is tall—thin but not lanky—and has a slow, wide smile. His hair is a riotous cloud of curls when he leaves it loose. I will admit, his look made me curious about how he thought about Blackness in Veracruz, but it was not his look alone. It was also his occupation.

We had met through son jarocho. He is a member of a well-known and respected son jarocho group and, near the end of my fieldwork, he began to offer workshop classes as well. In short, his activities in the fandanguero community have left him well versed, rehearsed, and practiced not just in the musical genre but in third root discourse, as well. I can only imagine the number of cultural events for which he stood stage left as he and his group waited for their moment to initiate the fandango portion of the evening. He has been present onstage as his group used their platform to educate their audience about the third root of son jarocho. He has led students through chord progressions and perhaps has even fielded questions about sones like "Los Negritos" or the meaning of *gurumbé*. All these experiences—in addition to this appearance—made me eager to sit down with Fidel. Eager, and upon listening to the recording of our chat, a little anxious.

I am struck by how nervous we both are. I laugh self-consciously when I feel I have asked a question indelicately. He shifts from half thought to half thought as he works his way into an opinion. I do not want to assume, and he does not want to offend, but the longer we chat the more comfortable we both get. In our long, winding conversation, he never identifies himself as Black, but he does name several family members as such. When I first asked Fidel about whether he considered himself to be *negro*, he deflected by mentioning his cousin. His cousin is also in the fandanguero community, so I knew him by sight, but not personally. According to Fidel, his cousin has "más raza," which literally translates to "more race." To justify this claim, Fidel mentions his cousin's mother is "negra-negra," with curly hair. The doubling of a descriptor emphasizes the trait. His cousin's mother is both dark-skinned and curly-haired. As a result, Fidel reasons his cousin has a stronger appearance as Black than he does.

He has mentioned his cousin to reference someone I know, but Fidel also focuses on his direct line of descent, which he says has "una raíz africana," or an African root. To prove this point, Fidel brings up his grandfather Antonio. Not only did he have musical talent, he was also negro-negro. The implication is that his family inherited not just their features but also their musical inclinations from this dark-skinned ancestor. In the middle of telling me about his grandfather, Fidel interjects that he himself is "now more diluted, no?" as an invitation for me to see why he did not readily see himself as Black, especially in comparison with his family members. Interestingly, he is even more equivocal when he touches on his mother. He eventually describes her as morena, after much consideration. When I ask him about his father, he immediately pronounces his father as having "rasgos africanos" (African features) and makes special mention of his father's height, which he describes as "altote," or very tall. He tells me his father was "two meters tall," which—like the doubling of a color descriptor—is a euphemism for very tall people, and not necessarily a literal claim to someone being over six and a half feet tall. By the time we had our conversation under the palm's shade, I was already familiar with these commonplace somatic allusions to Blackness. It is not that all tall, dark, or coily-haired people are Black, but rather that these are common traits among Black people. After all, Fidel is tall and darker than average, with a curly hair pattern. But Fidel is not Black.

Nevertheless, he acknowledges and does not try to diminish the African ancestry in his family. Sometimes he focuses on appearances like his cousin's dark-skinned mother or his father's notable height. Other times he speaks of intangibles, like his very dark grandfather passing along not just features but also musical abilities. All of this evidence shapes his relationship with his Blackness, which he varyingly terms a root, a trait, or a race. The most striking analogy, however, is that of the *pringa*.

"We all carry a *pringa* of Black, no?" he rhetorically asks me. I am unfamiliar with the term. To help me understand his meaning, Fidel offers the metaphor of throwing water on hot oil. In that scenario, the jumping oil would be a pringa. On the recording, you can hear me muttering the word to myself. In the corresponding field notebook, I wrote the word big, circled it, and added arrows just to be sure. His metaphor helped, but I knew then I wanted to look up the word in the dictionary to be sure I understood him. As we talk, Fidel switches to a more familiar metaphor. "We are all a mixture of coffee and milk," he tells me. "Some more coffee, some more milk."

Indeed, the "café con leche" metaphor is common in literature on race in Latin America, another way to describe mestizaje. For example, in Venezuela, the idea of "coffee with milk" became an iconic descriptor to capture the tonal variety that resulted from the generations of mixture. As Luis Angosto-Ferrández has argued, the term became popular in academic circles after the publication of Winthrop Wright's 1990 book *Café con Leche: Race, Class, and National Image in Venezuela*. While Wright borrowed the phrase from the Venezuelan public intellectual Andrés Eloy Blanco, who coined it in 1944, Angosto-Ferrández found the phrase had little use in contemporary Venezuela.[15] It is a striking metaphor. Veracruz's local coffee-and-milk drink, the *lechero*, is a tempting image to use when considering Blackness in the port. The fact that in the tableside preparation of the drink, one can add more coffee, but can never ask for less, is seductively evocative, as if it is a metanarrative about Blackness in Veracruz. Like the coffee in the *lechero*, the Blackness is both nonnegotiable and foundational. Yet he unconsciously returns to the imagery that makes the most sense to him—the *pringa*. *La pringa de la sangre negra*. The drop of Black blood.

Veracruzanos allude to their Black *raza, raíz, rasgos*, but especially their *pringa*. The metaphor of the pringa in an apt one. Like other notions of Black blood, it situates jarochos within broader understandings of legacies and nation. Metaphors of blood reveal ideas not just of the past but also the future. The royal "we" of his statement "Todos tenemos una pringa" requires us to consider how Blackness constitutes groupness as well as the afterlives and reconciliations of past racial logics. It was clear from our conversation that the "we" did not refer to all Mexicans, but rather to jarochos. The pringa, small though it may be, makes many things possible for inhabitants of Veracruz.

Allusions to Black blood in Veracruz are part of a broader project of belonging. While Blackness has been largely fashioned as outside or apart from Mexican identity, I find that Blackness, and specifically discursive ties to Black ancestry, binds locals together, not as a race but rather as a regional type—the jarocho. To have, or at least to acknowledge, a connection to Blackness is to strengthen the bonds of regional distinction. Therefore, Blackness is useful to their collective identity, even as it does not demand self-identification as Black. It is a shared possession that makes jarochos different.

As metaphorical blood, the pringa both avoids the ambiguity around personal African ancestry and renders the question moot. Karen and Barbara Fields have argued that metaphorical blood "always had everything to do with human groups." Blood is "an ancient metaphor of kinship and descent" that "inhabits the profoundest layer of mystique that humanity has carried with it from time immemorial" and therefore represents both "kin and kind."[16] For these reasons, blood and race are often interchangeable. As Sharon Patricia Holland states it, "a crude understanding of race is that it is always already that thing that happens in the blood."[17] However, while racialized, the pringa is not quite racial. Instead, it facilitates the collective imaginings of jarochos as avatars of Mexican Blackness. In that way, it is a project of belonging, but the contours of the groupness are regional rather than diasporic.

As a project of belonging, the blood signifies two sets of relations. One is through "real" biological connections at the level of family—for example, a blood relation. The second set of relations derives from identifying with others, having a sense of belonging to a group that is either imposed on someone or developed by choice. In my conversation with Fidel, he drew on both sets of relations, recalling his Abuelo Antonio, but also scaling up to jarochos in his statement that "we all carry a pringa of Black blood." Fidel's pringa epitomizes how notions of blood, foundational racial logics, and essentialisms create the slippages that allow for hereditary conceptions of Blackness to complicate more cultural understandings.

Fidel is not alone in this oscillation between the personal and the collective. Don Justo, a good friend of mine, would do the same. As a pensioner who used to work in the oil sector, he would spend his time telling tall tales, drinking dark drinks—coffee, Coca-Cola, and the occasional whiskey soda—and playing his jarana with friends. That is how we met, in son jarocho class. When he learned I was interested in the third root in Veracruz, he gestured between the two of us and said that he, too, "had the blood." He would point to his skin, to his curly hair, his nose, and say, "of course." A mutual friend, Chucho, would similarly claim to have Black blood running through his veins when I asked him whether he considered himself Afro-Mexican. While both would point to their bodies, their language would use the third-person plural.

Other people like El Vate Veracruzano, the cultural promoter, would go directly to the royal "we." Unlike Don Justo and Chucho, his pale skin and ginger stubble do not make for easy visual claims to Black ancestry. Instead, he has armed himself with a wealth of knowledge about the cultural inheritance he, as a jarocho, possesses. He has readied himself with lists of terms and foodstuffs that speak to African retentions. He is quick to point to local traditions like Carnival or the Christmas tradition called La Rama as evidence of the enduring African legacy in the city enjoyed by all jarochos. He cultivates imagery associated with Caribbeanness and happiness in his culture work. Early in our acquaintance, he told me, "We jarochos are the negritos mexicanos." In calling jarochos the Black Mexicans, he is not saying that jarochos are Afro-Mexicans. Rather, I take him as arguing that jarochos embody what at that time was the prevalent understanding of Mexican Blackness. As with Fidel, I wonder whether he now identifies as Afro-Mexican or whether there is a difference for him between claiming a group identity as negritos and an individual claim to being Black.

Among the jarochos, the idea of Black blood is not only creating a group belonging, but also signaling how racial logics sediment and evolve. Images of Black blood are quite familiar. To a US audience, the immediate association would be the one-drop rule, a racialized logic from the late nineteenth century that argues for hypodescent. It held that the progeny of mixture follows the category of the "most subordinate" ancestor. In the United States, that means that known Black ancestry is sufficient to make you Black. The imagery is culturally salient in the United States, but it is not universal.

In 2011 US scholar Henry Louis Gates Jr. created a PBS docuseries called *Black in Latin America*. The four episodes visited six countries across the region to introduce a US-based audience to lived manifestations of Blackness and Black identity different from their own. The first half of the final episode, subtitled "The Black Grandma in the Closet," focuses on Mexico. The title of the episode comes from a conversation he has with Mexican anthropologist Sagrario Cruz-Carretero during which she describes her family's history. As family photographs fill the screen, Cruz-Carretero recounts a conversation she once had with her grandfather when she asked him why he had never told her the family was Black. He responded that they were not Black but rather morenos. Continuing her story, she contextualizes this response by saying, "Of course he was aware that he was a Black man, but he rejected that identity. And I think this happens in most families, that you hide the Black grandma in the closet." Cruz-Carretero, one of the most vocal scholars of Afro-Mexico, was espousing a narrative of denial she found in her own family. Ancestry—specifically her Afro-Cuban ancestry—was, to her eyes, "downplayed" and hidden. Rather than seeing her grandfather's reasons for why he was not Black but rather moreno, she rephrased his words by saying that, while he rejected that identity, he was of course "aware that he was a Black man." He was aware, according to Cruz-Carretero, because of his ancestry. Because of "the Black grandma in the closet."[18]

In the documentary, the conversation ends with a lingering shot of a family photograph before cutting to an outdoor shot of Gates. He is alone in the picturesque town of Tlacotalpan as he delivers his final summation of the scene's point straight to camera before transitioning to a conversation about Yanga. Over B-roll of people in public spaces, the audience hears Gates's words, "In America, traditionally, if you had one drop of Black blood, you were Black. If the one-drop rule were to apply to Mexico, *all of* these people would be Black."[19] However, the one-drop rule does not apply to Mexico. The image, however, does exist but with different consequences.

In Latin America, the idea of a drop of Black blood is enmeshed with the Iberian concept of *limpieza de sangre*, or blood purity. As the late Maria Elena Martínez outlined, on the Iberian Peninsula, blood "became a vehicle through which all sorts of characteristics and religious proclivities were transmitted."[20] While the Iberian preoccupation with religious conversion was not as salient in the Americas, the logic of what blood could do and mean survived the Atlantic journey. The idea that blood carries essentialized traits both positive and negative, and that lineage is critical to understanding both who and how a person is, adapted to the American context. Impurity mapped onto African ancestry, becoming a stain passed on through the generations.

While the casta painting series of the late colonial moment were more aspirational than evidentiary, they nevertheless reveal the logic undergirding the impurity of Black ancestry. Whereas Indigenous blood could eventually "clear" within three generations of sustained mixture with Spaniards, no such return to "purity" was possible with the introduction of African lineage. Once African ancestry entered a family, it never left. Like the one-drop rule, though, these ideas were what Martinez calls "genealogical fictions," assumptions about blood and lineage that are not natural, but rather naturalized through policies, power struggles, and practices. As such, one had to prove—or disprove—their ancestry and lineage. The archives are filled with individuals having to demonstrate they rightfully belonged to the group identity they claimed. They did so through two sets of relations—through their family ties and through their social position. You see similar attempts in the present when individual jarochos legitimate their belonging to jarocho identity either through family ties of Black blood or through performing their social position, as we see in other chapters. However, much has changed since the colonial period, and the racial logics at hand to make sense of one's metaphorical blood have been indelibly affected by twentieth-century mestizaje.

Mestizaje is both the practice of intercultural and interracial mixture and the nation-building ideology—the all-inclusive ideology of exclusion, as Ronald Stutzman famously called it.[21] The Mexican political leader Jose Vasconcelos in his seminal work *La Raza Cósmica* (*The Cosmic Race*) theorizes, albeit briefly, about the Black blood of his cosmic race, which he believed would be the destiny of all humankind—a destiny earned through mixture and toward which Latin

Americans served as the vanguard. Vasconcelos believes "the Black may disappear" due to aesthetic eugenics, yet he gives space for "the drop put in our blood by the Black," which he characterizes as "eager for sensual joy, intoxicated with dances and unbridled lust."[22] For him, these are the scripts and traits carried in and through Black ancestry. This was their contribution to humanity on the way to what Vasconcelos considered a more perfect humankind. You will notice that the features he mentions, sensuality, joy, dance, and lust, are also the characteristics that the jarochos valorize as regional traits. Yet despite the centuries of mixture, the Black blood did not disappear; instead, it became a project of belonging—specifically, of belonging to Veracruz.

Fidel's image of jumping oil was helpful in the moment, but when I delved into the pringa's meaning and learned it could mean either a drop or a stain, I realized the pringa quite evocatively captures how people had been alluding to Blackness and their Black ancestry in my years of research in the city. As both a drop and a stain, the pringa represents two distinct racial logics, one originating from the colonial era with its preoccupation with establishing categorical difference despite ongoing mixture and another from the postrevolutionary moment, with its goal of creating a homogeneous national identity as Mexican despite the differences within the nation. Through the pringa, these logics exist within yet another racialized framework, that of multiculturalism, wherein Mexico's internal diversity is now a virtue rather than a sign of unsuccessful or incomplete acculturation. The pringa's continuing relevance within multiculturalism demonstrates that metaphorical reckonings of blood have afterlives beyond the historical context of their creation.

Yet the pringa and its logics did not arrive in the twenty-first century unchanged. As such, while Black ancestry was a stain that could never be cleared from the blood in the colonial moment, the staining quality in the contemporary moment speaks more to the idea that jarochos have this Black ancestry and therefore it can manifest in future generations. This modern-day *torna atrás* or throwback, is for the most part value neutral, which is not to diminish the ongoing consequences of Mexico's pigmentocracy. Nevertheless, the fatalism of the stain of Black ancestry is now discussed as a potential outcome rather than a curse. The following three encounters demonstrate different approaches to this conjecture and speculation about one's Black ancestry and its manifestation.

SPECULATIVE GENEALOGIES

Karen does not consider herself Black but holds a certain fascination about the rumored Black ancestry in her husband's family. Every time we reunite over hot *lecheros* (coffee-and-milk beverages) or cold *nieves* (water-based, ice cream–like desserts), Karen's face blossoms with her toothy grin as she retreads the same worn path of family lore and her personal connection to Blackness. She has yet to pin down the name of the small town where her husband's grandmother was born. Nevertheless, the legacy of this woman, fondly remembered as chinita-chinita and morena-morena, carries into the present and possibly the future. The memory of the dark-skinned woman with coiled hair meant that when my friend Karen was pregnant, her in-laws speculated about whether she was expecting a "little Black one." In the end, neither of Karen's two children resemble their paternal great-grandmother. They both have Karen's infectious smile, golden brown skin, and undulating hair. Nevertheless, Karen optimistically looks to the future. As she regularly assures me, "They say it skips a generation."

Karen's confidence in and positive outlook on skipped generations and the possibility for "a little Black one" in the future always reminds me of another conversation I once had about imagined futures. Unlike my yearslong friendship with Karen, I had just met my walking companion, Juancho. Despite the newness of our acquaintance, Juancho exuded the openness jarochos are famous for and launched into an anecdote from when his wife was pregnant.

Late in his wife's pregnancy, Juancho's mother took him aside for a candid conversation. She told him not to worry if the child came out darker skinned. "We have the blood in our family," she revealed. Juancho is moreno and has a very typical complexion among the jarochos. The term *moreno* encompasses a wide spectrum of browns, and many people fit the description. Some attribute their skin color to the strong tropical sun, others to ancestors long passed, and some do not bother to explain their permanently tanned complexion at all. Within families, skin tones vary widely as well, so the warning and reassurance from Juancho's mother is interesting. She took the opportunity to remember and pass on their family's past in anticipation of the new generation.

As we walked, he mused aloud that perhaps his great-grandfather or great-great-grandfather—some generation beyond his acquaintance—was Cuban. The mystery of where the blood came from did not trouble his easy acceptance of his mother's story. He told me he did not worry, and in the end, his child was not particularly darker than he or his wife. Regardless, Juancho remembers his mother's revelation that they have the blood. He now has the story of the unknown Black ancestor. Maybe one day in the future, he will also pull aside his child and reveal for them this latent Black blood that they have. It may skip generations, but its potential to manifest in the next one is always there. This is the colonial logic of limpieza de sangre put to a new twenty-first-century understanding of ancestry. Whereas in the past, people needed proof to establish their ancestry, in contemporary Veracruz Black ancestry often is a thing of conjecture. The impulse to identify ancestors known and unknown as an explanation for the future generation is a way to slot one's personal story into the common narrative of jarochos as possessing Mexico's Blackness. This idea of having Black blood rather than being Black also echoes the master narrative of mestizaje itself, as my conversation with a local historian made clear.

We were sitting in Ramón's recently inherited office above the Veracruz City Museum when he told me quite plainly, "you no longer find Black people in Veracruz." He gave his reasons. Chief among them was his belief that Afro-descendants intermixed early and often during the colonial period and the color disappeared. He identified facial and hair features that one can see in the general population, but he insisted that the color was gone. He offered himself as a case study. Ramón first characterized his moreno complexion as evidence of his African ancestry. He then assured me that while he kept his hair closely cropped, it would turn curly were he to let it grow long. Ramón attributed this hair texture to his father, whom he called *chino*, a descriptor for people with curly to tightly coiled hair, which is a popular allusion to Blackness. Nevertheless, he mused, his features were not as strong as in previous generations of his family. He then used me as an example to further explain his theory on why he saw the Black race as "genetically weak" when it came to mixture.

If I were to marry a *güero*, or white person, he told me that there would be a fifty-fifty chance that our child would be white. If that child also married a white person, my hypothetical grandchild would definitely be white. This generational attenuation is why he offered that there were features associated with Black people in the Port, but few people who were Black. It is possible Ramón was so certain that I would no longer find Black people in the Port because, as a historian, he knew how populated the city once was with people he would qualify as such. Their descendants remain in the city, as evidenced in the phenotypic vestiges he called "Negroid features."

There are many ways to read Ramón's candor. He does not deny Blackness or the African ancestry of either his personal history or jarochos in general. In fact, he makes a concerted effort to mention them as a reference point to his claim that you no longer find Black people in Veracruz. However, he is also promoting the utopic promise of mestizaje in that Afro-descendants of yore had successfully mixed away into the general population—a population that was perhaps moreno but was decidedly not Black. His theory that Black genes are more prone to dilution helps substantiate his idea about mixing out, though it is in direct contrast to Ellery's own family history, where the white genes were the ones to disappear. Ramón also has clear criteria for who qualifies as a Black person; or, rather, he has an opinion for what is not sufficient for such a qualification—ancestry.

Having ancestors, as close as a curly-haired father or as far as an imagined Cuban ancestor, did not make one Black. The distance was not the issue. Karen keeps in mind her grandmother-in-law's Blackness when thinking about the future progeny that would make her a grandmother. That child would be four generations removed from "the Black ancestor," after all. Certain features matter more than others. When looking to the past, height or musical abilities, like that of Fidel's father and grandfather, become signifiers of Black ancestry but not Black identity. Wide noses and certain hair textures often build the evidence for one's ancestry—especially when speaking on someone else's behalf. Even skin tone has its limits. Ellery's dark skin is only black for those who do not see well. Ramón's brown skin is a sign of superseded genes. Fidel's is from the sun.

Yet jarochos complicate the literature on discursive distancing. Disclaiming Black identity, but claiming Black ancestors, is not an attempt to diminish one's Blackness. While the means are the same, the ends are different. Discursive distancing is the tendency to temporally or geographically place Blackness at a remove, to distance away from the connotations—often negative—associated with Black identity as outside of the nation or as less modern. The emphasis on Caribbean links could be read as a spatially distancing move, for it argues that the true Black identity is there rather than in Mexico. Likewise, the common refrain that a grandfather, great-grandfather, or great-great grandfather was Black is also situating Blackness in the past. This could be read as temporal distancing. It is probable that many people in the city do so with these intentions. However, that is not the principal function of such stories. This is clear because when placing Blackness in their past, they do not leave it there.

Anthropologist Isar Godreau, in her work on the folklorization of Blackness in Puerto Rico, has argued that mentions of African heritage such as "roots," "veins," and "blood" are examples of discursive distancing because they demonstrate how "this legacy's contribution is understood as residing in a distant place that lies deep within one's body." You can see that in Fidel when he says that he is more "diluted," or when he calls his grandfather *negro-negro* and his mother *morena*, and says that he himself has Black blood. Each successive generation becomes less phenotypically "Black." You also see it with Ramón saying his features are less prominent than his father's features.

However, by looking at Black blood as a project of belonging—not to the racial category of Black, but rather to the regional identity of jarocho—placing Blackness in generations past is a strategic move. It seeks not to leave it in the past or deep in the body, but rather to give it a future. This is why pregnancies are moments to remember, and individual features serve as vestiges. To emphasize a present absence, to explain how and why jarochos are the way they are taught to be, is to leave space for it to manifest in the future—for it to phenotypically appear again. This future may not be cosmic, but it is provocative all the same.

AFRO-DESCENDANCY

One August day in 2016, I was on my way to visit the sisters Peregrino right in the heart of La Huaca. I approached from the south, walking along my old street of Emiliano Zapata, named after the famed revolutionary whose rumored Black ancestry was gaining more traction within discourse on Afro-Mexicans. As I turned right onto the Callejón Toña la Negra, I stopped to admire the new mural celebrating the neighborhood of La Huaca. The image was a large-scale version of

FIGURE 10. Street art modeled after the Cerveza Indio campaign featuring La Huaca as one of the iconic neighborhoods in Mexico. The mural is located at one end of the Callejón Toña la Negra and depicts two couples dancing, the colorful facades of the Barrio de la Huaca, and images of Toña la Negra and Agustín Lara. Photo by the author.

the new, limited-edition label for the beer brand Indio. It was part of the barrios campaign, which featured 150 different neighborhoods throughout the Republic as a way to celebrate the "authentic side of Mexico." Each label would carry the beer brand's iconic image of the Aztec emperor Cuauhtémoc alongside emblematic elements of their neighborhood (figure 10).[23]

La Huaca's version is a colorful homage to the neighborhood that features its iconic built environment, the famous musicians Toña la Negra and Agustín Lara, and two couples dancing below the brand's name. At the very top is a red banner with the neighborhood name La Huaca in orange and Veracruz named just below it. The multicolored wooden facades of the patio buildings flank the sides of the image, while Lara and Toña face in opposite directions on the same plane as the Aztec emperor. Lara has his famous scar on his face and is in a suit and tie, accessorized with a cigarette. Toña la Negra is in a red dress with white polka dots, with a smile on her face and a flower in her hair. The two dancing couples are in matching outfits—the men in white guayaberas with straw hats and the women in red dresses with their hair pulled back into buns. On the beer bottle label, the people—except for Lara—are a stylized pitch black with smiles on their faces. When the muralist reproduced the image for the neighborhood, the people became a more realistic brown color, though Lara is even paler than in the original image. The mural's debut coincided with the first Gorda and Picada Festival—the one where Blanca staunchly defended her fellow chilangos—and was a welcomed boon to the neighborhood association's touristic aspirations.[24]

I did not linger at the mural because I had a date with the Peregrinos. I had met them the night before around that plastic table, as their brother Toño regaled the table with nostalgic tales between singing the requested songs and demanded encores of the festivalgoers. He had come home to La Huaca from Mexico City, where he makes his living as a singer. Toño was a prodigal son and a minor celebrity—especially in comparison to their world-famous aunt, Toña la Negra, whose name graced the walkway, whose statue stood tall in said walkway, and now whose likeness featured on a wall at the end of that very same pedestrian path.

Born María Antonia del Carmen Peregrino Álvarez, she is most known by her stage name, Toña "the Black Woman." Prior to becoming famous, she performed with her brothers in the Trio Peregrino and was known simply as "La Peregrino" before her stage name—and life—changed in Mexico City.[25] She was the muse of Veracruzan composer Agustín Lara, and the association between the two is renowned, as reproduced in the mural and the close proximity of their statues in the walkway. The bolero singer was one of the prime representatives of "the popular soul of Veracruz" and helped feed "the sentimental education of the Mexican people."[26] She also helped educate Mexican people about their Afro-Caribbean heritage. As Frances Aparicio has argued, Toña la Negra not only vindicated Afro-Caribbean compositions, rhythms, and textures, she also "exhorted Mexican audiences to accept the African heritage of the Caribbean coast as a central element of their culture."[27] Through her presence and performances in music and film, she carved out space for Blackness within Mexican popular culture.[28] However, as mentioned during her statue unveiling in her hometown, she belongs to the soul of the jarocho people, who cannot live without that soul.[29] She is without a doubt the most famous person from the Barrio de la Huaca and one of the most celebrated Afro-Mexican personas. However, when I visited with her grandnieces, the Peregrinos, we also spoke of another famous member of the family—their father, David Rodríguez Peregrino, also known as El Negro Peregrino, a successful singer and leader of the group El Negro Peregrino y su Trío.

I sat with Lety in the small house in the middle of the callejón where they sell picadas made to order. She and her sister Laura were used to people coming to talk about their aunt and had aspirations for opening a museum in her honor. I was but one of many people with whom they had shared their personal memories of their paternal great-aunt. Although the naming customs resulted in Peregrino not being either of their last names, they answered to that name as the living links to her legend. Our conversation about Toña was engaging, but I was more fascinated with how Lety spoke about her father, his Blackness, and how it has influenced her understanding of race.

"What a beautiful Black man. I have never seen a more beautiful Black man. When I see a person of color like that, I feel something. I mean, I have a lot of respect for that type of person," she told me with a warm tone. Her father was "negro negro negro" with "pelo pasita," another phrase for kinky hair. None of his children turned out that way, though her older brother would chemically curl his hair in his youth. According to Lety, she was the most morena of his five children. Although she wished for a "negro" child, all of her own kids turned out "morenitos." Yet she is proud of their Black ancestry, which she says came from her father's mother. Lety's grandmother was the sister of Toña la Negra, and while Lety was unclear as to whether they were descendants of Africans or Cubans, she knew her grandmother's father was a Black man named Timoteo who was two meters tall.[30] When later I asked if this meant she considered herself Black, she rephrased the question and said Afro-descendant.

For Lety, all Black people are Afro-descendants, but not all Afro-descendants are Black.[31] The term *negro* was slippery in our conversation. After asking for clarification, she said features, skin tone, and hair all come together to distinguish someone as Black. When we first broached the topic of her father, she described him as "un negro," a Black man. She went on to describe him as "negro negro negro," which suggests she was referring to his physical appearance. Near the end, she referred to him as "de la raza negra," or of the Black race. This slight shift allowed her to bridge the Afro-descendant versus Black question. She also mentioned her aunt Toña la Negra as being of the Black race but made a point to clarify that she was actually morena and not very black complexion-wise. When I asked her how she would qualify me, she said that I am of the Black race as evident through my hair and my features, but I am a morena because of my complexion. Being of the Black race is different from being black. Being of the race is akin to Fidel's pringa; it is a legacy you possess regardless of whether you phenotypically express it. Nevertheless, that expression is still valued. It is why Ellery drew attention to his cafecito skin tone or Ramón focused on how curly his hair became when it grew out. It is why two-meters-tall grandfathers are a common trope and there is at times a longing or an anticipation that progeny to come will resemble ancestors of yore.

Lety's understanding of racial legacy is noteworthy because of her unique position as a known, though indirect, descendant of a famously Afro-Mexican figure. Both her great-aunt and her father used their Blackness in their stage names of Toña la Negra and El Negro Peregrino, respectively. Her brother's nickname alludes to the family's ancestry twice over; his given name is David Antonio Rodríguez García, though he professionally goes by Toño Peregrino. Toño not only is a nickname for his second name Antonio, it also alludes to his aunt's nickname for hers. In their branch of the family tree, the Peregrino last name ended with their father, yet he uses it to make clear the connection between him and the famous musicians in his family who came before him. His sisters who stayed in the Port likewise keep that association through community memory and answer to Las Peregrinos. That is to say, it is not a secret but rather a point of pride that they are descendants of people they and others think of as Afro-descendant. They are "of the Black race" by both features and reputation. They do not want to distance themselves from it, but rather take steps to emphasize the connection.

Importantly, Lety does not make her experience singular. Instead, she recruits her fellow porteños in her reckonings. As she told me when speaking of the past, "here, the people were black." To be clear, she is not saying all of the people were Black. Her mother, for example, she describes as "india" or Indigenous, and born and raised in La Huaca just like her father's family had been for at least three generations. Still, she told me, "Normally, the original peoples from the Port, we are of the Black race." Note the verb tenses. While the people in the Port were black before, they are currently of the Black race. Like Ramón, she points to mixture as justification for this change; like Ellery, she places Black ancestry as a key component to generational jarocho identity.

In many ways, the Peregrino family's relationship with Blackness has crucial parallels with that of jarochos collectively. Jarochos, too, are famously associated with their Black ancestry. It is an association they negotiate as they find their place in the contemporary moment. That reputation is why they are avatars of Mexican Blackness. They honor and celebrate that inherited legacy. They commemorate it just as surely as the Peregrino family seeks to develop a museum in their aunt's honor. Yet it is not a legacy left in amber. It is alive and lived. A festival like the one where I first met the family is an official demonstration of that legacy, but people do not wait for such occasions to enjoy it.

Jarochos' relationship with Blackness is about place as much as it is about race. It grounds them rather than limiting them. Toña la Negra's birthplace is crucial to her Blackness. She is representative of La Huaca's popular soul, a neighborhood hailed as the cradle of the city's Blackness. Likewise, Veracruz's stature as the birthplace of Mexican Blackness solidifies its association with the third root even as many people say there are no longer Black people there. This is because their identity as black— or even Black—does not dictate their identification with their local, proprietary Blackness. Instead, Blackness makes possible a sense of belonging to their jarocho identity. Just as place anchors this Blackness, time does as well. Ancestry, whether personal or generalized, links contemporary jarochos to previous ones that they may deem Blacker. It is also a claim to generational presence in a cosmopolitan city that has received visitors and transplants alike for over five hundred years. While there are Black people in the port of Veracruz, many more think of themselves as generations removed from the family member whom they would describe as black. Importantly, those generations, while often in the past, can also be in the future. This is because Blackness is an indelible mark. It is an authenticating one as well. The group to which people are seeking to belong is not a diasporic Afro-descended extended family, but the local, homegrown jarocho one.

As this chapter has shown, some individuals have or imagine more personal connections to the Blackness of the jarocho. Because the third root discourse has made Blackness a feature of the city's local color, some people further construct their sense of place and sense of home by recognizing their ancestry. However, ancestry is not necessarily a claim to identity. Being of African descent and self-recognizing as Afro-descendant are not synonymous for all peoples. This is a consequence of the unique recognition of Mexican Blackness that began in the 1980s and seems to have come to an end with the recognition of Black Mexicans. In the concluding chapter, we will recount the immediate reactions to this paradigm shift.

Conclusion

The Jarocho and the Afro-Mexican

In the early days of October 2014, a pillar of Veracruz's son jarocho community shared to my Facebook wall a flyer announcing the upcoming pilot study for the mid-census survey, the Encuesta Intercensal 2015. The shared image was part of the socialization campaign to prime the public for the first question in modern Mexican history to collect disaggregated data on the country's Afro-descendant population. The person who originally posted the flyer editorialized, "to demand recognition, you have to start with self-recognition. WE ARE BLACK PEOPLE! Please spread . . ." The jaranero did not add his own commentary to this missive, but he was in fact doing his part to spread the word. I did mine as well by sharing it with a group of tourism students at a private university in Veracruz. I had gone to them to speak about the third root and decided to incorporate the circulating image into my presentation. I wanted to do my part in raising awareness about this new step the government was taking. I did not anticipate sparking an existential question for the students. Yet I did, for at least one of them.

The official poster is a multilayered recruitment tool created to speak to people on different registers. It features nine diverse and multigenerational portraits of Mexican citizens in a three-by-three grid, creating a *Brady Bunch*–style blended family united under the newly official term *Afro-Mexican*. The photographed subjects stand before alternating backgrounds of concrete and foliage. Among the nine people are women and men, young and not so young. Their expressions range from happy to defiant, self-confident to self-satisfied. It was a familiar image to me for it was repurposed from a larger collage featured in the book *Afrodescendientes en México*, which was first published in 2012 by the National Council to Prevent Discrimination (CONAPRED) and the INAH and has since had a second edition.[1] Even for the unfamiliar, the portraits make a clear case for the diversity of people who are included in the term *afromexicano*. At the same time, this visual guide runs the risk of overly delimiting what an Afro-Mexican person may look like. Nine souls could not capture the range of ways of being Afro-Mexican. Perhaps this is why the poster includes group labels as well.

The words below the blended Afro-Mexican family portraits make explicit whatever the images imply. Directly below the images is a list of five group labels, each in their own typeface: *negro, morena, mascogo, costeña*, and *jarocho*. Each of the chosen terms has a connection to Mexican Blackness. *Negro* is a complicated term as it slips between a color label and a racial one. Beyond that, it can also serve as an insult or a term of endearment. As Laura Lewis has found, the term *moreno* has a particular significance in the Costa Chica region of Oaxaca and Guerrero. During her time in the field, locals preferred the term *moreno* to *negro*, considering it not only more polite but also more apt to highlight their mixed Afro-Indigenous heritage.[2] As we have seen, it also has a polite connotation in Veracruz and can euphemistically refer to Black ancestry. However, throughout the nation it broadly functions as a color category and descriptor. *Mascogos* are a small population in the northern state of Coahuila who are descendants of Black Seminoles who found protection, land, and rights across the US-Mexico border.[3] *Costeños* are generically anyone from the coast, though stereotypes exist such as an exaggerated accent of aborted consonant closings and ghosted syllables. Finally, there is the *jarocho*—an ethnoregional term that has an association with Blackness but is not limited to those who may identify with Blackness.

An ellipsis separates these five words from the claim "We are all Afro-Mexicans. If you recognize yourself, you count!" In smaller font, the poster informs its readers that between the seventh and eighteenth of October, the National Institute of Statistics and Geography (INEGI) would be visiting their residence to count them. The names of the sponsoring federal agencies stretched across the bottom of the poster: the Secretariat of the Interior (SEGOB) and its subsidiary CONAPRED, the Secretariat of Public Education and its then subsidiary CONACULTA, and the aforementioned INEGI. The poster made it seem so simple. It was anything but.

While people of African descent have existed in Mexico for over half a millennium, the Afro-Mexican category is a twenty-first-century invention. Previously existing labels like *jarocho* were recruited to the neologism *Afro-Mexican* just as surely as individuals were recruited to the category. Conceptual reworking of the Mexican population to (re-)include Afro-descendants happened via multi-sponsored publicity campaigns, the mid-census survey itself, and the media that announced its results. In what was the viewer to recognize herself? In the pictures? In the older terms like *morena* or *mascogo*, or in the new term *Afro-Mexican*? This was the dilemma facing one of the students that afternoon.

She was a young woman with fair skin, dark hair, and a scar on her cheek. Our brown eyes met as she made her way toward me at the end of my presentation. She had been an attentive face in the room, paying close attention when I spoke about the third root, the history of the term *jarocho*, the Caribbean culture of the city, and this new effort to count Afro-Mexicans. All of these things she mentioned as she asked me to help her figure out whether she counted as Afro-Mexican. She was born and raised in Veracruz, making her both a costeña and a jarocha. Her grandfather was Cuban, though she did not clarify whether he was a Cuban national let alone Afro-Cuban, or whether he was called Cuban because of his phenotype. Regardless, if this grandfather were Afro-descended, that ancestry did not express itself in her features. I was reminded of Mexican anthropologist Sagrario Cruz-Carretero's story of how she found her own Blackness through an encounter with Cuba.[4] She used the metaphor of sugar in coffee. It may not be visible, but it improves the final product. Maybe the inherited Blackness of this girl with the scar had been a palpable sense up to this point; maybe she had had only a mouthfeel for Blackness before there was a name and a call to recognize herself within it.

She had listened carefully to my discussion on the various African roots in Veracruz, the place she had been born. I imagine the Afro-Caribbean rhetoric I highlighted was as familiar as the budding political campaign captured by the poster was new. She had witnessed my nascent attempts to grapple with the broader questions those two arguments generate. But more than that, she had read the declarative "If you recognize yourself, you count" and ultimately decided that I could help her make that decision. I demurred. I told her the campaign relied on self-recognition. Who was I to give her permission or absolution one way or another to count herself as Afro-Mexican? A case could be made for either response.

The poster's juxtaposition of image and text cast a wide net in its attempt to recruit its viewers to the new term *Afro-Mexican*, but the criteria for self-recognition were not as evident as its makers presumed them to be. The brunette student's uncertainty and her desire for clarity best captured the scale at which shifts in multiculturalist policy are lived and processed. I was as curious as she was as to which metrics one uses to count oneself. Is it in the brown faces with features that look like mine that were displayed in the recruitment poster? Or is it in the family stories, like the young woman's mention of her dark-skinned Cuban grandfather, as if he vouchsafed for her claiming Afro-Mexican heritage as a light-skinned Veracruzana? Perhaps it is in the cultural practices that jarochos have revitalized to make clear their Afro-Caribbean bona fides. Is it in the combination of both? Is either cultural practice or genetic ancestry necessary, but not sufficient? In the newness of this label, what would justify someone's self-identification or the identification of someone else as Afro-Mexican? Had this woman always already been this term I had just introduced to her?

YES, IN PART

Over a year after the young woman asked if she counted, and with much fanfare, came the results of that advertised mid-census survey. In December 2015, INEGI announced that 1.38 million Mexicans, representing 1.2% of the total population, affirmatively answered the question, "Based on your culture, history, and traditions, do you consider yourself Black, that is to say Afro-Mexican or Afro-descendant?" As historian Ted Cohen has observed, such a question about Black identity in Mexico was contrary to Mexican racial formations for much of the twentieth century.[5] This question was a decided shift in racial politics. Its existence signaled Mexico's participation in the UN's International Decade for Peoples of African Descent (2015–24), and its responses would determine whether and how a question on Afro-descendancy would appear in the full census count in 2020. For activists, the count would be an important step in an ongoing quest for constitutional recognition and collective rights after decades of marginalization. Additionally, this first official question captured a state working through how it would define this population of people. After all, as Mara Loveman has succinctly put it, "censuses are not mirrors of demographic realities; they do not merely reflect existing lines of distinction within a given point in time." As such, they are "both stakes and instruments of politics."[6] As instruments of politics, they are calls with anticipated but unknown responses. The official question tells us much about Mexico's intentions, but also its presumptions.

This mid-census survey was the first articulation of Mexico's official approach to its Blackness, and the question itself shows its hand. In 2015 the question explicitly defined Black identity as a product of culture, history, and traditions. These are familiar grounds; those three aspects have been the purview of the third root movement since the late 1980s. In Veracruz, for example, their approach to Blackness explicitly has been through local culture, history, and practices, as discussed in the preceding chapters. What is more, the careful construction of the census question—to focus on "culture, history, and traditions"—discourages the conflation of phenotype with race. While the question does begin with the term *negro* before glossing it as Afro-Mexican or Afro-descendant, this *negro* is ethnic rather than racial. It echoes the best practices gleaned from the several Latin American states that have already worked to enumerate Afro-descendants before Mexico deigned to do so. This is the question heard by citizens and spread by news reporters. What has gotten less attention is that which was not intended for an audience— the interviewer's manual.[7]

In that document, you find paragraphs dedicated to educating the interviewer about the history of Afro-descendants in Mexico and guiding them on how to perform the new question in the field and to interpret the responses they may encounter. In the interviewer's manual, INEGI clarifies that they use the term *negro* because "in many regions of the country, Afro-Mexican or Afro-descendant people identify in that way." It goes on to explain that they are also identified as "negros mascogos, negros costeños o negros jarochos," making *Black* a modifying term for a regional label.[8] Note the difference between the manual and the poster advertising the questionnaire. Whereas the manual includes *Black* as a modifier for terms like *mascogo, costeño,* and *negro,* in the public-facing documentation these terms are glossed as Black, suggesting an equivalence rather than a particular type. In the manual, the instructions explicitly state that neither skin tone nor hair texture imply whether someone belongs in the category and reiterate the use of history, culture, and traditions instead of phenotype. The paragraph concludes by reminding the taker to respect how individuals self-identify.[9] While self-identification is now the standard, its pitfalls include the limited options set forth by the census itself, the ability for one respondent to represent an entire household, and the inability of census takers to indiscriminately ask and faithfully record an individual's answer.[10]

On the surface, the 2015 survey question grounded Blackness in culture, history, and traditions. In practice, it left room for ancestry, as well. During the interview, the census worker was to read the question slowly, without omitting any words, while listening for the words left unsaid. The manual makes clear that the census taker must ask the question on Afro-Mexican identity in every interview regardless of their presumptions about the presence of Afro-Mexicans in the region. It was also their job to confirm that the respondent understood the question is about Afro-Mexican identity, not just Mexican identity. This is the script the interview must follow. However, the interviewer still had an active interpretative role to play. They must pay attention to how the informant responds and record the answer according to the coded possibilities of "yes," "no," "yes, in part," and "does not know." While "yes" and "no" are self-explanatory, the manual dictates the circumstances that would warrant the latter two possibilities. If the informant were unaware of how someone else in the household would answer, the worker would mark "does not know." If the citizen equivocates, the census taker was to circle option 2, "yes, in part." The manual reads, "if they comment: 'could be because my father is, but my mother is not,' or 'I would say a little,' or something similar, that was coded as a partial affirmation." In that way, ancestry became a fourth criterion for enumerative purposes—but only a partial one.

Despite including the possibility, those data points went unreported. No infographics charted their number; no news reports boasted the information. If the purpose of the census was to create and count a group identity, how does the partial affirmation factor into that group? It is unclear how useful a partial affirmation would be for the state. Would the respondent agree with the idea of a partial affirmation? Why not a partial negation? Yes, in part could just have easily been, "no, in part." The idea of "parts" or partiality is itself an interesting choice. Why not "somewhat" or "to a certain degree"? Instead, "parts" resonates with an idea of a cosmic race made of bits and pieces of different originary races coalescing into this new being. This is, after all, the promise of mestizaje. However, when put through a multiculturalist frame, the image contorts to satisfy these somewhat divergent ends. For mestizaje, the answer for everyone could possibly be "yes, in part" because the wholeness of everyone is composed of parts of those who came before them. For the multiculturalist policy that preceded the census question, "yes, in part" is likewise an indiscriminate possibility. The promise of the national third root program, after all, held that that which is Mexican necessarily derives from the transculturation of indigenous, African, and European antecedents. Thus, yes, partially, the Mexican body is of African descent.

This, however, was not how the interviewer's manual trained the worker to assess whether the second option best captured an informant's response. Only mentioning familial ties would warrant this equivocal affirmation. The explicit criteria of culture, history, and traditions have already mapped onto Blackness for a generation. The cultural politics wrought from the third root movement, particularly in Veracruz, took pains to inform the general population that while they individually may not be Black, they have Blackness because of their local cultural practices, historical specificity, and revitalized traditions. Yet that was not the question asked in 2015. Stripped of its modifiers, the question asked the respondent if they thought of themselves as Black.

Constituting Afro-descended peoples in Mexico as an enumerable population is an example of what Ian Hacking calls "making up people." This is not to deny the centuries of existence of people of African descent in Mexico; rather, it emphasizes the newness of the category itself. New categories of people are often not just reflections of social change but also the reaction of new ways for people to be. He argues for a "dynamic nominalism," which is to say that the category and the categorized are coevally produced.[11] In *The Social Construction of What?*, Hacking further argues that "ways of classifying human beings interact with the human beings who are classified."[12] He calls this interaction a "looping effect" in which people of a certain kind change in response to their classification, what they believe themselves to be, and how their classification affects their treatment. In this age of the Afro-Mexican, the mid-census survey is but one call with an uncertain response. While over a million people affirmatively responded in 2015, the full census saw that number double, and the trend may continue upward. How respondents understood the question is less quantifiable. To ask if someone is "negro," a color label, and then immediately reconceive of it as a political category, like "Afro-descendant" or "Afro-Mexican," transforms a demographic question into something more abstract.

Afro-descendant has been the politically correct and most expansive term for Afro-Latin American peoples for over two decades. Activists across the region adopted the language in 2000 during their regional meeting in Santiago de Chile in preparation for the 2001 World Conference against Racism, Racial Discrimination, Xenophobia, and Related Intolerance (WCAR), held in Durban, South Africa. As the oft-quoted observation by Afro-Uruguayan leader Romero Rodríguez succinctly put it, "We entered Santiago as Black people and left as Afro-descendants."[13] This advocacy framework has united people across national lines and, in some cases, signaled the "genealogic relationship" between Africans and Afro-descendants within the same nation.[14] Since then, many Latin American nations have included this language in their censuses. Mexico followed suit in 2015 with the mid-census survey and in the full 2020 census count. However, note what Rodríguez observed. Those participants in Santiago and the people represented and sought to hail were already "Black." As Stuart Hall reminds us, one must learn to come into an identification.[15]

Decades prior to the historic survey, jarochos had been learning to associate their Blackness with their local identity rather than with a diasporic one. While they did experience what Hall calls a "politics of living identity through difference," Blackness was just one feature that helped clarify their position vis-à-vis the rest of the nation.[16] It was not the center of gravity for their group identity. In the end, nearly 5 percent of the port city's population in 2015 responded either wholly or partially as Afro-Mexican. The data and analyses possible from the enumerative turn have shaped and will continue to shape the ethnoracial politics of the city. Yet it is important to remember that the purpose of the census question was to determine who is Black in Mexico, not how Blackness manifests in Mexico.

INEGI changed the question on Black identity for the full 2020 census count. Rather than a contextual note, ancestry came to the forefront of the question. The question asked, "Based on your ancestors and according to your customs and traditions, do you consider yourself Afro-Mexican, Black, or Afro-descendant?"[17] Note the key differences. The criteria have changed. Whereas the sample survey based self-identification on culture, history, and traditions, the full census emphasized ancestors, customs, and traditions. Similarly, the first iteration created an equivalence between Black and Afro-Mexican or Afro-descendant. In the updated version, the question not only changed the listing order but also presented them as three options rather than as synonyms. There were changes in the responses, too. Unlike the 2015 version, the only possible responses were "yes" or "no." "Yes, in part," was no longer a possibility. Yet that does not mean a person would not equivocate when asked the question. However, there is no guidance as to how the interviewer should code a response beyond yes or no. It simply teaches that they must respect the response that is given.[18]

A yes or no question can provide a snapshot image of who self-identifies as Black once in a decade, but it cannot capture how people interpret or internalize that question or their response. Nor does it question the broader significance of

Mexican Blackness. Imagine the unshared conversations, the anecdotes no longer relevant if I were looking only for "Black" (or "black") people. Consider the richness and lessons learned from this unique approach to Blackness gone unexamined. In the liminal moment between recognizing Mexican Blackness and Black Mexicans, the jarochos had remade Blackness in their own image.

A RECALIBRATION

The census question is but a prominent demonstration of the ongoing negotiations of who and what counts as Black in Mexico. Just as the first question reflected the influence of the third root discourse, the second question is the state's attempt to fine-tune what exactly it is they are trying to determine with this information. The Afro-Mexican, officially, is an inchoate identity. Both the state and its citizens are still discovering what they mean by this. Mexicans of African descent have been a knowable reality in Mexico long before they were counted and before the invention of the Afro-Mexican. This is why previously existing labels like the *jarocho* were recruited neologisms just as surely as individuals were recruited to the category. The conceptual reworking of the Mexican population to (re-)include Afro-descendants happened via state-sponsored publicity, grassroots word of mouth, censual tools, and media reports. The first attempts cast a wide net. The invitation to join was broad—if you count yourself, you count. After 2015 proved the viability of the question, the narrative shifted, not to whether or not to count Afro-Mexicans, but to how best to capture and treat this population. Quantitative data demanded a different metric of belonging.

Prior to the 2020 full census, scholars Emiko Saldívar, Patricio Solís, and Erika Arenas believed the question needed revisions if it were to accurately enumerate the intended population. They compared the results of the 2015 survey with survey data from a different INEGI instrument from 2016, the Intergenerational Social Mobility Module (MMSI), which quantified the extent to which skin color affected opportunities and upward mobility from one generation to the next. While not as internationally lauded, this was also a historic survey. By using the eleven-point color scale created by the Project on Ethnicity and Race in Latin America (PERLA), it was the first survey to ask a question about skin tone and capture Mexico's pigmentocracy.[19] While Mexico is clear that phenotype is not an intended criterion for assessing whether one is Afro-Mexican, Saldívar and her team compared the two survey results because the MMSI asked a question based on "racial origins," alongside data on skin color.[20] They concluded that the 2015 question's "vague cultural references"—by which they meant the phrase "culture, history, and traditions"—as well as the uncommon terminology of *Afro-Mexican* or *Afro-descendant* contributed to sampling errors of inclusion and exclusion, respectively. They hypothesized that the cultural references could lead to errors because "there are people who can identify 'culturally' without belonging to these communities."

To capture better the historically marginalized population, they suggested a more direct question that omitted references to cultural origins.[21]

The idea of cultural references leading to errors is fecund. Errors imply an objective accuracy and authenticity that go against the reassurance that "If you count yourself, you count!" Yet errors also speak to the divergent goals of something like a demographic survey and something like identification. For both the state and activists, the enumeration of a bounded group for potential collective rights or reparative work would seek to minimize statistical errors. The recent shift in Mexico's approach to multiculturalism moves away from what sociologists Jonathan Warren and Christina Sue identified as the legacy of power-evasive multiculturalism. The earlier iterations of multiculturalism in Latin America were "not aimed at creating strong subaltern identities and communities but rather eliminating or submerging them to the broader communitarian identity of the hybrid nation."[22]

Critics of this wave of multiculturalism emphasize how this state-driven policy was a shallow attempt to look at internal differences, one that treated difference as mere folklore and ignored addressing substantive issues such as racism or inequity. It is, as George Yúdice outlined, an expedient approach to culture, treating it as a cultural resource at the disposal of the state.[23] In this way, the state harnesses a nation's diversity for its own ends, oftentimes upholding the hegemonic ideology of mestizaje. Thinking with education scholars Christine Sleeter and Carl Grant's concept of the "four Fs" approach to multiculturalism—that is, fairs, festivals, food, and folktales—Warren and Sue outline how this valorization of cultural difference works in fact to recenter the unmarked category as the norm. They also argue that this type of celebration of diversity is oftentimes superficial, reductionist, and cliché. In the end, culture becomes mere custom or folkloric practice, which ultimately allows the state to engage selectively with difference.[24] They describe how this selective engagement was one in which "Blacks and Indians were now counted, but only as supporting actors," actors who "supposedly gave dance, culinary arts, music and select words."[25] Warren and Sue identify this liberal, power-evasive multiculturalism as an early twentieth-century phenomenon and argue that a new version of multiculturalism arose in the 1980s and 1990s, one that is more explicitly antiracist, reform-oriented, and grounded in human rights. This periodization broadly aligns with the sweeping changes in the region that began around the quincentennial of Christopher Columbus's landing in the hemisphere and have gradually shifted to address the material concerns of marginalized populations.

The third root movement and its manifestation in Veracruz align quite clearly with the four Fs approach of fairs, festivals, food, and folktales. For the state, Mexican Blackness has been a cultural and historical phenomenon, rather than a racial one. It aligns with rather than challenges mestizaje. You see this in the racial reckonings of the third root's most ardent proponents. It is easy to see how acknowledging the Black root of Mexico avoids the work of addressing its Black present and future. However, this mode of analysis does not take into account what people have done with the official narrative. It does not address how people have grappled with what could have been otherwise a milquetoast gesture toward Mexico's Blackness.

In the interstitial period between culturally recognizing Mexican Blackness and constitutionally recognizing Afro-Mexicans, many people like those who animate this book made sense of their relationship to Blackness in ways that not only made sense to them but also vivified Blackness beyond mere fairs, festivals, food, and folktales. To qualify this as an error is in fact an error in perspective. It considers Mexican Blackness—and Blackness in general—first from a space of abjectness, marginalization, or lack, even as it seeks to celebrate and elevate Black people. As the recent years in Mexico have shown, it runs the risk of isolating Mexican Blackness as the purview of only Black Mexicans. Even Veracruz, with its rich legacy of Black popular culture, has succumbed to this tendency.

I first noticed this on a return visit in 2017 when I attended the inauguration of the twenty-first International Afro-Caribbean Festival. Within the former chapel space of IVEC, a dignitary on stage used the all too common phrase *our third root* in a new way. Rather than discussing the third root as a collective heritage, she began to highlight specific municipalities where the 2015 mid-census survey registered high percentages of self-recognized Afro-Mexicans. The collective possession of "our third root" was no longer shared culture but rather discrete populations within the state.

Earlier that year, two different state representatives proposed changing the Veracruz constitution to include language specifically related to Afro-Mexicans. Although from different political parties, both represented municipalities with large Afro-Mexican populations. In making their proposals, both politicians took protectionist stances on behalf of Afro-Mexicans while also presenting instances of Veracruz's Blackness as if they had been overlooked or appropriated by the general population. The first proposal advocated to amend article 5 to include language to "promote and protect" the "cultural and natural heritage" of the state's Afro-Mexican communities through public policy.[26] She argued that they have been overlooked by the government and in history books for not fitting into the classic understanding of mestizaje as an Indo-European process. The second politician, in making her appeal, demarcated a group distinction between we who enjoy the gifts of Afro-descendants—Carnival, cuisine, dance, and sones—and they whose rights are not recognized. She proposed an amendment to "promote and protect the development of Afro-Mexican communities, promoting their languages, cultures, customs, as well as their resources and special forms of social organization."[27] In their efforts to push forward political recognition, both ignored the cultural recognition that had been an ongoing state policy for decades. They also recast as afro many cultural policies that had previously been celebrated as jarocho in general. Rather than a cultural legacy shared by all, it became a gift from one contemporary group to another. This type of posturing makes for a good moral case for political recognition but is a stark departure from the previous understanding of Veracruz's third root. In the efforts to correct the marginalization of Afro-Veracruzanos, the centrality of Blackness to Veracruz's past, present, and potentially future is now at stake.

This has not been an ethnography of Afro-Mexicans, though some of the people who animate this story undoubtedly number among the 4.6 percent of the municipality's population that affirmatively answered the question on Black identity in 2020. Instead, it has been an exploration of how people have reckoned with the expectation that their local culture and identity were key iterations of Mexican Blackness. Whereas I first went to Veracruz curious about *los negros*, I ultimately fixated on *lo negro*, that which is Black, or Blackness itself. This distinction was not a contrivance but rather the logical conclusion to the lived reality of those engaged in jarocho publics. These people chose to fill their leisure time in activities that helped them be more themselves—that is to say, more jarocho. Since its creation, the jarocho has maintained an association with Blackness. Although no longer the derogatory term for Afro-Indigenous folk of the region, the Blackness never whitewashed away, even during the height of homogenizing mestizaje ideology. This perduringness made it an available cultural resource for late twentieth-century multiculturalist policy when the state began to remember and revalorize the African antecedents to Mexican culture and mixture. This they termed the third root, but in Veracruz, its importance as a regionalized distinguisher elevated it beyond a tertiary role. It became the link that bound the port city to the rest of the Afro-Andalusian Caribbean. It became the difference within the nation that made the city unique. In the process, the Blackness of the jarocho became expedient, crucial, and productive. However, it did not necessarily make jarochos Black. When the multiculturalist aims of the state shifted again to enumeration, rather than just valorization, this unique approach came to a head. The plural possessive of the "our third root" ethos in Veracruz has for a generation constituted a groupness around jarochoness rather than a national, let alone diasporic, group identity based on Blackness. As Afro-Mexicans gain rights and recognition, it is important to consider what conceptualizations of Mexican Blackness are lost in the process.

Jarochos understand their Blackness to be a product of their culture, history, and traditions. For decades, this has been the messaging disseminated by the state. Longer still has popular culture cultivated that linkage be it in sultry boleros or raucous festivals. Just as Black Mexicans are not new, neither is Mexican Blackness. Yet these two concepts have led overlapping but discrete lives. The multiculturalist approach in Veracruz maintained their distinction, but the national drive to enumerate Afro-Mexicans unceremoniously sutured the two together. "Yes, in part" may have been the way for the Census Bureau to capture people's allusions to Black ancestry, but jarochos in the Port have been primed to always already consider culture, history, and tradition as their avenue to their local manifestation of Mexico's third root. This is how people reckon with the expectation that they are a key site of Mexico's Blackness. With the new political recognition of the Afro-Mexican population, that calculus has begun to change.

Counting Afro-Mexicans was a radical shift away from the hegemonic belief of Mexico as merely a mestizo nation with Indigenous peoples. Afro-Mexicans are a product of the same mestizaje that forged Mexico's cosmic race, yet to become a political subject requires boundaries. Theorist E. Patrick Johnson suggests that "Blackness" does not belong to any singular group or person. Rather, it is "when blackness is appropriated to the exclusion of others, identity becomes political."[28] Because jarochos articulated their relationship to Mexican Blackness as a trait of their ethnoracial group identity, the exclusionary move was around jarocho-ness rather than Blackness itself. In other words, there were multiple ways to access Blackness—history, culture, traditions, ancestry—but Blackness was not the final destination. As Afro-Mexican identity continues to cohere as a political identity, the racialized reckonings of previous generations will have to contend with this shifting landscape.

The decades of deep engagement between jarocho identity and Mexican Blackness did not foment a strong political mobilization around Black identity in the Port. It did, however, offer many people a conceptual framework to think through the presumption of their Blackness. For locals involved in jarocho publics, they learned, embodied, editorialized, and performed their identification with Blackness on the way to being more jarocho. This alternative reckoning with Mexico's third root and the African diaspora in Latin America in general may have borne a local fruit, but it is sweet all the same.

Epilogue

New Views in the Port

I had always expected 2020 would be an inflection point in the story of Blackness in Veracruz. I based this assumption on the full census count and its political consequences; I had not anticipated a pandemic. As the world began to isolate, I wondered what would happen in Veracruz, where convivial spaces were the essence of sociality. I thought about Alfredo and his belief that people come together to sing and to dance as a way to face life. How would they face this new life alone? How would those musicians and vendors make a living without the crowds to whom they catered?

Like many communities, jarocho publics switched to the virtual realm when they could. The Afro-Caribbean Festival, for example, was simulcast online. Livestream concerts brought son jarocho or son music to living rooms. Places like IVEC uploaded public programming for the masses. These efforts helped tide people over until the public spaces of Veracruz could once again host mass gatherings, but they could never replace the conviviality of everyday life. In the interim, people had taken ill, had grown older, or had become wary of public spaces. Many pillars of the Port's various musical communities had passed away, altering the tenor of the city's soundscape.

When I returned to the Port in April 2022, the changes to the cultural scene preoccupied me. The loss of people and the shifts in habitus were the most immediately observed differences for communities that flourished in public, together. But there were also changes to the physical space. The current municipal administration's beautification project decided the permanent stage in the zócalo would better serve as a water feature. Now, the danzonera plays from a temporary stage right in front of City Hall. Dancers accommodated this change with an about-face, but the reorientation has severely limited the space for observers of the weekly danzón and how one traverses the main plaza. The biggest change I observed was to the Plazuela de la Campana. Whereas before, regulars lamented how the city had neglected the space, now the space had clear signs of municipal investment but no regulars. Beautification had brought more lighting to the outdoor space, but the death of Don Miguel had brought silence. No longer could you reliably enjoy free, live Afro-Antillean music four nights a week. The lights were on, but no one was home. The local color seemed duller to me.

In July 2023 I returned to the Port to finish writing this book. This time, I was prepared to embrace the changes in the cultural scene. Whereas before I focused on the loss, this time I was ready to appreciate the signs of resilience and perseverance. I took solace in my friend Chucho's belief that there would always be a "rinconcito" where people would come together and dance. I was not prepared, however, for a billboard I passed on my daily commute.

Allegedly, it was not a political campaign advertisement, though it had all the hallmarks of one during that campaign season. In Mexico, currently serving elected officials cannot hold their seat while campaigning for another one. When President Andres Manuel López Obrador reminded the politician of this norm, the politician maintained that these signs were not about his political aspirations but rather for a book he had written. Nevertheless, there was reason for censure; like the other billboards throughout the city, the politician's name dominated the sign.

Underneath his name rendered in all caps is the phrase "Thank you for making us visible!" In the top left quadrant of the billboard is a picture of the politician wearing a formal guayabera with gold embroidery flanking the placket. He has accessorized the look with a red neckerchief and straw hat. He is embracing two women who appear to be Afro-Mexican. One is *china-china* and wears a typical off-the-shoulder crocheted white top. The other woman is older, with her hair wrapped in an orange turban that matches her off-the-shoulder ruffled blouse. She wears a chunky necklace made of seashells and holds a woven basket in her hands. All three are smiling at the camera. I would later learn that this image was part of a larger photo shoot. As it would turn out, other advertisements featured them holding up their shackled and chained wrists. They are smiling in those, too.

Beside the trio is another quotation: "We afrojarochos exist because we resisted." (Given the rules of conjugation, one could reasonably read it as saying, "We exist because we resist." In any case, the temporal ambiguity seems fitting.) At the very bottom of the sign in barely legible font is the title of the book this campaign is allegedly promoting: *La Negritud en Veracruz, del Coyolillo al Sotavento* (Negritude in Veracruz, from Coyolillo to the Sotavento).

At first, I was struck by how this representation of Blackness could not have existed a decade ago, at the start of my travels to Veracruz. The "we" who exist because they resist(ed) is an appeal to groupness that is a product of a post-2020 census world. The text emphasizes the language of resistance and visibility, neither of which was mainstream in the rhetoric on Blackness in the Port in the years prior. It also suggests that Blackness in Veracruz was invisible until the politician wrote this book that none of the bookstores carried (I checked) and, I imagine, few had read.

In short, the billboard was audacious—both in its flouting of campaign rules and its declarations about Blackness in Mexico. For decades, jarochos have received declarative statements about their Blackness, but before they were cultural, not political. In this sign, I could not help but see Blackness a la Veracruzana being made anew.

Yet like a palimpsest, the vestiges of the old were legible alongside the new. Despite its decidedly political turn, this new approach to Blackness remained hyperlocal. The "we" referenced is afro*jarocho* rather than Afro-Mexican. Once again, the collective identity was regional rather than national, let alone diasporic. While the text emphasized resistance and newfound visibility, the visual cues were the same smiles and sartorial choices made familiar over the past decades. Even the title of the book the politician published highlighted places already imagined as Black spaces.

As much as the sign represented changes possible only with the political recognition of Afro-Mexicans, it also represented how locality remains the lens through which Blackness is lived. Place and race remain enmeshed in Veracruz. The tone of Blackness has shifted with the political landscape, but the color, it appears, remains local.

NOTES

PROLOGUE: A VIEW FROM THE PORT

1. All names of people are pseudonyms unless their speech or actions occurred publicly or in their official capacity.

2. See Alfredo Martínez Maranto, "Dios pinta como quiere. Identidad y cultura en un pueblo afromestizo," in *Presencia africana en México*, coord. Luz María Martínez Montiel (Mexico, DF: Consejo Nacional Para la Cultura y las Artes, 1994), 525–73. See also Marcus D. Jones and Charles Henry Rowell, eds., "Faces and Voices of Coyolillo, an Afromestizo Pueblo in Mexico," special issue, *Callaloo* 27, no. 1 (Winter 2004), https://www.jstor.org/stable/i201352.

3. See Odile Hoffmann, "De 'negros' y 'afros' in Veracruz," in *Atlas del patrimonio natural, histórico y cultural de Veracruz*, tomo 3, *Patrimonio Cultural*, ed. Enrique Florescano y Juan Ortiz Escamilla (Xalapa, Veracruz: Universidad Veracruzana, 2010), 127–40.

4. See Patrick J. Carroll, "Mandinga: The Evolution of a Mexican Runaway Slave Community, 1735–1827," *Comparative Studies in Society and History* 19, no. 4 (October 1977): 488–505, https://www.jstor.org/stable/178098; and Adela Amaral, "Social Geographies, the Practice of Marronage and the Archaeology of Absence in Colonial Mexico," *Archaeological Dialogues* 24, no. 2 (2017): 207–23.

5. *Reducciones* were a colonial-era social engineering project involving the mass displacement of Indigenous peoples for the primary goal of conversion. For more information, see William F. Hanks, *Converting Worlds: Maya in the Age of the Cross* (Berkeley: University of California Press, 2010).

6. For information, see "Africa in Mexico: A Special Section," ed. Charles Henry Rowell, *Callaloo* 29, no. 2 (2006): 396–512. For information on Alvarado especially, refer to Marcus D. Jones, Charles H. Rowell, Edgar Cano, and Rodolfo Figueroa Martinez, "Rodolfo Figueroa Martinez," *Callaloo* 29, no. 2 (2006): 401–16, https://doi.org/10.1353/cal.2006.0104.

7. Jennifer Anne Meri Jones, "'Mexicans Will Take the Jobs That Even Blacks Won't Do': An Analysis of Blackness, Regionalism and Invisibility in Contemporary Mexico," *Ethnic and Racial Studies* 36, no. 10 (2013): 1569, https://doi.org/10.1080/01419870.2013.783927.

8. Jones, "'Mexicans Will Take the Jobs,'" 1573.

9. Anthony Russell Jerry, *Blackness in Mexico: Afro-Mexican Recognition and the Production of Citizenship in the Costa Chica* (Gainesville: University Press of Florida, 2023), 22-50.

10. Christina A. Sue, "Racial Ideologies, Racial-Group Boundaries, and Racial Identity in Veracruz, Mexico," *Latin American and Caribbean Ethnic Studies* 5, no. 3 (2010): 273, https://doi.org/10.1080/17442222.2010.513829.

11. Here I am referring to the city. Because the city and the state share the same name, I will clarify when I am discussing the state; otherwise, all references should be assumed to be the city.

INTRODUCTION: BLACKNESS A LA VERACRUZANA

1. "En la Sociedad de castas del siglo XVIII, en particular en la región costera central de Golfo, 'jarocho' era un término despectivo para las personas mezcla de indio y negro. [...] El vocablo aludía, pues, a la actividad más característica de los afromestizos de dicha región: el trabajo, libre o esclavo, como vaqueros en las grandes haciendas ganaderas. [...] Hacia finales del siglo XVIII y en el XIX, dejó de ser un término despectivo y se usó para los mestizos del campo veracruzano de raíces europea, africana e indígena, con vertiente negra predominante. El 'jarocho' comenzó a reconocerse por su carácter alegre y bullanguero."

2. Michel-Rolph Trouillot, *Silencing the Past: Power and the Production of History* (Boston: Beacon Press, 1995).

3. While I heard about the sample survey in the fall of 2014 at the start of my long-term field study, the results did not come until after I had left Veracruz in the winter of 2015.

4. For monograph-length ethnographies of Afro-descendant populations in Mexico, see, for example, Gonzalo Aguirre Beltrán, *Cuijla: Esbozo etnográfico de un pueblo negro* (Mexico: Fondo de Cultura Económica, [1958] 1974); Laura Lewis, *Chocolate and Corn Flour: History, Race, and Place in the Making of "Black" Mexico* (Durham, NC: Duke University Press, 2012); Christina Sue, *Land of the Cosmic Race: Race Mixture, Racism, and Blackness in Mexico* (Oxford: Oxford University Press, 2013); and Jerry, *Blackness in Mexico*. For works focused on Afro-Mexican cultural production, see Anita González, *Afro-Mexico: Dancing between Myth and Reality* (Austin: University of Texas Press, 2010); Paulette Ramsey, *Afro-Mexican Constructions of Diaspora, Gender, Identity and Nation* (Kingston: University of the West Indies Press, 2016); and Hettie Malcomson, *Danzón Days: Age, Race, and Romance in Mexico* (Urbana: University of Illinois Press, 2023).

5. For example, Paulette Ramsey wrote of the third root in *Afro-Mexican Constructions of Diaspora, Gender, Identity, and Nation*: "This means that the *Nuestra Tercera Raíz* (Our Third Root) programme was highly unsuccessful since, as late as the twenty-first century, blacks still remain statistically undocumented" (13). That enumeration is the metric for success suggests crosswise expectations for the goals of the program.

6. See Peter Wade, "Multiculturalism y Racismo," *Revista Colombiana de antropología* 47, no. 2 (2011): 16.

7. For more on the distinction, see Stephan Palmié, *The Cooking of History: How Not to Study Afro-Cuban Religion* (Chicago: University of Chicago Press, 2013).

8. This argument appears throughout Stuart Hall's oeuvre. One key text would be his essay "Introduction: Who Needs 'Identity'?" in *Questions on Cultural Identity*, ed. Stuart Hall and Paul du Gay (London: Sage Publications, 1996), 2.

9. Lorgia García Peña, *Translating Blackness: Latinx Colonialities in Global Perspective* (Durham, NC: Duke University Press, 2022), 4–5.

10. Pierre Bourdieu and Loïc Wacquant, "On the Cunning of Imperialist Reason," *Theory Culture Society* 16, no. 41 (1999): 41.

11. Bourdieu and Wacquant, "On the Cunning," 44.

12. Rogers Brubaker, "Ethnicity without Groups," in *Ethnicity without Groups*, ed. Rogers Brubaker (Cambridge, MA: Harvard University Press, 2004), 8.

13. Indeed, Brubaker would argue that the category does not a group make. As he argues, if groups are about "a sense of solidarity, corporate identity, and capacity for concerted action," then a category "is at best a potential basis for group-formation or 'groupness,' but it is not itself a group" (12).

14. Christian Rinaudo, "Más allá de la 'identidad negra': mestizaje y dinámicas raciales," in *Mestizaje, diferencia y nación: Lo "negro" en América Central y el Caribe*, coord. Elisabeth Cunin (Mexico, DF: Instituto Nacional de Antropología e Historia; Mexico, DF: Centro de Estudios Mexicanos y Centroamericanos; Mexico, DF: Universidad Autónoma de Mexico-Centro de Investigaciones sobre América Latina y el Caribe; Mexico, DF: Institut de Recherche pour le Développement, 2010), 228.

15. Rinaudo, "Más allá de la 'identidad negra,'" 230.

16. Brubaker, "Ethnicity without Groups," 11–12.

17. More on this point in chapter 3.

18. To get a sense of the breadth and scope of recent works on contemporary Afro-Latin America, see Maria Fernanda Escallón, *Becoming Heritage: Recognition, Exclusion, and the Politics of Black Cultural Heritage in Colombia* (Cambridge: Cambridge University Press, 2023); Reighan Gillam, *Visualizing Black Lives: Ownership and Control in Afro-Brazilian Media* (Urbana: University of Illinois Press, 2022); Isar P. Godreau, *Scripts of Blackness: Race, Cultural Nationalism, and U.S. Colonialism in Puerto Rico* (Urbana: University of Illinois Press, 2015); Tianna S. Paschel, *Becoming Black Political Subjects: Movements and Ethno-racial Rights in Colombia and Brazil* (Princeton, NJ: Princeton University Press, 2018); Michael Birenbaum Quintero, *Rites, Rights and Rhythms: A Genealogy of Musical Meaning in Colombia's Black Pacific* (New York: Oxford University Press, 2018); Patricia de Santana Pinho, *Mama Africa: Reinventing Blackness in Bahia* (Durham, NC: Duke University Press, 2010); Kristina Wirtz, *Performing Afro-Cuba: Image, Voice, Spectacle in the Making of Race and History* (Chicago: University of Chicago Press, 2014).

19. Tanya Golash-Boza, "Does Whitening Happen? Distinguishing between Race and Color Labels in an African-Descended Community in Peru," *Social Problems* 57, no. 1 (2010): 139, https://doi.org/10.1525/sp.2010.57.1.138.

20. Sue, *Land of the Cosmic Race*, 5–7.

21. María Elisa Velázquez, introduction to *Debates históricos contemporáneos: africanos y afrodescendientes en México y Centroamérica*, coord. María Elisa Velázquez (Mexico, DF: Instituto Nacional de Antropología e Historia; Mexico, DF: Centro de Estudios Mexicanos

y Centroamericanos; Mexico, DF: Universidad Autónoma de Mexico-Centro de Investigaciones sobre América Latina y el Caribe; Mexico, DF: Institut de Recherche pour le Développement, 2011), 19.

22. Citlalli Domínguez, "Luz María Martínez Montiel, A Mexican Africanist, Pioneer in Afro-Mexican Studies," in *Routledge Handbook of Afro-Latin American Studies*, ed. Bernd Reiter and John Antón Sanchez (New York: Routledge, 2023), 610–13.

23. Jerry, *Blackness in Mexico*, 3. Akin to Charles Hale's questioning whether multiculturalism can menace, critics of the term *Afro-Mexican* focus on its neoliberal multicultural ethos. See Charles Hale, "Does Multiculturalism Menace? Governance, Cultural Rights and the Politics of Identity in Guatemala," *Journal of Latin American Studies* 34, no. 3 (2002): 485–524.

24. Ian Hacking, "Making Up People," in *Reconstructing Individualism: Autonomy, Individuality, and the Self in Western Thought*, ed. Thomas C. Heller, Morton Sosna, and David E. Wellbery (Stanford, CA: Stanford University Press, 1986), 222–36.

25. Sue, *Land of the Cosmic Race*, 14.

26. Sue, *Land of the Cosmic Race*, 7.

27. Jerry, *Blackness in Mexico*, 81.

28. Jerry, *Blackness in Mexico*, 39, 51.

29. María L. Amado, "The 'New Mestiza,' the Old *Mestizos*: Contrasting Discourses on Mestizaje," *Social Inquiry* 82, no. 3 (2012): 447, https://doi.org/10.1111/j.1475-682X.2012.00411.x.

30. Peter Wade, "Rethinking 'Mestizaje': Ideology and Lived Experience," *Journal of Latin American Studies* 37, no. 2 (2005): 239–57.

31. Ben Vinson III, *Before Mestizaje: The Frontiers of Race and Caste in Colonial Mexico* (New York: Cambridge University Press, 2018), 37.

32. Theodore W. Cohen, *Finding Afro-Mexico: Race and Nation after the Revolution* (Cambridge: Cambridge University Press, 2020), 4–5.

33. Diana Taylor, *The Archive and the Repertoire: Performing Cultural Memory in the Americas* (Durham, NC: Duke University Press, 2003), 98; Manuel R. Cuellar, *Choreographing Mexico: Festive Performances and Dancing Histories of a Nation* (Austin: University of Texas, 2022), 6.

34. Robert D. Rhode, *Setting in the American Short Story of Local Color, 1865–1900* (The Hague: Mouton, 1975), 13.

35. Kathryn B. McKee, "Local Color," in *The Companion to Southern Literature: Themes, Genres, Places, People, Movements, and Motifs*, ed. Joseph M. Flora and Lucinda H. MacKethan (Baton Rouge: Louisiana State University Press, 2002), 449.

36. Donald A. Dike, "Notes on Local Color and Its Relation to Realism," *College English* 14, no. 2 (1952): 82.

37. Rhode, *Setting in the American Short Story*, 14.

38. John Hartigan, "Translating 'Race' and 'Raza' between the United States and Mexico," *North American Dialogue* 16, no. 1 (2013): 29–30, https://doi.org/10.1111/nad.12001.

39. Hartigan, "Translating 'Race' and 'Raza,'" 29.

40. Lewis, *Chocolate and Corn Flour*, 85–118.

41. Juan Rejano, "La esfinge mestiza, 1939," in *Cien viajeros en Veracruz: Crónicas y relatos*, tomo 9, *1928–1983*, ed. Martha Poblett Miranda (Xalapa: Gobierno del Estado de Veracruz, 1992), 204.

42. Marilyn Grace Miller, *Rise and Fall of the Cosmic Race: The Cult of Mestizaje in Latin America* (Austin: University of Texas Press, 2004), 47.

43. Angela Castañeda, "Musical Migrations: Son Cubano a la Veracruzana," *Latin Americanist* 52, no. 1 (2008): 62, https://doi.org/10.1111/j.1557-203X.2008.00006.x.

44. Paul Gilroy, *The Black Atlantic: Modernity and Double Consciousness* (Cambridge, MA: Harvard University Press, 1995), 16.

45. Henk Driessen, "Mediterranean Port Cities: Cosmopolitanism Reconsidered," *History and Anthropology* 16, no. 1 (2005): 131, https://doi.org/10.1080/0275720042000316669.

46. See Keith Basso, "Wisdom Sits in Places: Notes on a Western Apache Landscape," in *Senses of Place*, ed. Steven Feld and Keith Basso (Santa Fe, NM: School of American Research Press, 1996), 54.

47. Basso, "Wisdom Sits in Places," 57.

48. See Jacqueline Nassy Brown's ethnography *Dropping Anchor, Setting Sail: Geographies of Race in Black Liverpool* (Princeton, NJ: Princeton University Press, 2005).

49. Scholars of Afro-Central America have been at the forefront of deepening our understanding of the racialization of space and the spatialization of race. See, for example, Lowell Gudmundson and Justin Wolfe, eds., *Blacks and Blackness in Central America: Between Race and Place* (Durham, NC: Duke University Press, 2010).

50. George Lipsitz, "The Racialization of Space and the Spatialization of Race: Theorizing the Hidden Architecture of Landscape," *Landscape Journal* 26, no. 1 (2007): 12.

51. Juliet Hooker, "Race and the Space of Citizenship: The Mosquito Coast and the Place of Blackness and Indigeneity in Nicaragua," in Gudmundson and Wolfe, *Blacks and Blackness in Central America*, 246.

52. Odile Hoffmann and Christian Rinaudo, "The Issue of Blackness and *Mestizaje* in Two Distinct Mexican Contexts: Veracruz and Costa Chica," *Latin American and Caribbean Ethnic Studies* 9, no. 2 (2014): 138–55, https://doi.org/10.1080/17442222.2013.874643.

53. Ian Hacking, *The Social Construction of What?* (Cambridge, MA: Harvard University Press, 2000), 34.

54. Godreau, *Scripts of Blackness*, 5.

55. Lily Hope Chumley and Nicholas Harkness, "Introduction: QUALIA," *Anthropological Theory* 13, no. 1/2 (2013): 239, https://doi.org/10.1177/1463499613483389.

56. Susan Gal, "Qualia as Value and Knowledge: Histories of European Porcelain," *Signs and Society* 5, no. 1 (Supplement 2017): S132, https://doi.org/10.1086/690108.

57. Cohen, *Finding Afro-Mexico*, 277.

58. Ben Vinson III, "Introduction: Black Mexico and the Historical Discipline," in *Black Mexico: Race and Society from Colonial to Modern Times*, ed. Ben Vinson III and Matthew Restall (Albuquerque: University of New Mexico Press, 2009), 7.

59. Shannon Lee Dawdy, *Patina: A Profane Archaeology* (Chicago: University of Chicago Press, 2016), 4.

60. Dawdy, *Patina*, 4.

61. Michael Warner, *Publics and Counterpublics* (Princeton, NJ: Princeton University Press, 2005), 65.

62. Peggy Phelan, *Unmarked: The Politics of Performance* (London: Routledge, 1993), 146.

63. *Afro-mestizo* is another term used in Afro-Mexican studies to refer to intermixed people. The *Afro* modifying *mestizo* is used to emphasize that the mixture involves all three originary races.

64. Taylor, *Archive and the Repertoire*, 28.

65. One of my dearest memories was the second summer I returned to Veracruz. When one person who was a regular but had since joined the group questioned my presence, other members corrected his assumption that I was a stranger. He quickly embraced me afterward, and I now consider him one of my dearest friends.

66. As a young, single woman in that space, my association with that group of men helped shield me from some unwanted attention.

67. Clifford Geertz, "Deep Hanging Out," *New York Review of Books*, October 22, 1998, https://www.nybooks.com/articles/1998/10/22/deep-hanging-out/.

68. For more information about the danzón scene in Veracruz, see Malcomson, *Danzón Days*.

69. Brubaker, "Ethnicity without Groups," 12.

70. Brubaker, "Ethnicity without Groups," 17.

71. I put these three terms together to reflect the language of the 2020 census, in which the terms *negro, afromexicana*, and *afrodescendiente* all appeared in the question soliciting self-recognition as such. I list all three in recognition that there are nuances between the terms. When discussing the governmental categorization, I will use the term *Afro-Mexican* since that is the state's favored neologism.

72. Palmié, *Cooking of History*, 8.

73. In the 2020 census, 4.6 percent of the local population identified themselves as Black. See chapter 5 for more on this quantitative data.

1. VERACRUZ AND ITS JAROCHO

1. "Necesitamos una chica entre 15 a 25 años de edad, morena de pelo en rizos, que sea la típica jarocha para protagonista de un video, nominen y ayúdennos a encontrarla."

2. "Por qué buscar al o la 'típica' jarocho. Por qué no mostrara la diversidad de formas de ser, pensar, sentir o parecer jarocho o jarocha."

3. "Por tanto será así, celebrando tmb la afrodescendencia que poco espacio tiene en los medios visuals e irónicamente tampoco en los videos de Veracruz."

4. "Pero igual tendríamos muuuchas críticas si la protagonista fuera rubia . . . me explico?"

5. Also significant here is El Vate's search for a jarocha rather than a jarocho. While the jarocho figure has been maligned for the majority of its existence, this denigration is also gendered. Women from Veracruz—jarochas—have not had the same negative association as their male counterparts.

6. B. Christine Arce, *México's Nobodies: The Cultural Legacy of the Soldadera and Afro-Mexican Women* (Albany: SUNY Press, 2017), 10.

7. William Hickling Prescott, *History of the Conquest of Mexico* (Boston: Phillips, Sampson and Co., 1856), 365.

8. Among the conquistadors were several creolized Afro-descendant peoples, the most famous among them being Juan Garrido. For more information on the Afro-descendant auxiliaries who participated in Spanish conquests, see Matthew Restall, "Black Conquistadors: Armed Africans in Early Spanish America," *The Americas* 57, no. 2 (2000), https://doi.org/10.1353/tam.2000.0015.

9. The location of the city of Veracruz would change three times in its first century of existence. The Spaniards relocated the original settlement from the beach where they disembarked north to a more hospitable area. This second founding was near the indigenous settlement Quiahuitzlan at what is now known as Villa Rica de la Vera Cruz. In 1525 it relocated to what is present-day La Antigua before finally returning to its current location at the turn of the seventeenth century. For more information, see Antonio García de León, *Tierra adentro, mar en fuera: El Puerto de Veracruz y su litoral a Sotavento, 1519–1821* (Xalapa: Fondo de Cultura Económica, Universidad Veracruzana, Secretarías de Educación del Estado de Veracruz, 2011).

10. For many years, that impression was not positive. Many visitors commented on the provincial nature of the city, the bad water, the buzzards, the weather, and the illness that ran rampant in the city. For examples, see the anthology *Cien viajeros en Veracruz: Crónicas y relatos*, comp. Martha Poblett Miranda (Xalapa: Gobierno del Estado de Veracruz, 1992).

11. Carl Christian Sartorius, *Mexico about 1850* (Stuttgart: F. A. Brockhaus Komm.-Gesch., 1961 [1858]), 1.

12. Frances Calderón de la Barca, *Life in Mexico* (Berkeley: University of California Press, 1982), 31, 33.

13. Frances Erskine Inglis, the Marquesa of Calderón de la Barca, was a Scottish-born noblewoman who was the wife of a diplomat. The historian William Prescott recommended that she publish her private correspondence from her two years in the country, which became the book *Life in Mexico*.

14. Calderón de la Barca, *Life in Mexico*, 40.

15. Heroic designations in Mexico serve to recognize historical events in defense of the nation. Veracruz is four times heroic. It earned its first badge of heroism for weathering the final expulsion of Spanish forces during the Mexican War of Independence. The second act of heroism commemorates the blockade, bombardment, and invasion by the French it experienced during the Pastry War of 1838–39. The last two heroic acts were from suffering two US interventions. The first occurred in 1847, when the United States laid siege to Veracruz during the Mexican-American War. The second US intervention was a seven-month occupation in 1914 during the Mexican Revolution.

16. Miguel Alemán Velazco, "Presentación," in *Veracruz y sus viajeros*, ed. Daniel Sánchez Scott (Gobierno del Estado de Veracruz, 2001), 7.

17. For more information on the sotavento region and its culture, see Alfredo Delgado Calderón, *Historia, cultura e identidad en el Sotavento* (Mexico, DF: CONACULTA, 2004).

18. Kwame Appiah, "Identity, Authenticity, Survival: Multicultural Societies and Social Reproduction," in *Multiculturalism: Examining the Politics of Recognition*, ed. Amy Gutman (Princeton, NJ: Princeton University Press, 1994), 155.

19. Hacking, *Social Construction of What?*, 34.

20. According to the editors of *Race and Performance*, a "useful past" (as opposed to a "usable past") sees the value of the past in terms of use rather than exchange. As they describe it, it is "the difference between consumption and collaboration." See "Tidying Up after Repetition," in *Race and Performance after Repetition*, ed. Soyica Diggs Colbert, Douglas A. Jones Jr., and Shane Vogel (Durham, NC: Duke University Press, 2020), 22.

21. For an extensive overview of the various theories on the meaning of the word *jarocho*, see Ricardo Pérez Montfort, *Expresiones populares y estereotipos culturales en México. Siglos XIX y XX. Diez ensayos* (Mexico, DF: CIESAS, 2007), 185–90.

22. José Miguel Macías, *Diccionario Cubano, etimológico, crítico, razonado y comprensivo* (Veracruz: Trowbridge, 1858), vii.

23. *Diccionario Cubano*, s.v. "jarocho."

24. Alfred H. Siemens, *Between the Summit and the Sea: Central Veracruz in the Nineteenth Century* (Vancouver: University of British Columbia Press, 1990), 157.

25. Andrew Sluyter, *Black Ranching Frontiers: African Cattle Herders of the Atlantic World, 1500–1900* (New Haven, CT: Yale University Press, 2012), 23.

26. Hipólito Rodríguez, "Veracruz: Del Puerto de la conquista al de la independencia y la modernidad," in *La Habana—Veracruz/Veracruz—La Habana: Las dos orillas*, coord. Bernardo Garcia and Sergio Guerra (Mexico: Universidad Veracruzana/Universidad de la Habana).

27. Sluyter, *Black Ranching Frontiers*, 24.

28. Jackie R. Booker, "Needed but Unwanted: Black Militiamen in Veracruz, Mexico, 1760–1810," *Historian* 55, no. 2 (Winter 1993): 259–76, https://www.jstor.org/stable/24449521.

29. See, for example, Peter Gerhard, "A Black Conquistador in Mexico," *Hispanic American Historical Review* 58, no. 3 (1978): 451–59, https://doi.org/10.1215/00182168-58.3.451. See also Restall, "Black Conquistadors."

30. Juan Ortiz Escamilla, "Las compañías milicianas de Veracruz. Del 'negro' al 'jarocho': La construcción histórica de una identidad," *Ulúa* 8 (July–December 2006): 10.

31. Gonzalo Aguirre Beltrán, *La población negra de México, 1519–1810: Estudio etnohistórico* (Mexico, DF: Educaciones Fuente Cultural, 1946), 216.

32. See Robert Schwaller, *Géneros de Gente in Early Colonial Mexico: Defining Racial Difference* (Tulsa: University of Oklahoma Press, 2016).

33. Norman Whitten Jr., "The Longue Durée of Racial Fixity and the Transformative Conjunctures of Racial Blending," *Journal of Latin American and Caribbean Anthropology* 12, no. 2 (2007): 356–83, https://doi.org/10.1525/jlat.2007.12.2.356.

34. Aguirre Beltrán, *Lo población negra*, 216.

35. Trouillot, *Silencing the Past*, 23.

36. Lucien Biart, *Tierra caliente: Escenas de costumbres mexicanas* (Madrid: Medina y Navarro, 1862), 15.

37. Pérez Montfort, *Expresiones populares*, 195.

38. Ben Vinson III, "Fading from Memory: Historiographical Reflections on the Afro-Mexican Presence," *Review of Black Political Economy* 33, no. 1 (2005): 59–72.

39. Pérez Montfort, *Expresiones populares*, 203–4.

40. Pérez Montfort, *Expresiones populares*, 204.

41. Laura G. Gutiérrez, "Afrodiasporic Visual and Sonic Assemblages," in *Decentering the Nation: Music, Mexicanidad, and Globalization*, ed. Jesús A. Ramos-Kittrell (Lanham, MD: Lexington Books, 2020), 3.

42. Antonio García de León, *Fandango: El ritual del mundo jarocho a través de los siglos* (Mexico, DF: CONACULTA, 2006), 31.

43. "Visiting Vera Cruz," *James A. FitzPatrick Traveltalks Shorts*, vol. 3, directed by James A. FitzPatrick (1946; Beverly Hills, CA: Warner Home Video, 2016), DVD.

44. McKee, "Local Color," 449.

45. Clifford Geertz, "Thick Description: Toward an Interpretive Theory of Culture," in *The Interpretation of Cultures: Selected Essays* (New York: Basic Books, 1973), 22–23.

46. Anita González, *Jarocho's Soul: Cultural Identity and Afro-Mexican Dance* (Dallas: University Press of America, 2004), 13.

47. Similar to the term *jarocho, chilango* has a negative connotation for some. A more neutral term would be *defeño*, someone from the Distrito Federal, which was officially renamed the Ciudad de Mexico (CDMX), or Mexico City, in 2016.

48. Literally, "Veracruz is an egg." Not to be confused with the call-and-response "Jarochos! A huevo!," which roughly translates to "Jarochos! Heck yeah!"

49. Christian Rinaudo, *Afromestizaje y fronteras étnicas: Una mirada desde el puerto de Veracruz,* trans. Lorraine Karnoouh (Xalapa, Veracruz: Universidad Veracruzana, 2012), 107–38.

50. Andrew Grant Wood, "Viva la Revolución Social!: Postrevolutionary Tenant Protest and State Housing Reform in Veracruz, Mexico," in *Cities of Hope: People, Protests, and Progress in Urbanizing Latin America, 1870-1930,* ed. Ronn F. Pineo and James A. Baer (Boulder, CO: Westview Press, 1998), 92.

51. Rafael Figueroa Hernández, *Toña la Negra* (CreateSpace Independent Publishing Platform, 2012), 18.

52. Antonio García de León, "Los patios danzoneros," *Del Caribe* no. 20 (1993): 40.

INTERLUDE: TENACIOUS ROOTS

1. *Múcara* stone is made from coral reefs. For more information, see T. J. Zamudio-Zamudio et al., "Characterization of 16th and 18th Century Building Materials from Veracruz City, Mexico," *Microchemical Journal* 74, no. 1 (February 2003): 83–91, https://doi.org/10.1016/S0026-265X(02)00172-8.

2. Michel de Certeau, *The Practice of Everyday Life* (Berkeley: University of California Press, 1984), 91.

2. THE LIVING PAST

1. Dawdy, *Patina,* 26.

2. Trouillot, *Silencing the Past,* 29.

3. Dawdy, *Patina,* 40–41.

4. Dawdy, *Patina,* 26, 45.

5. Malcomson, "Expediency of Blackness," 36.

6. Lewis, *Chocolate and Corn Flour,* 1–5.

7. Here Lewis is thinking with Norman E. Whitten and Arlene Torres's observation that adding the article *la* in front of *culture* elevates it to something "refined, European, civilized." Whitten and Torres also observe that this courtesy is not extended to Black culture. Norman E. Whitten and Arlene Torres, *Blackness in Latin America and the Caribbean,* vol. 1 (Bloomington: Indiana University Press, 1998), 4.

8. For a detailed discussion of the relationship between the archive and the repertoire, see Taylor, *Archive and the Repertoire.*

9. "Misión, Visión y Principios," Instituto Veracruzano de la cultura, accessed May 10, 2015, http://ivec.gob.mx/mision.php.

10. For more on the topic, see Juan Manuel de la Serna Herrera, "Indios, pardos, mulatos y negros esclavos. Lo cotidiano en el Puerto de Veracruz," in *Pautas de Convivencia étnica en la America Latina colonial: (indios, negritos, mulato, pardos y esclavos)* (Mexico, DF: Universidad Nacional Autónoma de Mexico, 2005).

11. Citlalli Domínguez, Alfredo Delgado, María Elisa Velázquez, and José Luis Martínez, *El Puerto de Veracruz y Yanga: Sitios de memoria de la esclavitud y las poblaciones Africanas y Afrodescendientes* (Mexico City: INAH, 2017), 7.

12. Cohen, *Finding Afro-Mexico*, 279.

13. "Casas de la cultura," Instituto Veracruzano de la cultura, accessed October 1, 2015, http://litorale.com.mx/ivec/subdirecciones48.php?id=48.

14. When I refer to IVEC as a location, this is the site to which I refer. The other locations will be referenced by their name—e.g., CEVART, Atarazanas, etc.

15. Elodie Marie Bordat, "Institutionalization and Change in Cultural Policy: CONACULTA and Cultural Policy in Mexico (1988–2006)," *International Journal of Cultural Policy* 19, no. 2 (2013): 222, https://doi.org/10.1080/10286632.2011.638980.

16. Luis Méndez y Berrueta, "Bonfil Batalla, Guillermo (1935–1991)," *The Blackwell Encyclopedia of Sociology* (February 2007): 1–5, https://doi.org/10.1002/9781405165518.wbeosbo40.

17. Cohen, *Finding Afro-Mexico*, 277.

18. Odile Hoffmann, "Negros y afromestizos en México: Viejas y nuevas lecturas de un mundo olvidado," *Revista Mexicana de Sociología* 68, no. 1 (January–March 2006), 114, https://www.redalyc.org/articulo.oa?id=32112598004.

19. Rinaudo, *Afromestizaje y fronteras étnicas*, 23.

20. Cohen, *Finding Afro-Mexico*, 276–77.

21. Rinaudo, *Afromestizaje y fronteras étnicas*, 67–71.

22. Hoffmann and Rinaudo, "Issue of Blackness and *Mestizaje*," 144–45.

23. Rinaudo, *Afromestizaje y fronteras étnicas*, 76–78.

24. Mateo Pazos Cárdenas, "Festival Internacional Afrocaribeño: Lo 'afro' en la construcción de identidades en Veracruz," *Revista Mexicana del Caribe*, no. 21 (January–June 2016), 145–46, https://doi.org/10.22403/UQROOMX/RMC21/05.

25. Rinaudo, *Afromestizaje y fronteras étnicas*, 67–68.

26. Pazos Cárdenas, "Festival Internacional Afrocaribeño," 146.

27. Pazos Cárdenas, "Festival Internacional Afrocaribeño," 145.

28. "Inaugura IVEC el XXVI Festival Internacional Afrocaribeño 2022," IVEC, accessed September 6, 2023, https://saladeprensa.veracruzcultura.com/principal/inaugura-ivec-el-xxvi-festival-internacional-afrocaribeno-2022/.

29. Despite the restrictions of the 2020 global pandemic, organizers were able to arrange a virtual festival in November 2020.

30. For a detailed historical analysis, see Yolanda Juárez Hernández, *Persistencias culturales afrocaribeñas en Veracruz* (Mexico: Gobierno del Estado de Veracruz, 2006).

31. Juárez Hernández, *Persistencias culturales afrocaribeñas*, 266–309.

32. Benedict Anderson, *Imagined Communities: Reflections on the Origin and Spread of Nationalism* (London: Verso, 2006), 7.

33. Stuart Hall, "Negotiating Caribbean Identity," in *New Caribbean Thought: A Reader*, ed. Brian Meeks and Folke Lindahl (Kingston: University of the West Indies Press, 2001), 25.

34. Hall, "Negotiating Caribbean Identity," 26.

35. Ralph Premdas, "Ethnicity and Identity in the Caribbean: Decentering a Myth" (working paper no. 234, Kellogg Institute for International Studies, University of Notre Dame, Indiana, 1996), 2.

36. Michel-Rolph Trouillot, "The Caribbean Region: An Open Frontier in Anthropological Theory," *Annual Review of Anthropology* 21 (1992): 21, https://www.jstor.org/stable/2155979.

37. "Festival Internacional del Desierto de los Leones," accessed October 28, 2020, https://www.facebook.com/festleones/.

38. Rafael Figueroa Hernández, *Son jarocho: Guía histórico-musical* (Xalapa, Veracruz: CONACULTA, 2007), 97–99.

39. For more on son jarocho's role in Mexican cinema, see Rafael Figueroa Hernández, "Mario Barradas and Mexican Cinema," in *Mario Barradas and Son Jarocho: The Journey of a Mexican Regional Music*, by Yolanda Broyles-González, Rafael Figueroa Hernández, and Francisco González (Austin: University of Texas Press, 2022), 131–48.

40. Taylor, *Archive and the Repertoire*, 21.

41. Alejo Carpentier and Alan West-Durán, "Music in Cuba," *Transition*, no. 81/82 (2000): 191, https://www.jstor.org/stable/3137455.

42. Carpentier and West-Durán, "Music in Cuba," 207.

43. Alexandro D. Hernández, "Hidden Histories of Resistance in Mexico's Son Jarocho," in *Sounds of Resistance: The Role of Music in Multicultural Activism*, vol. 2, ed. Eunice Rojas and Lindsay Michie (Santa Barbara, CA: Praeger, 2013), 476.

44. Carpentier and West-Durán, "Music in Cuba," 192.

45. Elena Deanda Camacho, "'El chuchumbé te he de soplar': Sobre obscenidad, censura y memoria oral en el primer 'son de la tierra' novohispano," *Mester* 35, no. 1 (2007): 68, https://doi.org/10.5070/M3361014661.

46. Deanda Camacho, "'El chuchumbé te he de soplar,'" 55.

47. Rubí Oseguera Rueda and Francisco García Ranz, "El repertorio tradicional de los sones jarochos de tarima: Práctica y uso actual," *Antropología: Interdisciplinaria del INAH*, no. 91 (2011): 125, https://revistas.inah.gob.mx/index.php/antropologia/article/view/2750.

48. Delgado Calderón, *Historia, cultura e identidad en el Sotavento*, 55.

49. Antonio García de León and Liza Rumazo, *Fandango: El ritual del mundo jarocho a través de los siglos* (Mexico, DF: CONACULTA, 2006), 54.

50. García de León and Rumazo, *Fandango*, 54.

51. Álvaro Alcántara López, *Dijera mi boca: Textualidades sonoras de un sotavento imaginado* (Mexico: CONACULTA, 2006), 61.

52. Personal recording, "una amalgama natural a través de la rítmica, a través de ese ritmo africano que también es nuestro. Porque nuestro ritmos también son afro."

53. Oseguera Rueda and García Ranz, "El repertorio tradicional," 125.

54. Martha Gonzalez, *Chican@ Artivistas: Music, Community, and Transborder Tactics in East Los Angeles* (Austin: University of Texas Press, 2020), 78. Gonzalez focuses on the

ethics and aesthetics of convivencia as praxis in Chicano/a "artivista" (activist/artistic) communities that focuses on relationships through music rather than products and leads to critical consciousness and community building.

55. Other well-known jaranero-academics include Antonio García de León, formerly of Zacamandú; Rubí C. Oseguera Rueda, formerly of Chuchumbé and Son de Madera; Juan Meléndez de la Cruz; and Jessica Gottfried. A similar dual role is that of promoters and jaraneros, such as Gilberto "El Mono" Gutierrez of Mono Blanco, Patricio Hidalgo of Afrojarocho, Rafael Vázquez of Grupo Estanzuela, and Juan Campechano of Mono Blanco.

56. Trouillot, *Silencing the Past*, 153.

57. Albert B. Lord, *The Singer of Tales* (Cambridge, MA: Harvard University Press, 2000 [1960]), 29.

58. Hall, "Negotiating Caribbean Identity," 37.

59. Elizabeth A. Povinelli, "Routes/Worlds," *e-flux journal* 27 (2011): 9.

3. PRACTICING INNATENESS

1. Stuart Hall, "What Is This 'Black' in Black Popular Culture?," *Social Justice* 20, no. 1/2 (Spring–Summer 1993): 111, https://www.jstor.org/stable/29766735.

2. Hall, "What Is This 'Black'?," 108.

3. Hall, "What Is This Black'?," 109.

4. Paul Gilroy, *Small Acts: Thoughts on the Politics of Black Cultures* (London: Serpent's Tail, 1993).

5. At the time of research, this was just shy of US$20.

6. Bordat, "Institutionalization and Change in Cultural Policy," 222.

7. Laura Lewis, "Blacks, Black Indians, Afromexicans: The Dynamics of Race, Nation, and Identity in a Mexican *Moreno* Community (Guerrero)," *American Ethnologist* 27, no. 4 (2000): 900, https://www.jstor.org/stable/647400.

8. Melba Ali Velázquez Mabarak Sonderegger, "El fandango jarocho y el movimiento jaranero: Un recorrido histórico," *Balajú: Revista de cultura y comunicación* 10 (2019): 4–30, https://doi.org/10.25009/blj.voi10.2566.

9. While I use the term *fandangueros* mostly to refer to participants in the folk tradition known as *fandangos*, there is also the term *jaraneros*. I use it here because Mono Blanco consists of musicians, while the term *fandanguero* is capacious enough to include passive participants in the collective music-making activity known as *fandango*.

10. Hale, "Does Multiculturalism Menace?"

11. Malcomson, "Expediency of Blackness," 45.

12. For a deeper analysis of how age factors into both the imaginary and the practice of the danzón, see Hettie Malcomson, "New Generations, Older Bodies: *Danzón*, Age and 'Cultural Rescue' in the Port of Veracruz, Mexico," *Popular Music* 31, no. 2 (2012): 217–30, https://www.jstor.org/stable/23325758.

13. Erandi García Cabrera, "El son de Los Negritos: Rescate e innovación," in *Entre la tradición y el canon: Homenaje a Yvette Jiménez Báez*, ed. Ana Rosa Domenella, Luzelena Gutiérrez de Velasco, and Edith Negrín (Mexico City: El Colegio de México, 2009), 165–78.

14. Here I am thinking with John Jackson's concept of racial sincerity. He argues that racial sincerity—as opposed to racial authenticity—encompasses the "liveness," the ad hoc,

the ad-libbing of everyday racial performances. According to Jackson, sincerity allows for a focus on intent rather than content. When thinking about choreography and a freestyling, the tension is between following steps and creating movement. See John Jackson, *Real Black: Adventures in Racial Sincerity* (Chicago: University of Chicago Press, 2005), 18.

15. Cuellar, *Choreographing Mexico*, 21.

16. Cuellar, *Choreographing Mexico*, 18.

17. Aimee Meredith Cox, *Shapeshifters: Black Girls and the Choreography of Citizenship* (Durham, NC: Duke University Press, 2015), 29.

18. Taylor, *Archive and the Repertoire*.

19. For a detailed exploration of jarocho dance style and the differences between its professional and its popular iterations, see González, *Jarocho's Soul*.

4. AFFECTATIONS

1. Frederick W. Turner, *A Border of Blue: Along the Gulf of Mexico from the Keys to the Yucatán* (New York: Henry Holt & Company, 1993), 253.

2. See Basso, "Wisdom Sits in Places," 54.

3. Appiah, "Identity, Authenticity, Survival," 155.

4. A notable exception is the Mascogos of the northern state of Coahuila. However, their origin story as Black Seminoles from the United States who relocated south of the US-Mexico border in the nineteenth century takes a decidedly different register from that of Afro-Mexicans or Afro-descendancy along the coasts. Pre–census data, the Costa Grande of Guerrero also earned inclusion in discussions of contemporary Afro-descendant populations in Mexico. For more, see *Afrodescendientes en México: Una historia de silencio y discriminación* (2012), by Mexicanists, scholars, and activists María Elisa Velázquez and Gabriela Iturralde Nieto. The book was published by CONAPRED, the Consejo Nacional Para Prevenir la Discriminación (National Council to Prevent Discrimination), as well as by INAH (Instituto Nacional de Antropologia e Historia / National Institute of Anthropology and History) and CONACULTA.

5. Hoffmann and Rinaudo, "Issue of Blackness."

6. Taylor, *Archive and the Repertoire*, 98.

7. Moritz Heck, *Plurinational Afrobolivianity: Afro-Indigenous Articulations and Interethnic Relations in the Yungas of Bolivia* (Bielefeld, Germany: Transcript Verlag, 2020), 155.

8. Livio Sansone, *Blackness without Ethnicity: Constructing Race in Brazil* (New York: Palgrave Macmillan, 2003).

9. Rinaudo, *Afromestizaje y fronteras étnicas*, 150–59.

10. Antonio Benítez-Rojo, *The Repeating Island: The Caribbean and the Postmodern Perspective* (Durham, NC: Duke University Press, 1992), 10.

11. Benítez-Rojo, *Repeating Island*, 10.

12. For more information, see Cohen, *Finding Afro-Mexico*, 190–221.

13. Hall, "Negotiating Caribbean Identity," 26.

14. Lila Ellen Gray, *Fado Resounding: Affective Politics and Urban Life* (Durham, NC: Duke University Press, 2013), 6.

15. Gobierno del Estado de Veracruz, "Ley del himno al estado de Veracruz de Ignacio de la Llave," *La Gaceta Oficial* (December 2, 2005).

16. Thomas Turino, "Nationalism and Latin American Music: Selected Case Studies and Theoretical Considerations," *Latin American Music Review* 24, no. 2 (Autumn–Winter 2003): 169–209, https://www.jstor.org/stable/3598738.

17. An argument could be made that "La bamba" is the more popular anthem of the city. For example, Ted Cohen details how in the 1940s, the son jarocho number became known as "[President Miguel] Alemán's hymn," "Veracruz's hymn," "our state's hymn," and "our jarocho hymn." See *Finding Afro-Mexico*, 170–71. Indeed, "La bamba" is ubiquitous in the city and used strategically at cultural events. However, unlike "Veracruz," "La bamba" does not specifically reference or eulogize the city.

18. In her analysis of mariachi and national identity, Mary-Lee Mulholland argues that suffering is "the most salient allusion" to Mexican culture. Mary-Lee Mulholland, "Mariachi, Myths and Mestizaje: Popular Culture and Mexican National Identity," *National Identities* 9, no. 3 (2007): 253.

19. Andrew Grant Wood, "On the Selling of Rey Momo: Early Tourism and the Marketing of Carnival in Veracruz," in *Holiday in Mexico: Critical Reflections on Tourism and Tourist Encounters*, ed. Dina Berger and Andrew Grant Wood (Durham, NC: Duke University Press, 2010), 93–94.

20. Andrew Grant Wood, "Carnaval en Veracruz: Celebraciones públicas, identidad y el inicio del turismo," *Ulúa* 3 (2004): 139–74.

21. Wood, "On the Selling of Rey Momo," 93.

22. Joel Cruz, "Colocan estructura metálica en el centro de Veracruz; da la bienvenida a la 'capital de la alegría,'" *XEU Noticias*, accessed July 7, 2024, https://xeu.mx/veracruz/887084/colocan-estructura-metalica-en-el-centro-de-veracruz-da-la-bienvenida-a-la-capital-de-la-alegria.

23. José Romero, *Danzonero* (Veracruz: Atracadero Films, NGA Producciones, Sociedad Baluarte, and Sistemas Contino, 2012).

24. Don Miguel García Cortés closed his business during the COVID-19 pandemic shutdown after nearly twenty-five years. He passed away in 2021, and the programming he sponsored has not returned. At last visit, in 2023–24, the space was periodically used for a wide variety of events sponsored by local government.

25. Godreau, *Scripts of Blackness*, 14.

5. SANGUINE BLACKNESS

1. Sue, "Racial Ideologies," 281–83.

2. Palmié, *Cooking of History*, 13.

3. Palmié, *Cooking of History*, 8.

4. Here I use the capitalized *Black* to encapsulate subject positions across various color labels. The capitalized *Black* is an umbrella term that includes phenotypic understandings of color—which includes skin tone, hair texture, and facial features—as well as more genealogical understandings as found in the term *Afro-descendant* or references to Afro-descendant ancestors.

5. For a detailed explanation of the colonial caste term *chino*, see Vinson, *Before Mestizaje*, 9–10. In it, he describes how by the eighteenth century, *chino* could mean various things, including an Asian person or someone who looked Asian, as well as someone brown or someone with Afro-indigenous ancestry. See also Marco Polo Hernández Cuevas, "The

Mexican Colonial Term 'Chino' Is a Referent of Afrodescendant," *Journal of Pan African Studies* 5, no. 5 (2012): 124–43. In contemporary Veracruz, I observed people described as chino based on their coiled hair texture, often associated with African ancestry, or their Asian (or appearance of Asian) ancestry.

6. Godreau, *Scripts of Blackness*, 37.

7. For a detailed analysis of pigmentocracy, see Edward Telles's *Pigmentocracies: Ethnicity, Race, and Color in Latin America* (Chapel Hill: University of North Carolina Press, 2014).

8. Sue, *Land of the Cosmic Race*, 2.

9. Sue, *Land of the Cosmic Race*, 7.

10. Telles, *Pigmentocracies*, 3.

11. Guillermo Trejo and Melina Altamirano, "The Mexican Color Hierarchy: How Race and Skin Tone Still Define Life Chances 200 Years after Independence," in *The Double Bind: The Politics of Race and Class Inequalities in the Americas*, ed. Juliet Hooker and Alvin B. Tillery Jr. (Washington, DC: American Political Science Association, 2016), 4.

12. "Se veía muy africano."

13. Anthony Jerry observed a similar linguistic practice in the Costa Chica. See Jerry, *Blackness in Mexico*, 38.

14. Christina Sue also had interlocutors who made similar claims. See the example of Silvia in Sue, *Land of the Cosmic Race*, 3.

15. Luis F. Angosto-Ferrández, "From 'café con leche' to 'o café, o leche': National Identity, *Mestizaje* and Census Politics in Contemporary Venezuela," *Journal of Iberian and Latin American Research* 20, no. 3 (2014): 392, https://doi.org/10.1080/13260219.2014.995876.

16. Karen E. Fields and Barbara J. Fields, *Racecraft: The Soul of Inequality in American Life* (London: Verso, 2012), 50–52.

17. Sharon Patricia Holland, *The Erotic Life of Racism* (Durham, NC: Duke University Press, 2012), 3.

18. The capitalization used in this anecdote is intentional as well as indicative of the slippage between black as a color label and Black as an ethnoracial, collective identity. While the connotation inherent in the grandfather's use of the term *negro* is unclear in Cruz Carretero's retelling of the encounter, her statement "Of course he was a Black man" reads as a political identity claim more than a color descriptor.

19. "Mexico and Peru: The Black Grandma in the Closet," *Black in Latin America*, dir. Henry Louis Gates Jr. (PBS Distribution, 2011), DVD.

20. María Elena Martínez, *Genealogical Fictions: Limpieza de Sangre, Religion, and Gender in Colonial Mexico* (Stanford, CA: Stanford University Press, 2008), 26.

21. Ronald Stutzman, "El Mestizaje: An All-Inclusive Ideology of Exclusion," in *Cultural Transformations and Ethnicity in Modern Ecuador*, ed. Norman E. Whitten Jr. (Urbana-Champaign: University of Illinois Press, 1981), 45–94.

22. José Vasconcelos, *La Raza Cósmica / The Cosmic Race*, trans. Didier Tisdel Jaén (Baltimore: Johns Hopkins University Press, 1997), 23.

23. "Barrios Indio-El Lado auténtico de México," Latinspots.com, last accessed September 29, 2023, https://www.latinspots.com/sp/comercial/barrios-indio-el-lado-autntico-de-mxico/25958.

24. "Plasma INDIO el lado más auténtico de La Huaca en un mural," last accessed September 20, 2023, https://spaciorandom.wordpress.com/2016/08/08/plasma-indio-el-lado-mas

-autentico-de-la-huaca-en-un-mural/.

25. Figueroa Hernández, *Toña la Negra*, 23–24, 27.

26. Pérez Montfort, "El 'negro' y la negritud," 208.

27. Frances R. Aparicio, *Listening to Salsa: Gender, Latin Popular Music, and Puerto Rican Cultures* (Hanover, NH: University Press of New England, 1998), 175.

28. Marilyn Miller, "'The Soul Has No Color' but the Skin Does: *Angelitos Negros* and the Uses of Blackface on the Mexican Silver Screen, ca. 1950," in *Global Soundtracks: Worlds of Film Music*, ed. Mark Slobin (Middletown, CT: Wesleyan University Press, 2008), 248.

29. Marcela Prado Revuelta, *Desde el portal: Crónicas de Veracruz* (Mexico: Gobierno del Estado de Veracruz, 2009), 362.

30. According to biographer Rafael Figueroa, the Peregrino story in Mexico began with Severo Peregrino, a Haitian immigrant who was a direct descendant of enslaved Africans. He married a jarocha and had four children, one of whom was Timoteo, the father of Toña la Negra and grandfather of El Negro Peregrino. Figueroa Hernández, *Toña la Negra*, 15.

31. The capitalization of *Black* versus *black* is intentional. It serves to distinguish her understanding of *negro* as a physical descriptor rather than a subject position.

CONCLUSION: THE JAROCHO AND THE AFRO-MEXICAN

1. Velázquez and Iturralde Nieto, *Afrodescendientes en México*, 101.

2. Lewis, "Blacks, Black Indians, Afromexicans," 899.

3. Rocío Gil, "The Mascogo/Black Seminole Diaspora: The Intertwining Borders of Citizenship, Race, and Ethnicity," *Latin American and Caribbean Ethnic Studies* 9, no. 1 (2014): 26, https://doi.org/10.1080/17442222.2013.843826.

4. Henry Louis Gates Jr., *Black in Latin America* (New York: New York University Press, 2011), 59, 64–65.

5. Cohen, *Finding Afro-Mexico*, 15.

6. Mara Loveman, *National Colors: Racial Classification and the State in Latin America* (Oxford: Oxford University Press, 2014), 8–9.

7. There is little difference between the 2015 and 2020 manuals in regard to explanatory material for the Afro-descendancy question.

8. Instituto Nacional de Estadística y Geografía (INEGI), *Censo de Poblacion y Vivienda 2020. Manual del entrevistador del cuestionario básico. Enumeración* (2021), 263.

9. INEGI, *Encuesta Intercensal 2015. Manual del entrevistador* (Mexico, 2014), 113–14.

10. Telles, *Pigmentocracies*, 9–10.

11. Hacking, "Making Up People," 228.

12. Hacking, *Social Construction of What?*, 31.

13. Cristian Báez Lazcano, "Reflections on the Afro-Chilean Social Movement," *ReVista: Harvard Review of Latin America* 18, no. 2 (2018), https://revista.drclas.harvard.edu/reflections-on-the-afro-chilean-social-movement/.

14. Paola C. Monkevicius and Marta M. Maffia, "Memory and Ethnic Leadership among Afro-Descendants and Africans in Argentina," *African and Black Diaspora: An International Journal* 8, no. 2 (2014): 191, https://doi.org/10.1080/17528631.2014.908546.

15. Stuart Hall, "Old and New Identities, Old and New Ethnicities," in *Culture, Globalization and the World-System: Contemporary Conditions for the Representation of Identity,*

ed. Anthony D. King (Minneapolis: University of Minnesota Press, 1997), 55.

16. Hall, "Old and New Identities," 57.

17. "Por sus antepasados y de acuerdo con sus costumbres y tradiciones, ¿(nombre) se considera afromexicano(a), negro(a), o afrodescendiente?"

18. INEGI, *Censo de Población y Vivienda 2020*, 262–64.

19. Leo Perlata, "El INEGI reveló nuestra pigmentocracia," *HuffPost Mexico*, accessed July 20, 2017, www.huffingtonpost.com.mx/leo-peralta/el-inegi-revelo-nuestra-pigmentocracia _a_22488829/.

20. Emiko Saldívar, Patricio Solís, and Erika Arenas, "Consideraciones metodólogicas para el conteo de la población afromexicana en el Censo 2020," *Conyuntura Demográfica*, no. 14 (2018): 48.

21. Saldívar, Solís, and Arenas, "Consideraciones metodólogicas," 50–52.

22. Jonathan Warren and Christina Sue, "Comparative Racisms: What Anti-racists Can Learn from Latin America," *Ethnicities* 11, no. 1 (2011): 44, https://doi.org/10.1177 /1468796810388699.

23. George Yúdice, *The Expediency of Culture: Uses of Culture in the Global Era* (Durham, NC: Duke University Press, 2004).

24. Warren and Sue, "Comparative Racisms," 43.

25. Warren and Sue, "Comparative Racisms," 45.

26. Congreso del Estado de Veracruz, "Propone Yazmín Copete proteger la cultura de afrodescendientes radicados en Veracruz," comunicación social comunicado: 0426, May 23, 2017, accessed April 3, 2020, https://www.legisver.gob.mx/boletines/boletinesLXIV /BOLETIN0426.pdf.

27. Congreso del Estado de Veracruz, "Pide Dunyaska acabar con discriminación contra comunidad afrodescendiente," comunicación social comunicado: 0614, July 25, 2017, accessed April 3, 2020, https://www.legisver.gob.mx/boletines/boletinesLXIV /BOLETIN0614.pdf.

28. E. Patrick Johnson, *Appropriating Blackness: Performance and the Politics of Authenticity* (Durham, NC: Duke University Press, 2003), 2.

BIBLIOGRAPHY

Aguirre Beltrán, Gonzalo. *Cuijla: Esbozo etnográfico de un pueblo negro.* Mexico, DF: Fondo de Cultura Económica, [1958] 1974.

———. *La población negra de México, 1519–1810: Estudio etno-histórico.* Mexico, DF: Educaciones Fuente Cultural, 1946.

Alcántara López, Álvaro. *Dijera mi boca: Textualidades sonoras de un sotavento imaginado.* Estado de Mexico: Criba Taller Editorial, 2006.

Alemán Velazco, Miguel. "Presentación." In *Veracruz y sus viajeros*, edited by Daniel Sánchez Scott. Mexico: Gobierno del Estado de Veracruz, 2001.

Amado, María L. "The 'New Mestiza,' the Old *Mestizos*: Contrasting Discourses on *Mestizaje.*" *Sociological Inquiry* 82, no. 3 (2012): 446–59. https://doi.org/10.1111/j.1475-682X .2012.00411.x.

Amaral, Adela. "Social Geographies, the Practice of Marronage and the Archaeology of Absence in Colonial Mexico." *Archaeological Dialogues* 24, no. 2 (2017): 207–23. https://doi.org/10.1017/S1380203817000228.

Anderson, Benedict. *Imagined Communities: Reflections on the Origin and Spread of Nationalism.* London: Verso, 2006.

Angosto-Ferrández, Luis F. "From 'café con leche' to 'o café, o leche': National Identity, *Mestizaje* and Census Politics in Contemporary Venezuela." *Journal of Iberian and Latin American Research* 20, no. 3 (2014): 373–98. https://doi.org/10.1080/13260219.2014 .995876.

Aparicio, Frances R. *Listening to Salsa: Gender, Latin Popular Music, and Puerto Rican Cultures.* Hanover, NH: University Press of New England, 1998.

Appiah, Kwame. "Identity, Authenticity, Survival: Multicultural Societies and Social Reproduction." In *Multiculturalism: Examining the Politics of Recognition*, edited by Amy Gutman, 149–64. Princeton, NJ: Princeton University Press, 1994.

Arce, B. Christine. *México's Nobodies: The Cultural Legacy of the Soldadera and Afro-Mexican Women.* Albany: SUNY Press, 2017.

Báez Lazcano, Cristian. "Reflections on the Afro-Chilean Social Movement." *ReVista: Harvard Review of Latin America.* https://revista.drclas.harvard.edu/reflections-on -the-afro-chilean-social-movement/.

Basso, Keith. "Wisdom Sits in Places: Notes on a Western Apache Landscape." In *Senses of Place,* edited by Steven Feld and Keith Basso, 53–90. Santa Fe, NM: School of American Research Press, 1996.

Beezley, William H. *Mexican National Identity: Memory, Innuendo, and Popular Culture.* Tucson: University of Arizona Press, 2008.

Benítez-Rojo, Antonio. *The Repeating Island: The Caribbean and the Postmodern Perspective.* Durham, NC: Duke University Press, 1992.

Bennett, Herman. *Colonial Blackness: A History of Afro-Mexico.* Bloomington: Indiana University Press, 2009.

Biart, Lucien. *Tierra caliente: Escenas de costumbres mexicanas.* Madrid: Medina y Navarro, 1862.

Booker, Jackie R. "Needed but Unwanted: Black Militiamen in Veracruz, Mexico, 1760–1810." *Historian* 55, no. 2 (Winter 1993): 259–76. https://www.jstor.org/stable/24449521.

Bordat, Elodie Marie. "Institutionalization and Change in Cultural Policy: CONACULTA and Cultural Policy in Mexico (1988–2006)." *International Journal of Cultural Policy* 19, no. 2 (2013): 222–48. http://dx.doi.org/10.1080/10286632.2011.638980.

Bourdieu, Pierre, and Loïc Wacquant. "On the Cunning of Imperialist Reason." *Theory Culture Society* 16, no. 41 (1999): 41–58. https://doi.org/10.1177/026327699016001003.

Brown, Jacqueline Nassy. *Dropping Anchor, Setting Sail: Geographies of Race in Black Liverpool.* Princeton, NJ: Princeton University Press, 2005.

Broyles-González, Yolanda. *Mario Barradas and Son Jarocho: The Journey of a Mexican Regional Music.* Austin: University of Texas Press, 2022.

Brubaker, Rogers. "Ethnicity without Groups." In *Ethnicity without Groups,* edited by Rogers Brubaker, 7–27. Cambridge, MA: Harvard University Press, 2004.

Calderón de la Barca, Frances. *Life in Mexico.* Berkeley: University of California Press, 1982.

Carpentier, Alejo, and Alan West-Durán. "Music in Cuba." *Transition* no. 81/82 (2000): 172–228. https://www.jstor.org/stable/3137455.

Carrera, Magali M. *Imagining Identity in New Spain: Race, Lineage, and the Colonial Body in Portraiture and Casta Paintings.* Austin: University of Texas Press, 2003.

———. "Locating Race in Late Colonial Mexico." *Art Journal* 57, no. 3 (1998): 36–45. https://doi.org/10.1080/00043249.1998.10791891.

Carretero-Cruz, Sagrario. "Yanga and the Black Origins of Mexico." *Review of Black Political Economy* 33, no. 1 (June 2005): 73–77. https://doi.org/10.1007/s12114-005-1034-6.

Carroll, Patrick. *Blacks in Colonial Veracruz: Race, Ethnicity, and Regional Development.* Austin: University of Texas Press, 2001.

———. "Mandinga: The Evolution of a Mexican Runaway Slave Community, 1735–1827." *Comparative Studies in Society and History* 19, no. 4 (October 1977): 488–505. https:// www.jstor.org/stable/178098.

Castañeda, Angela. "Musical Migrations: Son Cubano a la Veracruzana." *Latin Americanist* 52, no. 1 (2008): 55–71. https://doi.org/10.1111/j.1557-203X.2008.00006.x.

Chávez-Hita, Adriana Naveda. *La esclavitud africana en las haciendas azucareras de Córdoba, 1690–1839.* Xalapa: Universidad Veracruzana-Centro de Investigaciones Históricas, 1987.

Chumley, Lily Hope, and Nicholas Harkness. "Introduction: QUALIA." *Anthropological Theory* 13, no. 1/2 (2013): 3–11. https://doi.org/10.1177/1463499613483389.

Clark, Paul C., Jr., and Edward H. Moseley. "D-Day Veracruz, 1847—A Grand Design." *Joint Forces Quarterly* (Winter 1995–96): 103–15.

Cohen, Theodore W. *Finding Afro-Mexico: Race and Nation after the Revolution.* Cambridge: Cambridge University Press, 2020.

Congreso del Estado de Veracruz. "Pide Dunyaska acabar con discriminación contra comunidad afrodescendiente." Comunicación social 0614. July 25, 2017. Accessed April 3, 2020. https://www.legisver.gob.mx/boletines/boletinesLXIV/BOLETIN0614.pdf.

———. "Propone Yazmín Copete proteger la cultura de afrodescendientes radicados en Veracruz." Comunicación social 0426, May 23, 2017. Accessed April 3, 2020. https://www.legisver.gob.mx/boletines/boletinesLXIV/BOLETIN0426.pdf.

Cox, Aimee Meredith. *Shapeshifters: Black Girls and the Choreography of Citizenship.* Durham, NC: Duke University Press, 2015.

Cruz, Joel. "Colocan estructura metálica en el centro de Veracruz; da la bienvenida a 'la capital de la alegría.'" *XEU Noticias.* Accessed July 7, 2024. https://xeu.mx/veracruz/887084/colocan-estructura-metalica-en-el-centro-de-veracruz-da-la-bienvenida-a-la-capital-de-la-alegria.

Cuellar, Manuel R. *Choreographing Mexico: Festive Performances and Dancing Histories of a Nation.* Austin: University of Texas Press, 2022.

Davis, Adrienne D. "Identity Note Part One: Playing in the Light." *American University Law Review* 45, no. 3 (February 1996): 695–720.

Dawdy, Shannon Lee. *Patina: A Profane Archaeology.* Chicago: University of Chicago Press, 2016.

De Certeau, Michel. *The Practice of Everyday Life.* Translated by Steven Rendall. Berkeley: University of California Press, 1984.

Deanda Camacho, Elena. "'El chuchumbé te he de soplar': Sobre obscenidad, censura y memoria oral en el primer 'son de la tierra' novohispano." *Mester* 36 (2007): 53–71. https://doi.org/10.5070/M3361014661.

Del Palacio, Celia. "El Puerto de Veracruz durante la Guerra de Reforma." *La Palabra y el Hombre,* no. 10 (2009): 48–54.

Delgado Calderón, Alfredo. *Historia, cultura e identidad en el Sotavento.* Mexico, DF: CONACULTA, 2004.

Diccionario Enciclopédico Veracruzano. s.v. "jarocho, a." Accessed May 23, 2017. https://sapp.uv.mx/egv/diccionary_detail.aspx?article=jarocho.

Diggs Colbert, Soyica, Douglas A. Jones Jr., and Shane Vogel, eds. *Race and Performance after Repetition.* Durham, NC: Duke University Press, 2020.

Dike, Donald A. "Notes on Local Color and Its Relation to Realism." *College English* 14, no. 2 (1952): 81–88. https://doi.org/10.2307/371767.

Domínguez, Citlalli. "Luz María Martínez Montiel, A Mexican Africanist, Pioneer in Afro-Mexican Studies." In *Routledge Handbook of Afro-Latin American Studies,* edited by Bernd Reiter and John Antón Sanchez, 610–13. New York: Routledge, 2023.

Domínguez, Citlalli, Alfredo Delgado, María Elisa Velázquez, and José Luis Martínez. *El Puerto de Veracruz y Yanga: Sitios de memoria de la esclavitud y las poblaciones Africanas y Afrodescendientes.* Mexico City: INAH, 2016.

Driessen, Henk. "Mediterranean Port Cities: Cosmopolitanism Reconsidered." *History and Anthropology* 16, no. 1 (2005): 129–41. https://doi.org/10.1080/0275720042000316669.

Escallón, María Fernanda. *Becoming Heritage: Recognition, Exclusion, and the Politics of Black Cultural Heritage in Colombia.* Cambridge: Cambridge University Press, 2023.

Fabian, Johannes. *Power and Performance: Ethnographic Explorations through Proverbial Wisdom and Theater in Shaba, Zaire.* Madison: University of Wisconsin Press, 1990.

Festival Internacional del Desierto de los Leones. "About." Accessed October 28, 2020. https://www.facebook.com/festleones/.

Fields, Karen E., and Barbara J. Fields. *Racecraft: The Soul of Inequality in American Life.* London: Verso, 2012.

Figueroa Hernández, Rafael. *Son jarocho: Guía histórico-musical.* Xalapa, Veracruz: CONACULTA, 2007.

———. *Toña la Negra.* CreateSpace Independent Publishing Platform, 2012.

FitzPatrick, James A. "Visiting Vera Cruz." In *James A. FitzPatrick Traveltalks Shorts*, vol. 3. 1946; Beverly Hills: Warner Home Video, 2016. DVD.

Frierson, Karma F. "Enumerating Blackness: The Shifting Politics of Recognition in Mexico." In *Hemispheric Blackness and the Exigencies of Accountability*, edited by Jennifer Gómez Menjívar and Héctor Nicolás Ramos Flores, 163–80. Pittsburgh: University of Pittsburgh Press, 2022.

Gal, Susan. "Qualia as Value and Knowledge: Histories of European Porcelain." *Signs and Society* 5, no. 1 (2017): S128-53. https://doi.org/10.1086/690108.

García Cabrera, Erandi. "El son de los negritos: Rescate e innovación." In *Entre la tradición y el canon: Homenaje a Yvette Jiménez de Báez*, edited by Ana Rosa Domenella, Luzelena Gutiérrez de Velasco, and Edith Negrín, 165–78. Mexico City: El Colegio de México, 2009.

García de León, Antonio, and Liza Rumazo. *Fandango: El ritual del mundo jarocho a través de los siglos.* Mexico, DF: CONACULTA, 2006.

———. *El mar de los deseos. El Caribe afroandaluz historia y contrapunto.* Mexico City: Fondo de Cultura Económica, 2014.

———. "Los patios danzoneros." *Del Caribe* no. 20 (1993): 36–46.

———. *Tierra adentro, mar en fuera: El Puerto de Veracruz y su litoral a Sotavento, 1519–1821.* Xalapa: Fondo de Cultura Económica, Universidad Veracruzana, Secretarías de Educación del Estado de Veracruz, 2011.

García Díaz, Bernardo. "El Caribe en el Golfo: Cuba y Veracruz a fines del Siglo XIX y principios del XX." *Anuario X* (1995): 47–66.

García Peña, Lorgia. *Translating Blackness: Latinx Colonialities in Global Perspective.* Durham, NC: Duke University Press, 2022.

Gates, Henry Louis, Jr. *Black in Latin America.* New York: New York University Press, 2011.

———. "Mexico and Peru: The Black Grandma in the Closet." *Black in Latin America.* 2011. PBS Distribution. DVD.

Geertz, Clifford. "Deep Hanging Out." *New York Review of Books*, October 22, 1998. https://www-nybooks-com/articles/1998/10/22/deep-hanging-out/.

———. *The Interpretation of Cultures: Selected Essays.* New York: Basic Books, 1973.

Gerhard, Peter. "A Black Conquistador in Mexico." *Hispanic American Historical Review* 58, no. 3 (1978): 451–59. https://doi.org/10.1215/00182168-58.3.451.

Gil, Rocío. "The Mascogo/Black Seminole Diaspora: The Intertwining Borders of Citizenship, Race, and Ethnicity." *Latin American and Caribbean Ethnic Studies* 9, no. 1 (2014): 23–43. https://doi.org/10.1080/17442222.2013.843826.

Gillam, Reighan. *Visualizing Black Lives: Ownership and Control in Afro-Brazilian Media.* Urbana: University of Illinois Press, 2022.

Gilroy, Paul. *The Black Atlantic: Modernity and Double Consciousness.* Cambridge, MA: Harvard University Press, 1995.

———. *Small Acts: Thoughts on the Politics of Black Cultures.* London: Serpent's Tail, 1993.

Gobierno del Estado de Veracruz. "Ley del himno al estado de Veracruz de Ignacio de la Llave." *La Gaceta Oficial*, December 2, 2005.

Godreau, Isar P. "Folkloric 'Others': *Blanqueamiento* and the Celebration of Blackness as an Exception in Puerto Rico." In *Globalization and Race: Transformations in the Cultural Production of Blackness*, edited by Kamari Maxine Clarke and Deborah Thomas, 171–87. Durham, NC: Duke University Press, 2006.

———. *Scripts of Blackness: Race, Cultural Nationalism, and U.S. Colonialism in Puerto Rico.* Urbana: University of Illinois Press, 2015.

Golash-Boza, Tanya. "Does Whitening Happen? Distinguishing between Race and Color Labels in an African-Descended Community in Peru." *Social Problems* 57, no. 1 (2010): 138–56. https://doi.org/10.1525/sp.2010.57.1.138.

González, Anita. *Afro-Mexico: Constructions of Diaspora, Gender, Identity, and Nation.* Austin: University of Texas Press, 2010.

———. *Jarocho's Soul: Cultural Identity and Afro-Mexican Dance.* Dallas: University Press of America, 2004.

Gonzalez, Martha. *Chican@ Artivistas: Music, Community, and Transborder Tactics in East Los Angeles.* Austin: University of Texas Press, 2020.

Gray, Lila Ellen. *Fado Resounding: Affective Politics and Urban Life.* Durham, NC: Duke University Press, 2013.

Gudmundson, Lowell, and Justin Wolfe, eds. *Blacks and Blackness in Central America: Between Race and Place.* Durham, NC: Duke University Press, 2010.

Gutiérrez, Laura G. "Afrodiasporic Visual and Sonic Assemblages." In *Decentering the Nation: Music, Mexicanidad, and Globalization*, edited by Jesús A. Ramos-Kittrell. Lanham, MD: Lexington Books, 2020.

Hacking, Ian. "Making Up People." In *Reconstructing Individualism: Autonomy, Individuality, and the Self in Western Thought*, edited by Thomas C. Heller, Morton Sosna, and David E. Wellbery, 222–36. Stanford, CA: Stanford University Press, 1986.

———. *The Social Construction of What?* Cambridge, MA: Harvard University Press, 2000.

Hale, Charles. "Does Multiculturalism Menace? Governance, Cultural Rights and the Politics of Identity in Guatemala." *Journal of Latin American Studies* 34, no. 3 (2002): 485–524. https://doi.org/10.1017/S0022216X02006521.

Hall, Stuart. "Introduction: Who Needs Identity?" In *Questions on Cultural Identity*, edited by Stuart Hall and Paul du Gay, 1–17. London: Sage Publications, 1996.

———. "Negotiating Caribbean Identity." In *New Caribbean Thought: A Reader*, edited by Brian Meeks and Folke Lindahl, 24–39. Kingston, Jamaica: University of the West Indies Press, 2001.

———. "Old and New Identities, Old and New Ethnicities." In *Culture, Globalization and the World-System: Contemporary Conditions for the Representation of Identity*, edited by Anthony D. King, 41–68. Minneapolis: University of Minnesota Press, 1997.

———. "What Is This 'Black' in Black Popular Culture?" *Social Justice* 20, no. 1/2 (Spring-Summer 1993): 104–14. https://www.jstor.org/stable/29766735.

Hanks, William F. *Converting Worlds: Maya in the Age of the Cross*. Berkeley: University of California Press, 2010.

Hartigan, John. "Translating 'Race' and 'Raza' between the United States and Mexico." *North American Dialogue* 16, no. 1 (2013): 29–41. https://doi.org/10.1111/nad.12001.

Heck, Moritz. *Plurinational Afrobolivianity: Afro-Indigenous Articulations and Interethnic Relations in the Yungas of Bolivia*. Bielefeld, Germany: Transcript Verlag, 2020.

Hernández, Alexandro D. "Hidden Histories of Resistance in Mexico's Son Jarocho." In *Sounds of Resistance: The Role of Music in Multicultural Activism*, edited by Eunice Rojas and Lindsay Michie, 473–90. Santa Barbara, CA: Praeger, 2013.

Hernández Cuevas, Marco Polo. "The Mexican Colonial Term 'Chino' Is a Referent of Afrodescendant." *Journal of Pan African Studies* 5, no. 5 (2012): 124–43.

Hoffmann, Odile. "De 'negros' y 'afros' in Veracruz." In *Atlas del patrimonio natural, histórico y cultural de Veracruz*. Tomo 3, *Patrimonio Cultural*, edited by Enrique Florescano and Juan Ortiz Escamilla, 127–40. Xalapa, Veracruz: Universidad Veracruzana, 2010.

———. "Negros y afromestizos en México: Viejas y nuevas lecturas de un mundo olvidado." *Revista Mexicana de sociología* 68, no. 1 (January–March 2006): 103–35. https://www.redalyc.org/articulo.oa?id=32112598004.

Hoffmann, Odile, and Christian Rinaudo. "The Issue of Blackness and *Mestizaje* in Two Distinct Mexican Contexts: Veracruz and Costa Chica." *Latin American and Caribbean Ethnic Studies* 9, no. 2 (2014): 138–55. https://doi.org/10.1080/17442222.2013.874643.

Holland, Sharon Patricia. *The Erotic Life of Racism*. Durham, NC: Duke University Press, 2012.

Hooker, Juliet. "Race and the Space of Citizenship: The Mosquito Coast and the Place of Blackness and Indigeneity in Nicaragua." In *Blacks and Blackness in Central America: Between Race and Place*, edited by Lowell Gudmundson and Justin Wolfe, 246–77. Durham, NC: Duke University Press, 2010.

Instituto Nacional de Estadística y Geografía (INEGI). *Censo de Población y Vivienda 2020. Manual del entrevistador del cuestionario básico. Enumeración*. Mexico City, 2021.

———. *Encuesta Intercensal 2015. Manual del entrevistador*. Mexico City, 2014.

Instituto Veracruzano de la Cultura. "Casas de la cultura." Accessed October 1, 2015. http://litorale.com.mx/ivec/subdirecciones48.php?id=48.

———. "Inaugura IVEC el XXVI Festival Internacional Afrocaribeño 2022." Accessed September 6, 2023. https://saladeprensa.veracruzcultura.com/principal/inaugura-ivec-el-xxvi-festival-internacional-afrocaribeno-2022/.

———. "Misión, Visión y Principios." Accessed May 20, 2015. http://ivec.gob.mx/mision.php.

Jackson, John. *Real Black: Adventures in Racial Sincerity*. Chicago: University of Chicago Press, 2005.

Jerry, Anthony Russell. *Blackness in Mexico: Afro-Mexican Recognition and the Production of Citizenship in the Costa Chica*. Gainesville: University Press of Florida, 2023.

Johnson, E. Patrick. *Appropriating Blackness: Performance and the Politics of Authenticity*. Durham, NC: Duke University Press, 2003.

Jones, Jennifer Anne Meri. "'Mexicans Will Take the Jobs That Even Blacks Won't Do': An Analysis of Blackness, Regionalism and Invisibility in Contemporary Mexico." *Ethnic and Racial Studies* 36, no. 10 (2013): 1564–81. https://doi.org/10.1080/01419870.2013.783927.

Jones, Marcus D., and Charles Henry Rowell, eds. "Faces and Voices of Coyolillo, an Afromestizo Pueblo in Mexico." Special issue, *Callaloo* 27, no. 1 (Winter 2004). https://www.jstor.org/stable/i201352.

Jones, Marcus D., Charles H. Rowell, Edgar Cano, and Rodolfo Figueroa Martinez. "Rodolfo Figueroa Martinez." *Callaloo* 29, no. 2 (Spring 2006): 401–16. https://doi.org/10.1353/cal.2006.0104.

Juárez Hernández, Yolanda. *Persistencias culturales afrocaribeñas en Veracruz: Su proceso de conformación desde la Colonia hasta fines del siglo XIX*. Mexico: Gobierno del Estado de Veracruz, 2006.

Katze, Illona. *Casta Paintings: Images of Race in Eighteenth-Century Mexico*. New Haven, CT: Yale University Press, 2004.

Latinspots.com. "Barrios Indio-El Lado auténtico de México." Accessed September 29, 2023. https://www.latinspots.com/sp/comercial/barrios-indio-el-lado-autntico-de-mxico/25958.

Lewis, Laura. "Blacks, Black Indians, Afromexicans: The Dynamics of Race, Nation, and Identity in a Mexican *Moreno* Community (Guerrero)." *American Ethnologist* 27, no. 4 (2000): 898–926. https://www.jstor.org/stable/647400.

———. *Chocolate and Corn Flour: History, Race, and Place in the Making of "Black" Mexico*. Durham, NC: Duke University Press, 2012.

Lipsitz, George. "The Racialization of Space and the Spatialization of Race: Theorizing the Hidden Architecture of Landscape." *Landscape Journal* 26, no. 1 (2007): 10–23.

Lord, Albert B. *The Singer of Tales*. Cambridge, MA: Harvard University Press, 2000 [1960].

Loveman, Mara. *National Colors: Racial Classification and the State in Latin America*. Oxford: Oxford University Press, 2014.

Macías, José Miguel. *Diccionario Cubano, etimológico, crítico, razonado y comprensivo*. Veracruz: Trowbridge, 1858.

Madrid, Alejandro L., and Robin D. Moore. *Danzón: Circum-Caribbean Dialogues in Music and Dance*. New York: Oxford University Press, 2013.

Malcomson, Hettie. *Danzón Days: Age, Race, and Romance in Mexico*. Urbana: University of Illinois Press, 2023.

———. "The Expediency of Blackness: Racial Logics and Danzón in the Port of Veracruz, Mexico." In *Afro-Latin@s in Movement: Critical Approaches to Blackness and Transnationalism in the Americas*, edited by Petra R. Rivera-Rideau, Jennifer A. Jones, and Tianna S. Paschel, 35–60. New York: Palgrave Macmillan, 2016.

———. "New Generations, Older Bodies: *Danzón*, Age and 'Cultural Rescue' in the Port of Veracruz, Mexico." *Popular Music* 31, no. 2 (2012): 217–30. https://www.jstor.org/stable/23325758.

Martínez, María Elena. *Genealogical Fictions: Limpieza de Sangre, Religion, and Gender in Colonial Mexico*. Stanford, CA: Stanford University Press, 2008.

Martínez Maranto, Alfredo. "Dios pinta como quiere. Identidad y cultura en un pueblo afromestizo." In *Presencia africana en México*, coordinated by Luz María Martínez Montiel (Mexico, DF: Consejo Nacional Para la Cultura y las Artes, 1994), 525–73.

Mauss, Marcel. "Techniques of the Body." *Economy and Society* 2 (1973): 70–88. https://doi .org/10.1080/03085147300000003.

McKee, Kathryn B. "Local Color." In *The Companion to Southern Literature: Themes, Genres, Places, People, Movements, and Motifs*, edited by Joseph M. Flora and Lucinda Hardwick MacKethan, 449–42. Baton Rouge: Louisiana State University Press, 2002.

Meléndez Moré, Marleys Patricia. "Experiencias 'negras' y 'morenas.' Los procesos de adscripción de una comunidad afromexicana en Veracruz." In *Afros al Frente: Racismo, Resistencia y Lucha*, edited by Gerardo Cham, Gisela C. Fregoso, Wilfried Raussert, and Nicolas Rey, 63–90. Buenos Aires: CLACSO, 2024. https://doi.org/10.54871/ca24afid.

Méndez y Berrueta, Luis. "Bonfil Batalla, Guillermo (1935–1991)." *The Blackwell Encyclopedia of Sociology* (February 2007): 1–5. https://doi.org/10.1002/9781405165518.wbeosbo40.

Miller, Marilyn Grace. *Rise and Fall of the Cosmic Race: The Cult of Mestizaje in Latin America*. Austin: University of Texas Press, 2004.

———. "'The Soul Has No Color' but the Skin Does: *Angelitos Negros* and the Uses of Blackface on the Mexican Silver Screen, ca. 1950." In *Global Soundtracks: Worlds of Film Music*, edited by Mark Slobin, 241–57. Middletown, CT: Wesleyan University Press, 2008.

Monkevicius, Paola C., and Marta M. Maffia. "Memory and Ethnic Leadership among Afro-descendants and Africans in Argentina." *African and Black Diaspora: An International Journal* 8, no. 2 (2014): 188–98. https://doi.org/10.1080/17528631.2014.908546.

Mulholland, Mary-Lee. "Mariachi, Myths, and Mestizaje: Popular Culture and Mexican National Identity." *National Identities* 9, no. 3 (2007): 247–64. https://doi.org /10.1080/14608940701406237.

Ortiz Escamilla, Juan. "Las compañías milicianas de Veracruz. Del 'negro' al 'jarocho': Le construcción histórica de una identidad." *Ulúa* 8 (July–December 2006): 9–29. https:// doi.org/10.25009/urhsc.v0i8.1404.

Oseguera Rueda, Rubí, and Francisco García Ranz. "El repertorio tradicional de los sones jarochos de tarima: Práctica y uso actual." *Antropología: Interdisciplinaria del INAH*, no. 91 (2011): 123–27. https://revistas.inah.gob.mx/index.php/antropologia/article/view/2750.

Palmié, Stephan. *The Cooking of History: How Not to Study Afro-Cuban Religion*. Chicago: University of Chicago Press, 2013.

Paschel, Tianna. *Becoming Black Political Subjects: Movements and Ethno-racial Rights in Colombia and Brazil*. Princeton, NJ: Princeton University Press, 2018.

Pazos Cárdenas, Mateo. "Festival Internacional Afrocaribeño: Lo 'afro' en la construcción de identidades en Veracruz." *Revista Mexicana del Caribe*, no. 21 (January–June 2016): 140–71. https://doi.org/10.22403/UQROOMX/RMC21/05.

Pérez Montfort, Ricardo. "El 'negro' y la negritud en la formación del estereotipo del jarocho durante los siglos XIX y XX." In *Expresiones populares y estereotipos culturales en México. Siglos XIX y XX. Diez ensayos*, edited by Ricardo Pérez Montfort, 175–210. Mexico, DF: CIESAS, 2007.

Perlata, Leo. "El INEGI reveló nuestra pigmentocracia." *HuffPost Mexico*. June 20, 2017. www.huffingtonpost.com.mx/leo-peralta/el-inegi-revelo-nuestra-pigmentocracia_a _22488829/.

Phelan, Peggy. *Unmarked: The Politics of Performance*. London: Routledge, 1993.

Poblett Miranda, Martha, comp. *Cien viajeros en Veracruz. Crónicas y relatos*. Tomo 1–11. Xalapa: Gobierno del Estado de Veracruz, 1992.

Povinelli, Elizabeth A. "Routes/Worlds." *e-flux journal* 27 (2011): 1–12.

Prado Revuelta, Marcela. *Desde el portal: Crónicas de Veracruz.* Mexico, DF: Gobierno del Estado de Veracruz, 2009.

Premdas, Ralph. "Ethnicity and Identity in the Caribbean: Decentering a Myth." Working paper no. 234. Kellogg Institute for International Studies, University of Notre Dame, Indiana, 1996.

Prescott, William Hickling. *History of the Conquest of Mexico.* Boston: Phillips, Sampson, and Co., 1856.

Quintero, Michael Birenbaum. *Rites, Rights and Rhythms: A Genealogy of Musical Meaning in Colombia's Black Pacific.* Oxford: Oxford University Press, 2018.

Ramsey, Paulette. *Afro-Mexican Constructions of Diaspora, Gender, Identity, and Nation.* Kingston, Jamaica: University of the West Indies Press, 2016.

Rejano, Juan. "La esfinge mestiza, 1939." In *Cien viajeros en Veracruz: Crónicas y relatos,* tomo 9, *1928–1983,* edited by Martha Poblett Miranda, 199–222. Xalapa: Gobierno del Estado de Veracruz, 1992.

Restall, Matthew. "Black Conquistadors: Armed Africans in Early Spanish America." *The Americas* 57, no. 2 (2000): 171–205. https://doi.org/10.1353/tam.2000.0015.

Rhode, Robert D. *Setting in the American Short Story of Local Color, 1865–1900.* The Hague: Mouton, 1975.

Rinaudo, Christian. *Afromestizaje y fronteras étnicas: Una Mirada desde el Puerto de Veracruz.* Translated by Lorraine Karnoouh. Xalapa, Veracruz: Universidad Veracruzana, 2012.

———. "Más allá de la 'identidad negra': Mestizaje y dinámicas raciales." In *Mestizaje, diferencia y nación: Lo "negro" en América Central y el Caribe,* coordinated by Elisabeth Cunin, 225–66. Mexico, DF: Instituto Nacional de Antropología e Historia; Mexico, DF: Centro de Estudios Mexicanos y Centroamericanos; Mexico, DF: Universidad Autónoma de Mexico-Centro de Investigaciones sobre América Latina y el Caribe; Mexico, DF: Institut de Recherche pour le Développement, 2010.

Rodríguez, Hipólito. "Veracruz: Del Puerto de la conquista al de la independencia y la modernidad." In *La Habana—Veracruz / Veracruz—La Habana: Las dos orillas,* coordinated by Bernardo García and Sergio Guerra, 65–86. Mexico: Universidad Veracruzana / Universidad de la Habana, 2002.

Romero, José. *Danzonero.* 2012. Veracruz: Atracadero Films, NGA Producciones, Sociedad Baluarte, and Sistemas Contino.

Saldívar, Emiko, Patricio Solís, and Erika Arenas. "Consideraciones metodológicas para el conteo de la población afromexicana en el Censo 2020." *Coyuntura Demográfica,* no. 14 (2018): 47–54.

Sansone, Livio. *Blackness without Ethnicity: Constructing Race in Brazil.* New York: Palgrave Macmillan, 2003.

Sartorius, Carl Christian. *Mexico about 1850.* Stuttgart: F. A. Brockhaus Komm.-Gesch., 1961 [1858].

Santana Pinho, Patricia de. *Mama Africa: Reinventing Blackness in Bahia.* Durham, NC: Duke University Press, 2010.

Schwaller, Robert. *Géneros de Gente in Early Colonial Mexico: Defining Racial Difference.* Tulsa: University of Oklahoma Press, 2016.

Serna Herrera, Juan Manuel de la. "Indios, pardos, mulatos y negros esclavos. Lo cotidiano en el Puerto de Veracruz." In *Pautas de Convivencia étnica en la América Latina colonial: (indios, negritos, mulato, pardos y esclavos)*, coordinated by Juan Manuel de la Serna Herrera, 91–110. Mexico: Universidad Nacional Autónoma de México: Centro Coordinador y Difusor de Estudios Latinoamericanos: Gobierno del Estado de Guanajuato, 2005.

Siemens, Alfred H. *Between the Summit and the Sea: Central Veracruz in the Nineteenth Century*. Vancouver: University of British Columbia Press, 1990.

Sluyter, Andrew. *Black Ranching Frontiers: African Cattle Herders of the Atlantic World, 1500–1900*. New Haven, CT: Yale University Press, 2012.

Spacio Random. "Plasma INDIO el lado más auténtico de La Huaca en un mural." Accessed September 20, 2023. https://spaciorandom.wordpress.com/2016/08/08/plasma-indio-el-lado-mas-autentico-de-la-huaca-en-un-mural/.

Stutzman, Ronald. "El Mestizaje: An All-Inclusive Ideology of Exclusion." In *Cultural Transformations and Ethnicity in Modern Ecuador*, edited by Norman E. Whitten Jr., 45–94. Urbana-Champaign: University of Illinois Press, 1981.

Sue, Christina A. *Land of the Cosmic Race: Race Mixture, Racism, and Blackness in Mexico*. Oxford: Oxford University Press, 2013.

———. "Racial Ideologies, Racial-Group Boundaries, and Racial Identity in Veracruz, Mexico." *Latin American and Caribbean Ethnic Studies* 5, no. 3 (2010): 273–99. https://doi.org/10.1080/17442222.2010.513829.

Taylor, Diana. *The Archive and the Repertoire: Performing Cultural Memory in the Americas*. Durham, NC: Duke University Press, 2003.

Telles, Edward. *Pigmentocracies: Ethnicity, Race, and Color in Latin America*. Chapel Hill: University of North Carolina Press, 2014.

Trejo, Guillermo, and Melina Altamirano. "The Mexican Color Hierarchy: How Race and Skin Tone Still Define Life Chances 200 Years after Independence." In *The Double Bind: The Politics of Race and Class Inequalities in the Americas*, edited by Juliet Hooker and Alvin B. Tillery Jr., 1–14. Washington, DC: American Political Science Association, 2016.

Trouillot, Michel-Rolph. "The Caribbean Region: An Open Frontier in Anthropological Theory." *Annual Review of Anthropology* 21 (1992): 19–42. https://www.jstor.org/stable/2155979.

———. *Silencing the Past: Power and the Production of History*. Boston: Beacon Press, 1995.

Turino, Thomas. "Nationalism and Latin American Music: Selected Case Studies and Theoretical Considerations." *Latin American Music Review* 24, no. 2 (Autumn–Winter 2003): 169–209. https://www.jstor.org/stable/3598738.

Turner, Frederick W. *A Border of Blue: Along the Gulf of Mexico from the Keys to the Yucatán*. New York: Henry Holt & Company, 1993.

Vasconcelos, José. *La Raza Cósmica / The Cosmic Race*. Translated by Didier Tisdel Jaén. Baltimore: Johns Hopkins University Press, 1997.

Velázquez, María Elisa. Introduction to *Debates históricos contemporáneos: Africanos y afrodescendientes en México y Centroamérica*. Coordinated by María Elisa Velázquez, 13–31. Mexico, DF: Instituto Nacional de Antropología e Historia; Mexico, DF: Centro de Estudios Mexicanos y Centroamericanos; Mexico, DF: Universidad Autónoma de Mexico-Centro de Investigaciones sobre América Latina y el Caribe; Mexico, DF: Institut de Recherche pour le Développement, 2011.

Velázquez, María Elisa, and Gabriela Iturralde Nieto. *Afrodescendientes en México: Una historia de silencio y discriminación*. Mexico, DF: Consejo Nacional para Prevenir la Discriminación, 2012.

Velázquez Mabarak Sonderegger, Melba Ali. "El fandango jarocho y el movimiento jaranero: Un recorrido histórico." *Balajú: Revista de cultura y comunicación* 10 (2019): 4–30. https://doi.org/10.25009/blj.v0i10.2566.

Vincent, Ted. "The Blacks Who Freed Mexico." *Journal of Negro History* 79, no. 3 (Summer 1994): 257–76. https://www.jstor.org/stable/2717506.

Vinson, Ben, III. *Bearing Arms for His Majesty: The Free-Colored Militia in Colonial Mexico*. Stanford, CA: Stanford University Press, 2002.

——. *Before Mestizaje: The Frontiers of Race and Caste in Colonial Mexico*. New York: Cambridge University Press, 2018.

——. "Fading from Memory: Historiographical Reflections on the Afro-Mexican Presence." *Review of Black Political Economy* 33, no. 1 (2005): 59–72.

——. "Introduction: Black Mexico and the Historical Discipline." In *Black Mexico: Race and Society from Colonial to Modern Times*, edited by Ben Vinson III and Matthew Restall, 1–18. Albuquerque: University of New Mexico Press, 2009.

Wade, Peter. "Multiculturalismo y Racismo." *Revista Colombiana de antropología* 47, no. 2 (2011): 15–35. https://doi.org/10.22380/2539472X.956.

——. "Rethinking 'Mestizaje': Ideology and Lived Experience." *Journal of Latin American Studies* 37, no. 2 (2005): 239–57.

Warner, Michael. *Publics and Counterpublics*. Princeton, NJ: Princeton University Press, 2005.

Warren, Jonathan, and Christina A. Sue. "Comparative Racisms: What Anti-racists Can Learn from Latin America." *Ethnicities* 11, no. 1 (2011): 32–58. https://doi.org/10.1177/1468796810388699.

Whitten, Norman E., Jr. "The Longue Durée of Racial Fixity and the Transformative Conjunctures of Racial Blending." *Journal of Latin American and Caribbean Anthropology* 12, no. 2 (2007): 356–83. https://doi.org/10.1525/jlat.2007.12.2.356.

Whitten, Norman E., Jr., and Arlene Torres, eds. *Blackness in Latin America and the Caribbean*. Vol. 1. Bloomington: Indiana University Press, 1998.

Wirtz, Kristina. *Performing Afro-Cuba: Image, Voice, Spectacle in the Making of Race and History*. Chicago: University of Chicago Press, 2014.

Wood, Andrew Grant. "Carnaval en Veracruz: Celebraciones públicas, identidad y el incio del turismo." *Ulúa* 3 (2004): 139–74.

——. "Four Times Heroic." *Peace Review* 10, no. 4 (1998): 613–17. https://doi.org/10.1080/10402659808426213.

——. "On the Selling of Rey Momo: Early Tourism and the Marketing of Carnival in Veracruz." In *Holiday in Mexico: Critical Reflections on Tourism and Tourist Encounters*, edited by Dina Berger and Andrew Grant Wood, 77–106. Durham, NC: Duke University Press, 2010.

——. "Viva la Revolución Social!: Postrevolutionary Tenant Protest and State Housing Reform in Veracruz, Mexico." In *Cities of Hope: People, Protests, and Progress in Urbanizing Latin America, 1870–1930*, edited by Ronn F. Pineo and James A. Baer, 88–128. Boulder, CO: Westview Press, 1998.

Yúdice, George. *The Expediency of Culture: Uses of Culture in the Global Era.* Durham, NC: Duke University Press, 2004.

Zamudio-Zaudio, T. J., A. Garrido-Alfonseca, D. Tenorio, and M. Jiménez-Reyes. "Characterization of 16th and 18th Century Building Materials from Veracruz City, Mexico." *Microchemical Journal* 74, no. 1 (February 2003): 83–91. https://doi.org/10.1016/S0026-265X(02)00172-8.

INDEX

academics, in revitalization of son jarocho, 61, 63, 65–66, 78

African, vs. Black, use of terms, 12

African contribution, use of term, 12

African diaspora, 8, 10, 12, 17, 26, 120, 148

Africanity, 8, 10, 99

African Presence in México, The (exhibition), 5

Afro-Andalusian Caribbean, 14, 22, 54, 97, 147

Afro-Antillean music, 67, 105–7

Afrobolivianity, 98

Afro-Caribbean Festival. *See* International Afro-Caribbean Festival

Afro-Caribbean heritage: vs. Afro-Mexican heritage, 16; embrace of, vs. Black identity, 3; meaning and use of term, 9, 12, 60; in Veracruzan Blackness, 16–18

Afrocaribeño. *See* International Afro-Caribbean Festival

Afro-Cuban dance. *See* danzón

Afro-descendants: vs. Black people, 134–35; meaning and use of term, 9–13; as preferred term in Latin America, 142–43; in Spanish conquest and colonization, 32, 36–37, 158n8. *See also* Afro-Mexicans

Afrodescendientes en México, 137–38

afrojarochos, 48–50, 150–51

afromestizos, 2, 6, 12, 157n63

Afro-Mexicans (Afro-descendant Mexicans): vs. Afro-Caribbeans, 16; vs. Black Mexicans, 13; in census surveys (*see* census); critics of term, 12–13, 156n23; geographic distribution of, 2; meaning and use of terms for, 9–14; political recognition of, 3, 7–8, 10, 146–47; recruitment into category of, 137–39

Afro-Mexican studies, history of, 10–13, 19

Aguirre Beltrán, Gonzalo, 11–12, 19, 37

Ajón, Ramona, 39

Alcántara, Sigfrido, 106

Alcántara López, Álvaro, 63, 66

alegría, 97. *See also* happiness

Alemán Velasco, Miguel, 33

Alma de Veracruz (group), 106, 114

Alvarado, 2

Amapa, 2

ancestry. *See* Black ancestry; Cuban ancestry

Andalusian Caribbean, 54. *See also* Afro-Andalusian Caribbean

Anderson, Benedict, 60

Angosto-Ferrández, Luis, 124

anthems, 101, 166n17

anti-Blackness, 26–27, 120–21

antojitos, 44, 133

Aparicio, Frances, 133

appearance. *See* physical appearance

Appiah, Kwame, 98

appropriation, 26, 74–75

Arce, B. Christine, 32

archives: of Afrocaribeño, 50–51; bodies as, 89; of Inquisition, 62–63; national, 62; and repertoire, 50, 62–63, 89–90

Arenas, Erika, 144–45
art, Black, 75
Asociación de Vecinos del Barrio de La Huaca, 31
Atlantic, Black, 16–17
authenticity: and appropriation, 74–75; in popular culture, 43–44; racial, 164n14

ballet folklórico, 88–89, 90, 92
Barrio de La Huaca. *See* La Huaca
Basso, Keith, 17
Before Mestizaje (Vinson), 14
Benítez-Rojo, Antonio, 99
Biart, Lucian, 37, 39
Black: capitalization of term, 12, 166n4, 167n18, 168n31; in census surveys, 13, 27, 141; as color label vs. racial identity, 11, 121, 134, 138, 167n18; feeling and acting vs. being, 98–99; meaning and use of term, 9–12, 166n4
Black ancestry, 119–36; Afro-descendancy and, 134–35; in blood, 124–31; in census surveys, 141–43; impact on identity, 119–21; in skin color, 122–23, 130–31
Black art, 75
Black Atlantic, 16–17
Black identity: vs. Blackness, 3, 8–9; chasing, 2–3; culture, history, and traditions as criteria for, 27, 140–44; meaning and use of term, 10; urban/rural divide in, 2
Black in Latin America (docuseries), 126–27
Black Mexicans: vs. Afro-Mexicans, 13; bonds between Indigenous peoples and, 68; claims about lack of in Veracruz, 1–3, 130; geographic distribution of, 1–3; meaning and use of term, 10–11, 13. *See also* Afro-Mexicans
Blackness: in absence of Black people, 75, 98; vs. Africanity, 8; vs. Black identity, 3, 8–9; as Caribbean, 11; without ethnicity, 99; as foreign, 56–57; hegemonic, 9; identifying *with* vs. *as*, 8, 13, 18, 26; as inheritance, 9; in jarocho identity, 3, 7, 147–48; as local color, 14–19, 41; meaning and use of term, 9, 13–14; and mestizaje, 7, 19; Mexicanness in relation to, 7, 13–14; as qualia, 18; as regional, 16; terminology of, 9–14. *See also* Veracruzan Blackness
Blackness in Mexico (Jerry), 13
Black popular culture, 74–75
Black race (raza negra), 134–35
Black stereotypes, 74, 97
Black towns, 30
Blanchard, P. P., 6
Blanco, Andrés Eloy, 124

blood: in belonging, 125–28, 131; Black ancestry in, 124–31; interchangeability of race and, 125; metaphor of drop of, 124–28; metaphor of rhythm in, 80; purity of, 127, 129
Boca del Río, 47, 102, 103, 105
bodies, as archives, 89
Bolivia, 98
Bonfil Batalla, Guillermo, 53
Bordat, Elodie, 52
Bosé, Miguel, 103
Bourbon Reforms, 37
Bourdieu, Pierre, 9
Brazil, 99
Brown, Jacqueline Nassy, 17
Brubaker, Rogers, 10–11, 155n13
Buena Vista Social Club (band), 39

Caballo Viejo, El, 112–14
cafecitos, 121–22
Café con Leche (Wright), 124
"café con leche" metaphor, 124
Café de la Parroquia, 101
Café La Merced, 1, 110
Calderón de la Barca, Frances (Frances Erskine Inglis), 33, 159n13
Camacho, Eleana Deanda, 62
Campana, La. *See* Plazuela de la Campana
Cantarell, Emilio, 39
Caribbean: Afro-Andalusian, 14, 22, 54, 97, 147; vs. Afro-Caribbean, meaning of, 60; Blackness as, 11; diversity of, 61; in lo caribeño, 10, 11, 16; in third root, 11; in Veracruzan Blackness, 16, 30; Veracruz as part of, 53–54, 57–58, 60–61. *See also* Afro-Caribbean
Carnival, in Veracruz, 45, 96, 102–5
Carpentier, Alejo, 62
Castañeda, Angela, 16
casta system, 6, 14, 37, 38, 43, 69
cattle, 36
censorship, in Inquisition, 62–63
census and mid-census surveys of 2015 and 2020, 137–48; Black ancestry in, 141–43; Black population as percentage in, 3, 140, 143, 147, 158n73; culture, history, and traditions criteria of, 27, 140–45, 147–48; first use of Afro-Mexican category in, 3, 7, 137; impacts of, 23, 25; interviewer's manual for, 140–42, 168n7; multiple terms for Black identity in, 13, 138, 140, 143, 158n71; pilot study poster for, 137–40, 141; possible responses to, 140–44; publication of results of, 140
Centro Cultural Atarazanas, 50–51

Centro Veracruzano de las Artes (CEVART), 50
Chacalapa, 2
Chalchihuecan, 32
Chaunu, Huguette, 54
Chaunu, Pierre, 54
chilangos, 42–43, 133, 161n47
chinos, 120, 129, 130, 150, 166n5
Choreographing Mexico (Cuellar), 89
choreography, in talleres, 79, 81–82, 87–91, 87*fig*.
chuchumbé, el (dance), 62
Chumley, Lily Hope, 18
Cien viajeros en Veracruz (anthology), 33
City Museum of Veracruz, 5–7; on jarochos, 6–7, 36; renovation of, 54; on slavery, 54
classes. *See* talleres
clothing, jarocho: in talleres, 88–89, 91–92; in El Vate's videos, 41; white, 6, 38, 40, 88–89
Coahuila, 138, 165n4
Cohen, Theodore, 14, 18–19, 51, 53, 140, 166n17
colonization. *See* Spanish conquest and colonization
color, local, Blackness as, 14–19, 41
color, skin: Black ancestry in, 122–23, 130–31; Black as color vs. racial identity, 11, 121, 134, 138, 167n18; hierarchy of, 121–22, 144; "irregular," 62; of jarochos, 31–32, 38–40; meaning and use of term, 11; of morenos, 122, 129–30; in pigmentocracies, 122, 144; vs. race, 11, 140–41; and social mobility, 144–45
CONACULTA. *See* National Council for Culture and Arts
CONAPRED. *See* National Council to Prevent Discrimination
conquest. *See* Spanish conquest
constitution, Mexican, 3
constitution, Veracruzan, 146–47
contredanse, 74
convivencia, 43–44, 66, 97
Cortés, Hernán, 32
Costa Chica, 77, 98, 138
Costa Grande, 165n4
costeños, 6, 138, 141
cover charges, 112, 114
COVID-19 pandemic, 149–50, 162n29, 166n24
cowboy culture, 6, 36
Cox, Aimee, 89
Cruz-Carretero, Sagrario, 126, 139, 167n18
Cuba: in Festival de son Tradicional Veracruzano de Raiz Cubana, 59–60, 59*fig*.; IVEC forums on, 60; and jarochos in film, 39; location of, xv*map*; origins of el chuchumbé dance in, 62. *See also* danzón

Cuban ancestry, 126, 129–30, 134, 139
Cuellar, Manuel R., 14, 89
cultura, la, 49, 77, 161n7
cultural appropriation, 26, 74–75
cultural centers: IVEC's role in, 52; jarocho publics in, 19; location of, xv*map*, 52
cultural imperialism, 9
cultural policy of Mexico, 52–53
cultural scene, IVEC as agent in, 50–55
culture: in census survey of 2015, 27, 140–45; popular, 43–44, 74–75

dance and dancing: Black stereotypes about, 74; in colonial era, 62; government support for, 105–6, 114; happiness through public, 97, 105–15; paired, 63; sites of, xv*map*; workshops on (*see* talleres). See also *specific types*
dance partners, 113
danzón and danzoneros, 87*fig*.; author's involvement with, 24; as Black art form, 75; definition of, 22; in jarocho publics, 76; origins in Cuba, 78, 85–86; origins in La Huaca, 45; in performing groups, 78–79; talleres on, 76–79
Danzonera Manzanita (band), 114
Danzonero (documentary), 106
Dawdy, Shannon, 20, 48, 49
décimas, 65
defeños, 161n47
desjarretadera, 36
Diccionario cubana (Macías), 35
Dictamen, El (newspaper), 103
Dike, Donald, 14–15
discipline, in talleres, 86–90
distancing: discursive, 131; racial, 3, 26, 35, 69; temporal, 131
domestic workers, 51
Driessen, Henk, 16–17
drums, 64–65

effortlessness, 75
El CaSon cultural center, 66
El Coyolillo, 2
elective Africanity, 99
El Puerto, 1. *See also* Veracruz (city)
emplacement, 18
English country dance, 85–86
esfinge mestiza, La (Rejano), 16
essentialism, 43, 74–75, 98
ethnicity: Blackness without, 99; political recognition of Afro-Mexican as, 3, 7–8, 10; process of emergence of categories of, 10

ethnographic problems, 25
ethnoracial identity, jarocho as, 37, 40, 69, 74, 148
ethnoregional identity, jarocho as, 32, 69, 74, 138
euromestizos, 12
expropriation, 74–75

Facebook, 31–32, 33
fado, 100
fandangos: in anthem of Veracruz, 101; author's
    involvement with, 23–24; at Festival de la
    Gorda y Picada, 44; in film, 39; hosted by
    Mono Blanco, 61–66, 78; meaning and use
    of term, 164n9; popular vs. real, 39. See also
    son jarocho
fandangueros: vs. danzoneros, 78–79; in film,
    39; in jarocho publics, 76; meaning and use
    of term, 22, 65, 164n9. See also son jarocho;
    talleres
festivals: Carnival, 45, 96, 102–5; Festival de
    la Gorda y Picada, 44, 133; Festival de
    son Tradicional Veracruzano de Raiz
    Cubana, 59–60, 59fig.; in La Huaca, 44–45;
    International Festival of the Desert of the
    Lions, 61–62; nostalgia in, 44. See also
    International Afro-Caribbean Festival
fictions, genealogical, 127
fictive kin, 69
Fields, Barbara, 125
Fields, Karen, 125
Figueroa Hernández, Rafael, 45, 61, 65, 66, 77,
    168n30
film, jarochos in, 38–40
Finding Afro-Mexico (Cohen), 14
first root, 16
FitzPatrick, James A., 40
folklorization, of son jarocho, 65
Fonoteca Nacional, 58–59
food festivals, 44
foreign, Blackness as, 56–57
four Fs approach to multiculturalism, 145–46

García Cabrera, Erandi, 84
García Cortés, Miguel, 109–10, 112–15, 150,
    166n24
García de León, Antonio, 54
García Peña, Lorgia, 9
Garrido, Juan, 158n8
garrocha, 36
Gates, Henry Louis, Jr., 126–27
Geertz, Clifford, 42
gender: of jarochas, 32, 158n5; of taller teachers, 79
genealogical fictions, 127

genetics, and Black ancestry, 122, 130
gente de color (people of color), 2, 121
Gilroy, Paul, 16
Godreau, Isar, 17–18, 115, 131
Golash-Boza, Tanya, 11
González, Anita, 42
Gonzalez, Martha, 66, 164n54
gorditas, 44
Gottfried, Jessica, 66
government. See Mexico; specific institutions
Grant, Carl, 145
Gray, Lila Ellen, 100
group identity, race vs. color in, 11
groupism, 10, 15, 155n13
groupness, 10–11, 15, 24, 124–25, 147, 150, 155n13
Guerrero, 37, 49, 77, 98, 138
gurumbé, 84–85
Gutiérrez, Laura G., 39
Gutiérrez Silva, Gilberto "El Mono," 62–65

Hacking, Ian, 142
hair: Black ancestry in, 122–25, 129–30; chino,
    129, 130, 150; in jarocho stereotype, 31–32
Haiti, 85
Hall, Stuart, 8, 60–61, 70, 74–75, 100, 143
happiness of jarochos, 96–116; during Carnival,
    96, 102–5; in lyrics, 99–102; as obligation,
    96–97, 105; as performance, 96, 98; through
    public dancing, 97, 105–15; regionalized
    Blackness and, 98–99; stereotype of, 6, 97; as
    work, 97–98
Harkness, Nicholas, 18
Hartigan, John, 15
Heck, Moritz, 98
hegemonic blackness, 9
herding, 35–36
heritage, meaning and use of term, 10
Heroic Veracruz, 33, 159n15
hierarchy: color, 121–22, 144; racial, 119
Holland, Sharon Patricia, 125
Hooker, Juliet, 17
Huaca, La. See La Huaca
hypodecent, one-drop rule of, 126–27

Iberian Peninsula, 127
identity: vs. heritage, meaning and use of
    terms, 10; and representation, 100.
    See also specific types
imperialism, cultural, 9
INBAL. See National Institute of Fine Arts and
    Literature
Indigenous heritage, 38, 138

Indigenous peoples: bonds between Black people and, 68; enslavement of, 68; as mestizos, 6, 14; as mulatos, 37; purity of blood of, 127

Indio (beer), 132, 132*fig.*

indiomestizos, 12

INEGI. *See* National Institute of Statistics and Geography

Inglis, Frances Erskine. *See* Calderón de la Barca, Frances

innateness, 80–84

Inquisition, 62–63

Instituto Nacional de Antropología e Historia (INAH). *See* National Institute for Anthropology and History

Instituto Veracruzano de la Cultura (IVEC). *See* Veracruz Institute of Culture

Intergenerational Social Mobility Module (MMSI), 144–45

interlocutors, 153n1; Alberto, 82; Alfredo, 67–70, 97, 100, 115, 149; Alicia, 82; Andrés, 99–100; Angel, 82; Blanca, 42–44, 133; Carla, 111–12; Carlos, 82; Celia, 88, 91; Chucho, 82, 84, 110–11, 115, 125–26, 150; Elena, 81; Ellery, 121–22, 131, 135; El Vate Veracruzano, 31–32, 34, 40–42, 126, 158n5; Enrique, 82; Esme, 81, 85, 91; Fidel, 122–26, 128, 130–31, 134; Flor, 81, 87–88, 89; Fran, 81; Gabriel, 82; Guillermo, 82; Javier, 50–52; Jorge, 81, 90; Juana, 82–85, 88–91; Juancho, 129; Julia, 51–52; Justo, 82, 84, 125–26; Karen, 128–30; Lena, 82; Lino, 81; Luna, 81, 113; Manuel, 82, 84, 90; Nico, 82–84, 88–90; Óscar, 109–11; Pablo, 81–83, 85–92; Ramón, 38–40, 130–31, 135; Ricardo, 1–4; Robert, 117–18; Rosita, 82, 88–90

interludes, 29, 47, 72, 94–95, 117–18

International Afro-Caribbean Festival (Afrocaribeño), 54–58; of 2011, 24, 55–56, 56*fig.*; of 2012, 56; of 2015, 66, 99; of 2016 (canceled), 57–58; of 2017, 146; of 2020, 149, 162n29; of 2022, 55; academic programs of, 51, 55, 57, 58; archives of, 50–51; Blackness as foreign in, 56–57; government role in, 54–55, 57–58; mission of, 51, 55; posters for, 21*fig.*, 55–56

International Decade for Peoples of African Descent, UN, 140

International Festival of the Desert of the Lions, 61–62

"irregular color," 62

IVEC. *See* Veracruz Institute of Culture

Jackson, John, 164n14

jara, 35–36

jaranero movement, 61, 65, 77

jaraneros, 61–66

jarocho(s), 30–46; afrojarocho past of, 48–50; Black identity of, lack of, 3, 7; Blackness as tool of, 98; Blackness in identity of, 3, 7, 147–48; in casta system, 6, 37, 38, 43, 69; changes in signifiers of, 37–42; vs. chilangos, 42–43, 161n47; City Museum on, 6–7, 36; clothing of, 6, 38, 40, 41; diversity of, 31–32; etymology of term, 6, 34–37; happiness of (*see* happiness); Indigenous heritage of, 38; meaning and use of term, 6, 33–34, 69, 138; negative associations of men vs. women as, 158n5; performing identity of, 40–46; physical appearance of, 31–32, 38–40; as racial vs. regional identity, 3–4, 6–7, 32, 69; recruitment into Afro-Mexican category, 138–39; reputation of, 80, 96–98; "typical," 31–34 (*see also* stereotype)

jarocho publics, 19–25; Blackness in, 22–23; gathering places for, 19–22; language and discourse of, 19–22; main groups of, 22; meaning and use of term, 19–20, 76; racial distancing and, 69; shared practices of, 19–22; in talleres, 76

jarocho sones. *See* son jarocho

Jerry, Anthony, 2–3, 12–14

Johnson, E. Patrick, 148

Jones, Jennifer Anne Meri, 2

joy. *See* happiness

Juventud Sonera (band), 99–100

karaoke, 101

kin: fictive, 69; in metaphors of blood, 125

La Antigua, 159n9

La Huaca: Blackness in, 17, 45; festivals in, 44–45; history of neighborhood, 44–45; mural in, 132–33, 132*fig.*; Peregrino family in, 131–35

Land of the Cosmic Race (Sue), 13

Lara, Agustín, 101–2, 132–33, 132*fig.*

lassoing, 36

learning aids, 79

learning, through leisure, 75, 84–86. *See also* talleres

lecheros, 124

leisure: happiness and, 97; learning through, 75, 84–86

Lewis, Laura, 15–16, 49, 77, 161n7

Life in Mexico (Calderón de la Barca), 159n13

limpieza de sangre, 127, 129

Linati, Claudio, 6

Lipschutz, Alejandro, 121
Lipsitz, George, 17
liveliness, 96–98
liveness, 89–90, 164n14
lo africano, 12
lo afro, 10, 11, 12
local color, Blackness as, 14–19, 41
local color genre of writing, 14–15, 41–42
lo caribeño, 10, 11, 16
lo negro, 10, 12, 147
looping effect, 17–18, 34, 142
López Obrador, Andres Manuel, 150
Lord, Albert B., 70
Loveman, Mara, 140
lyrics: of anthem of Veracruz, 101; of "El Chuchumbé," 62–63; and happiness, 99–102; learning, 90

Macías, José Miguel, 35
Malcomson, Hettie, 49, 80
maps, xv
marginalized voices, in archives, 63
maroons, 1–2
Martinez, Maria Elena, 127
Martínez Montiel, Luz María, 12, 53–54
mascogos, 138, 141, 165n4
mass media, jarochos in, 38–39
memory, 70, 100
mestizaje (racial mixture): Black blood in, 127, 129–30; "café con leche" metaphor for, 124; in La Huaca, 45; meaning and use of term, 13–14; vs. mulataje, 16; tripartite, 49; understandings of Blackness in, 7, 13–14, 19
mestizos, 6
Mexican census. See census
Mexican nationalism: Blackness and, 13–14; in lyrics, 101; role of culture in, 52–53
Mexicanness, Blackness in relation to, 7, 13–14
Mexican Revolution, 38, 53
Mexico: cultural policy of, 52–53; national anthem of, 101; National Archives of, 62; state role in third root, 50–59; state support for music in public spaces, 105–6, 114
Mexico City, chilangos from, 42–43, 133, 161n47
Miguel. See García Cortés, Miguel
militias, 36–37
MMSI. See Intergenerational Social Mobility Module
Mono Blanco (band), 61–66, 78
morenos: meaning and use of term, 15, 138; skin color of, 122, 129–30
Morrison, Toni, 75

movimiento jaranero. See jaranero movement
múcara stone, 47, 161n1
mulataje, 16
mulato pardo, 37
mulatos, 6, 12, 16, 37
Mulholland, Mary-Lee, 166n18
multiculturalism: four Fs approach to, 145–46; limitations of, 8, 145; origins of, 49; pringa in, 128
murals, 132–33, 132fig.
music: Black stereotypes about skills in, 74; happiness through, 97; in public spaces, government support for, 105–6, 114–15. See also lyrics; specific genres
music festivals. See specific festivals
music workshops. See talleres

national anthem, Mexican, 101
National Archives, 62
National Council for Culture and Arts (CONACULTA), 53–54, 138
National Council to Prevent Discrimination (CONAPRED), 137–38
National Institute for Anthropology and History (INAH), 51, 53, 137
National Institute of Fine Arts and Literature (INBAL), 53
National Institute of Statistics and Geography (INEGI), 138, 140–41, 143–44
nationalism. See Mexican nationalism
negritos, 1
negritos mexicanos, 121, 126
negritude movements, 100
Negritud en Veracruz, La (book), 150–51
negro(s): in census surveys, 138, 140–41, 158n71; as color label vs. racial identity, 11, 121, 134, 138, 168n31; meaning and use of term, 2, 11–12, 121; vs. morenos, 15, 138. See also Afro-Mexicans; Black
Negro Peregrino y su Trío, El (group), 133
Neighbors' Association of La Huaca, 31
New Spain, 32, 36–37, 62
nonblackness, 13
nonracism, 121
nostalgia, 44, 92, 101
Nuestra Tercera Raíz. See "Our Third Root"

Oakland Museum of California, 5
Oaxaca, 2, 37, 98, 138
one-drop rule, 126–27
Ortiz Escamilla, Juan, 36–37
"Our Third Root" program, 53–54, 64

Pacific Coast, 15, 18–19, 98
paired dance, 63
Palmera, La, 88
Palmié, Stephan, 8, 25, 119–20
pandemic, COVID-19, 149–50, 162n29, 166n24
Pardavé, Joaquin, 39
Parque Zamora, 114
past, the: afrojarocho, 48–50; flourishing of, 67–71; presentation of, 61–67; restoration of, 48; useful, 35, 159n20
Pazos Cárdenas, Mateo, 55
people of color, 2, 121
percussion, 64–65
Peregrino family, 133–35, 168n30. *See also* Toña la Negra
Pérez Fraga, Luis Antonio, 104
Pérez Montfort, Ricardo, 38
perfection, through practice, 75
performance: in Blackness, 14; happiness as, 96, 98; of jarocho identity, 40–46; by jarocho publics, 22; by talleres, 90–93; talleres in origins of performing groups, 78–79
PERLA. *See* Project on Ethnicity and Race in Latin America
physical appearance (phenotypes): of Afro-Mexicans, diversity of, 31–32, 137–38; color as shorthand for, 11; in jarocho stereotype, 31–32, 38–40; vs. race, 140–41; and social mobility, 144–45. *See also* color; hair
picadas, 44
pigmentocracies, 122, 144
place: African sounding names for, 2; local colorist writing on, 14–15, 41–42; in racialization, 15, 17; in Veracruzan Blackness, 14–19
Plazuela de la Campana, 55, 59*fig.*; Don Miguel's role in, 109–10, 112–15, 166n24; after pandemic, 150; public dancing in, 105–15, 108*fig.*, 113*fig.* See also *specific events*
población negra de México, La (Aguirre Beltrán), 19
popular culture: authenticity in, 43–44; Black, 74–75
Port, the: as nickname, 1; in Veracruzan Blackness, 16–17. *See also* Veracruz (city)
Portugal, 100
Povinelli, Elizabeth, 70
practice, perfection through, 75
Pregoneros del Recuerdo (band), 24, 59*fig.*, 67, 72
Premdas, Ralph, 61
Prescott, William, 32, 159n13
pringa, 124–28

Project on Ethnicity and Race in Latin America (PERLA), 121, 144
protest songs, 63
pseudonyms, 153n1. *See also* interlocutors
Psy, 104–5
public squares, 19
pueblos negros, 30
purity, blood, 127, 129

qualia, Blackness as, 18
Quiahuitzlan, 159n9

race: Black (raza negra), 134–35; vs. color and phenotype, 11, 140–41; denial of existence in Mexico, 121; interchangeability of blood and, 125; as social construction, 15; space in relation to, 17–18
racial authenticity, 164n14
racial distancing, 3, 26, 35, 69
racial fluidity, 11
racial hierarchy, 119
racial identity, vs. color label, *negro* as, 11, 121, 134, 138, 168n31
racialization: place in, 15, 17; of space, 17–18
racial localization, 15–19
racial scripts, 28, 93, 115
racial sincerity, 89, 164n14
racism, denial of existence in Mexico, 121
Ramsey, Paulette, 154n5
Raza Cósmica, La (Vasconcelos), 127–28
raza negra, 134–35
reducciones, 2, 153n5
regional identities: Blackness as, 16; jarocho as, 3–4, 6–7, 32, 69; other Mexican, 34
Rejano, Juan, 16
repertoire, and archives, 50, 62–63, 89–90
repetition, 76–79
representation, and identity, 100
reputation, of jarochos: happiness in, 96–98; innateness in, 80
rescate, 22, 48–49, 59, 90
resistance, 150–51
Rhode, Robert D., 15
rhythm, innateness of, 80–82
Rinaudo, Christian, 10, 45, 53–56, 99
Rivero Guillén, René, 39
Rodríguez, Hipólito, 36
Rodríguez, Romero, 143
Rodríguez García, David Antonio, 134–35
rumba, 39, 62
rural areas: Black identity in, 2; slavery in, 51

Saldívar, Emilo, 144–45
salsa dancing, 111–12
San Juan de Ulúa, 32–33
San Nicolás, 15–16, 49
Sansone, Livio, 99
Sartorius, Carl, 33
Schwaller, Robert, 37
scripts, racial, 28, 93, 115
Scripts of Blackness (Godreau), 17–18
Secretariat for Public Education (SEP), 53, 138
Secretariat of Culture, 53
Secretariat of the Interior (SEGOB), 138
selective memory, 100
self-identification: as Afro-Mexican, 57, 137–40;
    Black ancestry in, 119–20; as jericho, 33–34.
    See also census; *specific identities*
Seminoles, 138, 165n4
SEP. *See* Secretariat for Public Education
Siemens, Alfred H., 35
sincerity, racial, 89, 164n14
Siwy Machalica, Ryszard, 101
skin color. *See* color
slavery: City Museum on, 54; Indigenous
    peoples in, 68; in "Our Third Root," 54; in
    Veracruz, 51
Sleeter, Christine, 145
Sluyter, Andrew, 36
social clubs, talleres as, 79
social construction of race, 15
Social Construction of What?, The (Hacking), 142
social mobility, 144–45
social stratigraphy, 49
Sol (beer), 102, 103
Solís, Patricio, 144–45
son cubano. *See* son music
sones (musical pieces), 61–66; "El Camotal,"
    64; "El Chuchumbé," 62–64; "El Conejo,"
    88; "El Toro Zacamandú," 63, 64*fig.*; "El
    Zapateado," 83–84; "La Bamba," 88, 166n17;
    "La Guacamaya," 62, 91; "La Iguana," 66; "Los
    Negritos," 84; *sones de artesa,* 49; *sones de
    montón,* 88, 91; *sones de pareja,* 63
songs: "El Esclavo," 67, 70, 100; "Gangnam Style,"
    105; "La Cumbancha," 101; "Lindo Veracruz,"
    92; protest, 63
son jarocho: author's involvement with, 23–24;
    as Black art form, 75; folklorization of, 65;
    Mono Blanco in revitalization of, 61–66;
    talleres in revitalization of, 76–79. *See also*
    fandangueros
son music (son cubano, son montuno, son
    veracruzano): in anthem of Veracruz, 101;

at festivals, 44–45, 59; future of, 110–11;
    innateness of rhythm and, 80; of Pregoneros
    del Recuerdo, 59*fig.*, 72; public dancing
    to, 105
son veracruzano. *See* son music
sotavento region, 34, 36
sound archive. *See* Fonoteca Nacional
space, race in relation to, 17–18
Spanish conquest and colonization: Afro-
    descendant peoples in, 32, 36–37, 158n8;
    Andalusia in, 54; dances in, 62; in origins of
    Veracruz, 32–33
Spanish heritage, in jarocho imagery, 40
stereotypes, Black, 74, 97
stereotypes, jarocho, 31–34; happiness in,
    6, 97; jarocho publics' embrace of, 19;
    physical appearance in, 31–32, 38–40;
    postrevolutionary evolution of, 38;
    resistance to, 31. *See also* happiness
stringed instruments, 64–65
Stutzman, Ronald, 127
style, 75
Sue, Christina, 2–3, 11, 13–14, 119, 121, 145
sweet potatoes, 64

talleres (workshops), 74–93; cost of, 76;
    discipline in, 86–90; functions of, 76;
    innateness in, 80–84; learning through
    leisure in, 75, 84–86; performances of,
    90–93; performing groups originating
    in, 78–79; in revitalization of local
    tradition, 76–80; social interaction
    in, 79; teachers of, 79; third root in,
    76–80, 85
Taylor, Diana, 14, 23, 62, 90, 92
Teatro de la Reforma, 57
temporal distancing, 131
temporal slippages, 67–70
tenement housing, 45
tercera raíz. See third root
terminology, of Blackness, 9–14
third root (*la tercera raíz*), 48–71; in
    Afrocaribeño, 54–58; Caribbean in, 11,
    53–54, 57–58, 60–61; vs. first root, 16;
    government roles in, 50–59; limitations of
    multiculturalism in, 8; meaning and use
    of term, 3, 7–8, 12; Mono Blanco in, 61–66;
    origins of concept, 8, 12, 49; in talleres,
    76–80, 85; temporal slippages in, 67–70
Tierra Brava (film), 39
Toña la Negra, 132–35, 132*fig.*
Torres, Arlene, 161n7

tourism, in Veracruz: during Carnival, 96, 102–5; and happiness, 96–97; history of, 33, 159n10; from Mexico City, 42; performances of jarocho identity in, 40, 42–43; in Veracruzan identity, 31; videos promoting, 38, 40
"Travel Talks" (short films), 40
tripartite mestizaje, 49
Trouillot, Michel-Rolph, 7, 48, 61, 69
Turino, Thomas, 101
Turner, Frederick, 97

UNESCO, 2, 51, 53
United Nations (UN), 140
United States, one-drop rule in, 126–27
urban areas: Black identity in, 2; slavery in, 51
useful past, 35, 159n20

Vasconcelos, Jose, 127–28
Velázquez, María Elisa, 11–12
Venezuela, 124
Veracruzan Blackness, 5–29; Afro-Caribbean heritage in, 16–18; in La Huaca, 17, 45; identifying *with* vs. *as* Black in, 8, 13, 18, 26; in jarocho identity, 3, 7, 147–48; jarocho publics in, 19–25; as local color, 14–19, 41; terminology of, 9–14; as tool for jarochos, 98. *See also* jarocho(s)
veracruzanos, vs. jarochos, 38–39
"Veracruz" (ballad), 101
Veracruz (city): anthem of, 101, 166n17; census results for, 143, 147; claims about lack of Black people in, 1–3, 130; current condition of downtown, 47; dancing and cultural sites in, xv*map*; five hundredth anniversary of, 31–32, 40; founding of, 32–33; location of, xv*map*, 32–33, 159n9; nicknames of, 1, 6, 33; pandemic effects in, 149–50; as part of Caribbean, 53–54, 57–58, 60–61; population of, 19, 43; shared name with state, 30, 154n11; small-town feel of, 43–44; wall around, 44–45
Veracruz (state), xv*map*; anthem of, 101; Black towns in, 30; constitution of, 146–47; shared name with city, 30, 154n11
Veracruz Center for the Arts (CEVART), 50
"Veracruz: The Cultures of the Gulf and the Caribbean at 500 Years" forum, 54

Veracruz Institute of Culture (IVEC), 50–55; academic forums of, 44, 52, 54, 57–58, 60; as agent in cultural scene, 50–55; author's involvement with, 24; buildings of, 21*fig*., 50; diversity of programs of, 52; establishment of, 52, 54; forums on food at, 44; jarocho publics associated with, 20; mission of, 51–52; in *movimiento jaranero*, 61; music festivals of, 58–60, 59*fig*.; staff of, 64; El Vate and, 31. *See also* International Afro-Caribbean Festival
"Veracruz Is also Caribbean" forum, 54
Veracruz y sus viajeros (Veracruz and its travelers), 33
videos: promoting tourism, 38, 40; by El Vate Veracruzano, 31–32, 40–42
Villa Rica de la Vera Cruz, 159n9
Vinson, Ben, III, 14, 19, 166n5
"Visiting Veracruz" (travel film), 40
volováns, 44

Wacquant, Loïc, 9
Wade, Peter, 14
War for Independence, 6
Warner, Michael, 20
Warren, Jonathan, 145
WCAR. *See* World Conference against Racism
"What Is This 'Black' in Black Popular Culture?" (Hall), 74–75
white clothing, 6, 38, 40, 88–89
Whitten, Norman E., 161n7
Wood, Andrew Grant, 103
workshops. *See* talleres
World Conference against Racism, Racial Discrimination, Xenophobia, and Related Intolerance (WCAR), 143
Wright, Winthrop, 124

Xalapa and xalapeños, 34, 43

Yanga, 1–2, 51
Yúdice, George, 145

zacamandú (dance), 63, 64*fig*.
zambos, 37
zócalo (main plaza), public dancing in, 105–6, 107*fig*., 114–15. See also *specific events*

Founded in 1893,
UNIVERSITY OF CALIFORNIA PRESS
publishes bold, progressive books and journals
on topics in the arts, humanities, social sciences,
and natural sciences—with a focus on social
justice issues—that inspire thought and action
among readers worldwide.

The UC PRESS FOUNDATION
raises funds to uphold the press's vital role
as an independent, nonprofit publisher, and
receives philanthropic support from a wide
range of individuals and institutions—and from
committed readers like you. To learn more, visit
ucpress.edu/supportus.